D1562219

incest & influence

incest & influence

THE PRIVATE LIFE OF BOURGEOIS ENGLAND

ADAM KUPER

HARVARD UNIVERSITY PRESS

Cambridge, Massachusetts, and London, England

2009

Printed in the United States of America

Library of Congress Cataloging-in-Publication Data
Kuper, Adam.
Incest and influence : the private life of bourgeois England / Adam Kuper.
p.   cm.
Includes bibliographical references and index.
ISBN 978-0-674-03589-8 (alk. paper)
1. Consanguinity—England—History—19th century.
2. Cross cousin marriage—England—History—19th century.
3. Incest—Social aspects—England—History—19th century.
4. Domestic relations—England—History—19th century.
5. Middle class—England—History—19th century.
6. Elite (social sciences)—England—History—19th century.   I. Title.
HQ1026.K87 2009
306.85086'22094209034—dc22   2009016139

For Leila, Jesse, Joel, and Leo

Acknowledgments

This is my third book with Harvard University Press, and for the third time I have enjoyed the support and encouragement of Michael Fisher, the most loyal and understanding of editors, and benefited from the sympathetic expertise of Mary Ellen Geer, a wonderful copy editor. A major award from the Leverhulme Trust gave me time to get this project going. Jytte Klausen, Simon Kuper, Horace Freeland Judson, and Simon Gillett read a draft of this book, and Roderick Floud, Dan Jacobson, and Richard Kuper read several chapters. They all made many, often irritatingly acute criticisms, obliging me to undertake major revisions. Sam-Pablo Kuper was a patient resource at the Darwin Correspondence Project. Hannah Lamprecht provided invaluable assistance in assembling and analyzing genealogies. Julie M. Hartley prepared the diagrams.

Contents

Darwin's Marriage

Charles Darwin had been thinking about marriage—although not to anyone in particular—since returning to England after his five-year voyage on the *Beagle*. In July 1838 he took a sheet of paper, wrote "This is the Question" at the top, and divided it into two columns. "*Marry*" he wrote at the head of one column, "*Not Marry*" at the head of the other. He then laid out a balance sheet of arguments for and against.[1]

The arguments in favor were solid if unromantic. "Children—(if it Please God)—Constant companion, (& friend in old age) who will feel interested in one,—object to be beloved & played with.—better than a dog anyhow.—Home, & someone to take care of house—Charms of music & female chit-chat.—These things good for one's health.—*but terrible loss of time.*—"

Yet the bachelor life had its charms. "Freedom to go where one liked—choice of Society & *little of it.* Conversation of clever men at clubs—Not forced to visit relatives, & to bend in every trifle.—"

And marriage had its drawbacks: "—to have the expense & anxiety of children—perhaps quarrelling—*Loss of time.*—cannot read in the Evenings—fatness & idleness—Anxiety & responsibility—less money for books &c—if many children forced to gain one's bread. —(But then it is very bad for ones health to work too much)."

And where would he make a home? "Perhaps my wife wont like London; then the sentence is banishment & degradation into indolent, idle fool—." But the alternative was dismal. "Imagine living all one's day solitarily in smoky dirty London House.—Only picture to yourself a nice soft wife on a sofa with good fire, & books & music perhaps—Compare this vision with the dingy reality of Grt. Marlbro' St."

At the bottom of the "Marry" column he set down his conclusion: "Marry—Mary—Marry Q. E. D."

Then he moved on to the next question:

> It being proved necessary to Marry
> When? Soon or Late

On this he had consulted his father, Dr. Robert Darwin. "The Governor says soon for otherwise bad if one has children—one's character is more flexible—one's feelings more lively & if one does not marry soon, one misses so much good pure happiness—". No putting it off then. "Never mind my boy—Cheer up—One cannot live this solitary life, with groggy old age, friendless & cold, & childless staring one in ones face, already beginning to wrinkle.—never mind, trust to chance—keep a sharp look out—There is many a happy slave—".[2]

That settled, another very important question had to be faced. Whom should he marry? Lodging with his bachelor brother, Erasmus, in London, Charles had a few diffident flirtations. His father worried that he was showing an interest in the dauntingly intellectual Harriet Martineau. But Charles quickly decided that he wanted to marry a daughter of his favorite uncle, his mother's brother, Jos Wedgwood. Only one of Jos's daughters was unmarried and about the right age: this was the youngest Wedgwood daughter, Emma, who was a year older than Charles.

Emma was not only his first cousin; she was also his sister-in-law. Her oldest brother, Joe, had married Charles's sister Caroline in 1837. And other romances had been rumored between the young Wedgwoods and Darwins. According to Charles's sisters—who kept him up to date as he voyaged around the world—their elder brother Erasmus had shown an interest in Emma herself, and perhaps also in her two older sisters.[3] And three of Emma's brothers had been very attentive to Darwin's sister Susan.

Charles's courtship was awkward. He nerved himself to visit Emma at the Wedgwood home at Maer later that same July. They had a good talk, but he did not commit himself. Then in the first week of November, anxious and headachy, he returned and proposed. Emma was astonished that it all happened so quickly. Rather to Charles's surprise she accepted at once, but they were both still

Darwin's marriage.

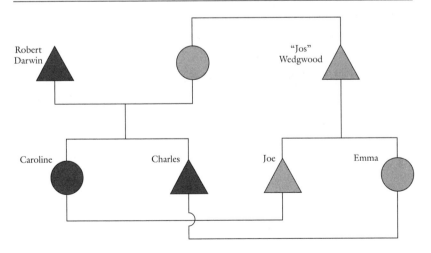

so overwrought when they confronted the family that one of the Wedgwood aunts was convinced that Emma must have turned him down.[4]

When Darwin wrote to his Cambridge mentor, Charles Lyell, to announce his engagement, he emphasized the family links. "The lady is my cousin, Miss Emma Wedgwood, the sister of Hensleigh Wedgwood [Darwin's special friend at Cambridge, well known to Lyell], and [Emma is also the sister] of the elder brother who married my sister, so we are connected by manifold ties, besides on my part by the most sincere love and hearty gratitude to her for accepting such a one as myself."[5]

The engagement did not come as a surprise to either family. "I knew you would be a Mrs Darwin," one of her psychic Wedgwood aunts wrote to Emma, adding that she was grateful to Charles for saving her from Erasmus.[6] Emma's father—Charles's uncle—wept with joy when Charles asked his permission for the marriage. "I could have parted with Emma to no one for whom I would so soon and so entirely feel as a father," he wrote to Robert Darwin, "and I am happy in believing that Charles entertains the kindest feelings for his uncle-father." He and his friend would now be quits: "You lately gave up a daughter—it is my turn now."[7] It was a match, Emma herself remarked, "that every soul has been making for us, so we could not have helped it if we had not liked it ourselves."[8]

They were married on the 29th of January, 1839. John Allen Wedgwood, vicar of Maer, officiated. He was first cousin to both Charles and Emma.

Introduction

*J*osiah Wedgwood, the grandfather of both Charles and Emma Darwin, pretended to be so busy that he could not say what he really was about. "I scarcely know, without a great deal of recollection, whether I am a Landed Gentleman, an Engineer, or a Potter, for indeed I am all three, & many other characters by turns. Pray heaven I may settle to something in earnest at last . . ."[1] In fact, Josiah was a distinguished specimen of a new breed of Englishmen. He was one of those who seized the opportunities offered by the most rapidly growing, the fastest-changing country in Europe. The new men made their way in the towns and cities, which were expanding at a dizzying rate as economic activity—and population—shifted from the countryside to new centers of production, from farms and workshops to factories.

Between 1751 and 1841, the population of Britain shot up from 6 million to 15 million.[2] The population of London doubled in size between the 1780s and the 1850s. With 2.5 million inhabitants, it was two and a half times the size of Paris, the next largest European city. Other cities expanded even more rapidly over the same period—not the old-world cathedral cities like Lincoln, Norwich, or York but the new industrial centers: Birmingham grew from 71,000 inhabitants to 233,000, Manchester from 75,000 to 303,000, Liverpool from 82,000 to 376,000.[3]

The changes were cumulatively massive, but they were less sudden, perhaps less pervasive, than was once thought. Economic historians now tend to downplay the rate of growth of productivity and GNP during the nineteenth century. Some prefer to avoid the term "industrial revolution" and even question the relative importance of the new industries and technologies.[4] D. N. McCloskey has suggested that it was not the Age of Cotton or the Age of Steam, but an age of improvement. Certainly the improvement, or transformation, was gradual.[5] Nor was there a steady advance; there were recurrent booms and busts, and periods of economic stagnation.

Nevertheless, after a generation of war the defeat of Napoleon opened up unprecedented opportunities in international trade, in finance, and in industry. Costly wars had spurred the development of new financial institutions and instruments—savings banks, discount houses, and the London Stock Exchange. The City of London created the world's greatest money market and securities market.[6] When peace came, industry could exploit new techniques that had been developed since the late eighteenth century. Coal and iron production soared. By 1850 Britain was exporting more pig iron and bar iron than was produced by the other European countries put together. In 1873, iron production in Britain matched the combined production of the United States and the rest of Europe.[7] Steam powered new industries. Old industries changed their ways. By the 1870s, British industry employed 42 percent of the workforce, compared to less than 30 percent in Germany and 25 percent in the United States.[8]

Entrepreneurs, bankers, and merchants became increasingly numerous, rich, and influential. Like Josiah Wedgwood, these men did not always fit comfortably into the old social structure, but society was changing. Gradually they colonized a distinctive social space, once something of a no-man's-land, between the middle class—clerks, tradesmen, and farmers—and the landed elite. An urban upper-middle class was emerging in England: a bourgeoisie.[9] Both terms, "bourgeoisie" and "class," require some explanation, even some excuse. I tend to prefer "bourgeoisie" to "upper-middle class" because the term suggests an urban identity and, more particularly, because it describes an elite within a modern capitalist society. The looser description, upper-middle class—or upper-middle classes—covers both bourgeoisie and country gentry.

Some bourgeois families might have links with the gentry, even with the aristocracy, yet their situation was very different. While the traditional upper classes inherited land and social prestige, the urban new men generally had neither. To be sure, there had always been rich merchants. Financiers typically emerged from a merchant background, and were drawn into banking by way of advancing credit to their suppliers. But industrialists often started from scratch. "All the great manufacturers that I have ever known," remarked Matthew Boulton, a friend of Josiah Wedgwood, "have begun in the world with very little capital."[10]

The professions also changed and expanded. Increasingly regulated and prestigious in the nineteenth century,[11] they opened up to intelligent outsiders at the same time as opportunities appeared in finance and industry. There were barriers, however—not least snobbery. James Stephen (1733–1779), the founding father of a great nineteenth-century lineage of professional men, intermittently maintained a shady law practice, but the benchers—the senior members—of the Middle Temple blackballed him on the grounds of his "want of birth, want of fortune, want of education, and want of temper."[12] A generation later, it was easier for the sons of financiers, merchants, and industrialists to make their way in the higher reaches of the law and medicine. Alongside the new clans of bankers, merchants, and industrialists there emerged dynasties of barristers and judges, clergymen and bishops, and high civil servants, as aristocratic patronage became less pervasive.

And then there were the intellectuals. They recast the natural and social sciences, questioned theological doctrines, debated public policy in the language of philosophy, and made the novel the great art form of their class. They emerged largely from within this professional milieu, although writers, scientists, and visionary engineers could also come from nowhere, at least in the late eighteenth and early nineteenth centuries. According to Leslie Stephen, "There is probably no period in English history at which a greater number of poor men have risen to distinction."[13] Women as well could make their names as writers and social reformers.

These were the elements of the bourgeoisie. Was it a social class? The term "class" carries a freight of ideological use and abuse, heavier even than the term "bourgeoisie." In the Marxist tradition, class refers in the first place to shared economic interests. At its simplest, even crudest, a class of capitalists is opposed to a class of workers. Most English capitalists were bourgeois, but some aristocrats grew rich from deposits of coal, or from land development in urban areas. In any case, the bourgeoisie cannot be defined simply with reference to economic functions. Civil servants, clergymen, headmasters, lawyers, doctors, accountants, and intellectuals—or at least the higher echelons of these professions—were often drawn from the same families as the businessmen. They intermarried, associated together, and came to recognize that they were the same kind of people.

Rather than a class in Marxist terms, the bourgeoisie was perhaps more precisely a status group. Certainly it became one, although it took some time for a national identity to crystallize. Drawn from a wide range of social backgrounds, engaged in a variety of occupations, the urban elites were divided at first by politics and, even more sharply, by religion. Merchants and industrialists took different sides in the great nineteenth-century debates on free trade. Nonconformists, Catholics, and Jews suffered legal discrimination and were barred from the universities and from Parliament. Interfaith marriages were discouraged.

There were also marked regional variations, especially between the bankers and brokers of the City of London and the northern industrialists. At first the urban elites were local. Well-off families in Manchester, Birmingham, Liverpool, and Leeds intermarried among themselves, and initially they were active mainly in the politics of their own cities.[14] Indeed, W. D. Rubinstein has argued that there were two distinct urban "middle classes" in the first half of the nineteenth century. The financiers of the City of London were likely to be Tory in politics and Anglican in religion, though often favoring the reformist, evangelical wing of the church. Their main business was making loans to governments, home or foreign; they did not provide substantial support to industry until the last decades of the century. The northern industrialists, in contrast, tended to be liberal in politics and often belonged to minority churches.[15] And they had to develop local banks and, later, stock exchanges.

Yet these divisions within the bourgeoisie may be exaggerated. In the early nineteenth century bankers could also be brewers, like the Barclays. Medical men might do some banking on the side, or might invest in industry and in canals and railways, like Dr. Robert Darwin, the father of Charles Darwin. High civil servants could be public intellectuals, like John Stuart Mill and Thomas Babington Macaulay. Roles were relatively unspecialized, and men could spread themselves over a variety of activities. Even intellectuals and businessmen shared common interests.

Josiah Wedgwood was a member of the Lunar Society of Birmingham.[16] While hardly typical, this club exemplifies the links between industry, science, and the professions. Some of the leading

Lunar Men were liberal intellectuals, like the educational theorist Richard Lovell Edgeworth, or Darwin's grandfather, Erasmus Darwin, a doctor, poet, and pioneering evolutionist. They admired the French Enlightenment, even sympathized at first with the Revolution, but they believed in marrying science, technology, and industry and were among the first to invest in the canals and railways that transformed Britain's communications.

The Lunar Men were enthusiastic participants in an "Industrial Enlightenment."[17] Josiah Wedgwood himself pioneered the industrial production of pottery. Another enterprising businessman, Josiah's friend Matthew Boulton, was a Lunar Man, together with his partner, James Watt, who contributed to the development of the steam engine. So too was the ironmonger and armaments maker Samuel Galton, who with his father funded the research of another member, the radical chemist James Priestley, who discovered oxygen, opening the way to new smelting techniques. Wedgwood's business associate Thomas Bentley encouraged Priestley's experiments with electricity. Josiah urged them to make their discoveries "more extensively usefull," even if he gently mocked their exuberance: "What daring mortals you are! To rob the thunderer of his Bolts,—and for what?—no doubt to blast the oppressors of the poor and needy . . . But peace to ye mortals! . . . Heaven's once dreaded bolt is now called down to amuse your wives and daughters—to decorate your tea-boards and baubles."[18]

Whatever their initial divisions may have been, these urban elites were on the rise. Their economic weight was growing. So too was their influence in public affairs. The landed interest remained powerful throughout the nineteenth century, but political power drifted, slowly but inexorably, to the cities, and within the cities to the bourgeoisie. Beginning in 1832, successive Reform Bills increased urban representation in Parliament. Fifty-two percent of MPs were professional men, mainly lawyers, in the Parliament that convened in 1886. Over 30 percent of members had substantial business interests.[19]

As the bourgeoisie consolidated, its members came to recognize one another by various conventions and signs, subtle but—to them —obvious enough. Increasingly they moved in the same circles, and intermarried by preference. In the first decades of the nineteenth century it was the City of London families that sent their boys to public schools, to be educated alongside the aristocracy. Later in the century the public schools were reformed, and they were patronized by the provincial bourgeoisie. Gradually, a common national identity crystallized.

As the bourgeoisie became more homogeneous, it became more exclusive. By the second half of the nineteenth century even talented outsiders were unlikely to break into their social circles, or to marry their daughters.[20] Recognized, by themselves and others, as a status group, they came to be called—and called themselves—ladies and gentlemen. Noel Annan observed that "the word, gentleman, in Victorian times became a subject of dialectical enquiry and nerve-racking embarrassment, as readers of Charlotte Yonge and Trollope know."[21] Nonetheless this self-definition marked them off—in principle at least—from the general run of middle-class shopkeepers and clerks. The frontier with the upper class was less strictly policed. Bourgeois gentlefolk might deplore the extravagance and immorality of the landed aristocracy, yet they valued certain upper-class traits —a country background, outdoor pursuits, good manners, chivalry.

A stigma was attached to trade, and the sons of successful entrepreneurs were sometimes tempted to make themselves over as country gentry. Josiah Wedgwood's sons and grandsons left the day-to-day management of the pottery to their Byerley cousins. Younger Wedgwood men bought country houses, married into the gentry, abandoned the Unitarian chapel for the established church, and patronized the arts, providing subsidies to Coleridge and Wordsworth.

The amateur spirit was prized. The aristocratic Captain Fitzroy engaged Charles Darwin as a "gentleman naturalist" on the *Beagle*. Darwin was not reimbursed for the five years he spent at sea, but he was the only man on board who shared the captain's quarters and his table. Charles and his brother, Erasmus Darwin, as well as several of their Wedgwood cousins, enjoyed the leisured existence of gentlemen, funded by capital settled on them by their families. "Now I am so completely a gentleman, that I have sometimes a little difficulty to pass the day; but it is astonishing how idle a three weeks I have passed," Darwin wrote to J. D. Hooker in 1859, as he completed *The Origin of Species*.[22] A German admirer who visited Down House toward the end of Darwin's life remarked, "In his appearance and in his pleasant, affable behaviour and his movements he is completely the English country gentleman, and hardly anything would reveal his profession."[23]

A disproportionate number of bourgeois came from nonconformist or Quaker families, although they tended to defect to the Church of England as they rose in the world. But it was possible to be a gentleman and a skeptic, like Darwin himself, and like most of the Wedgwood men (though not the women). The same German visitor to Down House asked his coachman about the great man. "'I don't know nothing bout hem, Sar,' he said in the splendid Kent dialect. 'Ha es en enfidel, Sar, yes, an enfidel, an infidel! And the people say he never went to church! But he is a gentleman, Sar, he is a gentleman, if ever anyone was, and he lives like a gentleman.'"[24]

Religious convictions were challenged, sometimes shattered, in the second half of the nineteenth century, yet a gentleman still had his code. He was courteous, principled, and prudent. "I now believe in nothing, to put it shortly," Leslie Stephen came to confess, "but I do not the less believe in morality, etc., etc., I mean to live and die like a gentleman if possible."[25] His older brother, James Fitzjames Stephen, spelled out what this meant. He was "resolved to do my duty, in the hope that it would turn out to have been my duty."[26]

PERHAPS ABOVE all, it was the family life of the bourgeoisie that was distinctive, although just what was so distinctive about it has been the subject of much debate. Historians once believed that the traditional English family was a sprawling, multi-generational corporation. Ideally, perhaps typically, three generations and several married couples with their children would live together. Servants and apprentices were counted in with the family. The household operated as a corporation, staffing a small farm or a craft workshop or a modest store. Then, with urbanization and industrial development, a man's work was detached from his home. Among the middle classes, and increasingly in proletarian families, married women seldom went out to work.

Not generally a productive entity now, the household remained the unit of consumption. People worked, saved, and invested above all in order to sustain their immediate families. The state gradually assumed many functions of the extended family, looking after the aged, the unemployed, and the education of the young.

This long-established view of the pre-industrial family was challenged by Peter Laslett and the Cambridge Group for the History of Population on one strategic issue. In studies published in the 1970s and 1980s, they demonstrated that the nuclear family household had been the norm at least since the sixteenth century, in Britain if not throughout Europe.[27] The age at which people married and the size of the family fluctuated with the ups and downs of the economy, but for centuries the typical British household seldom included kin beyond the immediate two-generation family of parents and children.

There is, of course, a difference between a family and a household.[28] While household structure was rather stable over time, on some measures at least, historians nevertheless tend to agree that the modern family, certainly the middle-class family, was fundamentally different from the families of the pre-industrial world.

In a controversial but hugely influential book, *The Family, Sex and Marriage in England 1500–1800*, published in 1977, Lawrence Stone identified a great secular transformation that was fully achieved by about 1800. Particularly in the growing industrial towns and cities, and especially in the middle classes, the character of the nuclear family changed. Husband and wife were supposed to love each other. Children were more likely to survive infancy, and they were cherished and nurtured in a fashion that would have been foreign to earlier generations.[29] Brothers and sisters were encouraged to form close relationships. Privacy was increasingly prized. Individualism became more pronounced, although, as J. L. Flandrin put it, it was an "individualism within the bosom of the family."[30]

The modern nuclear family had at last taken shape. Family sentiment was concentrated within a narrower circle. For those who were called the "middling" sort of people, the inner, nuclear family was now the most reliable source of value and meaning.

FOLLOWING LASLETT's and Stone's pioneering studies, the changing structure of the English family became a fashionable subject of research. Controversies erupted. Schools formed. Michael Anderson distinguished two main historiographical trends, the "household economics approach" of the Cambridge Group and a "sentiments approach" like that of Lawrence Stone.[31] A decade later in the early 1990s, Jane Turner Censer confirmed the "informal division of family historians into two major camps"—the numerate camp of the economists and demographers, and its less rigorous rival, which emphasized *mentalités* and psychological factors and drew on memoirs, diaries, and works of fiction.³² (Historians of the novel are now among its leading practitioners.)³³

The "sentiments" school attracted feminist historians, who paid particular attention to the status of women and the relationship between husband and wife. While confirming the rise of companionate marriage, they pointed out that men and women were treated very differently. In the nineteenth century female chastity was insisted upon, and women did not generally earn an income, even if they might exercise considerable influence in family affairs.

Nevertheless, young women in upper-middle-class circles were seldom put under serious pressure to marry against their will. Parents could not dictate terms, if only because love was generally agreed to be a necessary condition for marriage (although not, perhaps, a sufficient reason). To be sure, there were competing notions of true love. Not everybody approved of the romantic ideal. Passion was not entirely respectable, and the infatuations of the young were treated with suspicion. Like Jane Austen, parents tended to emphasize the importance of mutual affection, understanding, and respect. Love would grow on this foundation, and it would be lasting.³⁴

Parents who disapproved of a proposed marriage might try to exercise a veto, but with no guarantee of success. It was easier to persuade a couple to accept a lengthy engagement until the young woman was a little older, or the young man's financial situation had improved. In any case, the average age at marriage was higher among the upper-middle class than in the general population, and it tended to increase in the course of the nineteenth century, going up from around thirty for men to over thirty-three.³⁵

These ground rules gave some scope for romance, but they left ample room for a cool review of other considerations. At a minimum, a prospective husband had to be able to support his wife—ideally, in the clichéd phrase, in the style to which she had become accustomed. At the same time, wealthy parents were expected to settle sufficient capital on a young couple to assure their financial security and independence. Both sets of parents would normally provide roughly equal support.[36]

A well-to-do father would also see to it that his daughter did not become financially dependent on her husband after marriage. In common law, a married woman's property and earnings passed under the control of her husband. However, in the eighteenth century, courts of equity allowed a father to set up a trust that secured a daughter's capital while she enjoyed the income. Prenuptial settlements began to be used by the middle classes,[37] and they became more common in the nineteenth century. According to Pat Jalland, by the middle of the century one English wife in ten enjoyed the security of a trust fund.[38] Daughters might also inherit property and capital. In four out of five cases, the estate was divided fairly equally among all children on the death of their parents. Daughters were usually provided with income in trust, although they were sometimes given shares in family businesses.[39]

Trust funds, however, were the privilege of women from prosperous families. While "the daughters of the rich enjoyed . . . the considerable protection of equity," the Victorian constitutional historian A. V. Dicey remarked, "the daughters of the poor suffered under the severity and injustice of the common law."[40] In 1870 Parliament allowed married women control over their own earnings, and in 1882 all wives were given rights over property they brought into the marriage, granting them at last, as Dicey noted, "nearly the same rights as every English gentleman had for generations past secured under a marriage settlement for his daughter on her marriage."[41]

ALTHOUGH THE emotionally charged nuclear family became the nerve center of domestic life, broader networks of kin were still significant—in some ways more significant than ever.[42] Siblings remained close even after marriage, and adult brothers and sisters often formed joint households.⁴³ The bond between sisters was commonly even more intense and enduring. Like Charles Darwin's sisters, women threw themselves into planning marriages for their brothers, and then for the next generation of nephews and nieces. In consequence, uncles and aunts were important figures in the life of nineteenth-century English people, certainly in upper-middle-class families, and cousins grew up in friendly intimacy.

Free to mix unchaperoned, cousins readily fell in love. And they often married, usually with the approval of their families. Cousin marriage "was a way of safeguarding the domestic circle against change," Claudia Nelson remarks. "In a society that prized companionate marriage and tended to be suspicious of the outsider, keeping matrimony within the family helped to ensure that partners would understand each other and get along with their in-laws."⁴⁴

For similar reasons, brothers-in-law and sisters-in-law made suitable marriage partners. Emma Wedgwood was not only Charles Darwin's cousin but also his sister-in-law. Two of Jane Austen's brothers married two Lloyd sisters, and her novels feature a number of similar arrangements. In *Emma*, the heroine marries Mr. Knightley, who is the elder brother of her sister's husband. The heroine of *Sense and Sensibility*, Elinor, marries her brother-in-law, Edward Ferrars.

More generally, there was a preference for marriages that sustained an intimate and valued relationship between two families. As Valerie Sanders comments, "The ideal marriage in the Victorian novel adopts into the family someone who is almost a member of the family already."⁴⁵ Friends and close associates were easily turned into kin, as in-laws or godparents.

And marriages bound whole families together. "I protest against the opinions of those sentimental people who think that marriage concerns only the two principals," wrote Charles Darwin's cousin, Francis Galton; "it has in reality the wider effect of an alliance between each of them and a new family."[46] If a marriage between two families paid off, yielding financial ties or simply friendship and intimacy, there was an incentive to reinforce the connection by further marriages.. A network of marriages might weave together not two but three or even more families, sometimes giving rise to tightly-knit clans like the Wedgwood-Darwins.

Such marriages between relations were remarkably common among the upper-middle classes in England. "I have received some statistics from the R[egistrar] G[eneral]," George Darwin noted in an 1874 letter to his father, Charles Darwin, "& find that cousin marriages are at least 3 times as frequent in our rank as in the lower!"[47] Among people born into the great bourgeois clans of nineteenth-century England, like the Darwin-Wedgwoods, more than one marriage in ten was with a first or second cousin, as the table below shows.[48] Marriages between brothers- and sisters-in-law were equally frequent. Taken together, roughly one marriage in five was within the family circle.

Birth dates (men)	Married men and women	Couples who are 1st and 2nd cousins	Percentage of individuals who are 1st and 2nd cousins
before 1790	289	12	8.3%
1791–1820	132	8	12.1%
1821–1850	106	5	9.4%
1851–1880	68	4	11.8%
after 1880	28	0	0

This pattern of marriage came to an end, with the long nineteenth century itself, in the catastrophe of the First World War. But it had lasted for some hundred and fifty years, and it shaped the new bourgeoisie.

THEIR PREFERENCE for in-marriage distinguished the rising bourgeoisie from the ordinary run of urban middle-class families, but it had something in common with the practices of the upper classes.

Nevertheless, bourgeois marriage strategies were quite distinct from those of the aristocracy, let alone royal families.

Royal marriages were arranged, and the choice was restricted. This was because they mattered so very much. They were part of the machinery of foreign relations—moves in a great diplomatic game. If an alliance flourished, a cousin marriage might reinforce it. European royal genealogies were therefore studded with cousin marriages. But the domestic relationships of the English royal family were very different from those of the typical bourgeois clan.

The first Hanoverian king of England, George I, was crowned in 1714. He had married a cousin, his father's brother's daughter, in 1682. In 1694 he accused her of adultery, divorced her, and exiled her to the castle of Ahlden, where she died thirty-two years later. Before their separation they had a son, whom his father disliked intensely, but who succeeded him on the British throne. George II had a terrible relationship in turn with his own son, the Prince of Wales, and when the Prince died he was cordially detested by the Prince's heir, who became George III. Intermittently mad, and to some degree responsible for the loss of the American colonies, George III carried on the Hanoverian tradition by feuding with his eldest son, the dissolute Prince of Wales. He was also unwilling to allow his daughters to marry. His sons, for their part, were reluctant to abandon their mistresses in favor of a foreign princess.

The Prince of Wales actually married his mistress, Mrs. Fitzherbert. She had been widowed twice and was moreover a Catholic, whose family was part of the aristocratic English Catholic cousinhood. But lacking the consent of his father and of Parliament, the Prince's marriage was invalid. In 1795, needing money and tired of his wife, he reluctantly agreed to marry his cousin Caroline, the daughter of his father's favorite sister. "One damned German Frau is as good as another," he is said to have remarked, but when his cousin arrived at court and they formally embraced he was so affronted by her smell that he had to call for brandy.[49] He stuck to brandy for the three days before the wedding. Nonetheless Caroline bore a daughter, Charlotte, nine months later. She had by then already left her husband, and after being accused of adultery she moved abroad, where she lived in a rather rackety style according to the small army of British spies who kept track of her doings. (Rumor had her dancing naked to the waist at a ball in Geneva, taking her own servant as a lover, and dallying with Napoleon's brother-in-law, the King of Naples, an enemy of Britain.) Caroline had limited access to her daughter; she once locked her in a closet with a suitor when she was sixteen, instructing the young people to amuse themselves.[50]

In 1820 her husband succeeded to the throne as George IV. He immediately petitioned Parliament to put Caroline on trial for treason, or at least to strip her of her privileges and grant him a divorce. For her part, Caroline demanded to be recognized as queen. She was humiliatingly refused entry to the coronation ceremony at Westminster Abbey. A few weeks later she fell ill and died.

In the meantime, Charlotte, the king's daughter by Caroline, had married Prince Leopold of Saxe-Coburg-Saalfeld, but she died in childbirth in 1817. The baby did not survive. A crisis loomed, since the new king began to show signs of insanity, like his father, and became a recluse. Impelled by Parliament, the king's four brothers, the Royal Dukes, now scrambled to ensure the continuity of the dynasty.

The Duke of York, the second and favorite son of George III, made a good marriage to a daughter of the King of Prussia, but there were no children and the couple soon separated. He served disastrously as a military commander, immortalized as The Grand Old Duke of York. He nevertheless became Commander in Chief, but was eventually obliged to resign when it came out that his mistress was selling commissions in the army. He died in 1827.

The next son of George III, the Duke of Clarence, reluctantly agreed to leave his devoted mistress of twenty years, Mrs. Jordan, and to marry a German princess. In 1830 he succeeded his brother as William IV. His marriage was a great success, his wife a paragon of domestic virtue. However, they had no children.

George III's fourth son, the Duke of Kent, had an unfortunate military career, like his brother the Duke of York. It came to an end when he precipitated a mutiny in the Gibraltar garrison in 1802. He was also obliged to put aside his mistress, with whom he had lived happily for twenty-eight years, in order to marry the sister of Prince Leopold, Charlotte's widower, in 1818. The couple had a daughter, Victoria, and historians now discount contemporary rumors that Kent was not in fact her father.

The youngest of the Royal Dukes, Ernest Augustus, Duke of Cumberland, of his own free will married a cousin, Friederike, a princess of Mecklenburg-Strelitz, in 1815. But even though Friederike was his cousin, she was not an acceptable consort. She had been twice widowed. Worse still, she had been pregnant when she married her second husband, and was in the process of divorcing him when he died. The mother of Ernest Augustus, Queen Charlotte, was distraught, and she never received Friederike after the marriage.[51] In any case, the union was childless.

And so it was Victoria, the daughter of the Duke of Kent, who came to the throne in 1837, following the death of William IV. On February 10, 1840, a year after Charles Darwin's wedding, Queen Victoria married Prince Albert of Saxe-Coburg and Gotha, who was her mother's brother's son. The Prime Minister, Lord Melbourne, did suggest that their close relationship might be a problem, but with his unreconstructed Regency tastes Melbourne was hardly in a position to sermonize. ("Spanking sessions with aristocratic ladies were harmless," Boyd Hilton remarks, "not so the whippings administered to orphan girls taken into his household as objects of charity, besides which he seemed strangely dependent on a sinister and low-born private secretary.")[52]

In any event, Melbourne's reservations were not widely shared.

The press was more concerned that Albert had no money and might be a fortune hunter. He was also younger than the queen, who surely required mature guidance.[53] But Victoria and Albert became a popular couple, honorary bourgeois, the very model of respectable matrimony, and the best possible advertisement for the marriage of cousins.

UNLIKE THE bourgeoisie, aristocrats tended to avoid marriages between brothers- and sisters-in-law.[54] Cousin marriage, however, was acceptable in aristocratic and gentry circles in the seventeenth and eighteenth centuries. It might even be regarded as a safe option. The Byron of the Restoration court, Lord Rochester, described a young man—"the heir and hopes of a great family"—coming to town. And "lest crossing of the strain / Should mend the booby breed, his friends provide / A cousin of his own to be his bride."[55]

Yet aristocrats had more choice than royals. Caste exclusiveness mattered, but marriages with middle-class heiresses became increasingly common. The proportion of marriages within the aristocracy itself dropped below one in four in the eighteenth and nineteenth centuries.[56] To be sure, a nobleman was not always obliged to choose between caste and cash. Marriage to an aristocratic cousin could pay off very nicely. Samuel Dugard, a seventeenth-century clergyman who married his cousin and wrote a treatise in favor of cousin marriage, commented approvingly that if an heiress married the son of her father's brother, this kept her estate "in her father's family."[57] Fully half of the aristocratic cousin marriages in the eighteenth century were between the children of two brothers.[58]

The children of a brother and sister married less frequently, and such marriages would not usually bring financial advantage to the groom. However, a contemporary of Dugard, Bishop Jeremy Taylor, argued that a woman might wish to arrange a marriage between her daughter and her brother's son in order to preserve "her father's name in her own issue, which she had lost in her own persona and marriage."[59] The children of two sisters very rarely married, but then neither property nor lineage would have been served by such a marriage. Indeed, Ruth Perry suggests that Jane Austen particularly approved of marriage between maternal cousins precisely because no property was involved.[60]

Yet however acceptable cousin marriage may have been in principle, and whatever particular benefits might follow, it was uncommon in practice in aristocratic circles in the eighteenth century, when only about one percent of aristocrats married their first cousins.[61] There was a sharp rise in the rate of cousin marriage among the aristocracy in the nineteenth century; Charles Darwin's son George found in the 1870s that 4.5 percent of aristocratic marriages were between first cousins.[62] The new popularity of cousin marriage actually coincided with the decline of marriages within the aristocracy. The younger sons of landowners, making careers in the army, the church, and the law, were now marrying into banking and professional families. The division between the bourgeoisie and the aristocracy was gradually eroding. Financiers and provincial merchants entered Parliament and might buy estates and country houses. Sons of self-made businessmen became lawyers, clergymen, or military officers, like the younger sons of the aristocracy or gentry. Boyd Hilton notes that "the growing fashion for landed offspring to take legal qualifications without ever intending to practise law . . . exemplifies the way in which some members of the old elite sought to appropriate the status symbols of their erstwhile challengers, rather than the other way around."[63] And as they became absorbed into the new bourgeoisie, aristocrats adopted bourgeois marriage practices, including a preference for cousin marriage.

THE POLITICAL networks of the eighteenth-century aristocracy, like the Whig Cousinhood, were succeeded by hundreds of the new bourgeois clans—in business and finance, in the professions, in the church, in local and national politics, and in intellectual life. But the bourgeoisie did not marry cousins in imitation of the aristocracy, let alone royalty. They were impelled by their own characteristic interests, informed by a distinctive pattern of family sentiment, governed by their own standards of decorum and morality.

The consequences were profound. Marriages between relatives sustained networks of kin. Veritable clans emerged and might persist for several generations—in the case of the Darwin-Wedgwoods for over a century, and they were not exceptional. These webs of relationships delivered enormous collateral benefits, shaping vocations, generating patronage, yielding information, and giving access to capital. A young man with such family connections began his career with a decisive advantage.

According to David Sabean, kinship networks were crucial to the rise of the nineteenth-century bourgeoisie in most European countries. He argued that "the new kin-constructed networks were the most important resource for capital accumulation and business enterprise, and contributed to the formation of classes and class cultures."[64] This was certainly true in England, perhaps especially in the provinces, where exclusion from the established church often bolstered family solidarity. As Pat Hudson notes,

> The leading business families throughout the Lancashire cotton area came primarily from nonconformist groups, their families bonded through intermarriage . . . The Lees and Armitages of Salford and the Boltons and Kershaws of Stockport and Manchester were linked by marriage . . . Similar family ties can be traced in Bolton and in Blackburn and Darwen, where family networks spread across cotton, engineering, and ironmaking over several generations. . . . The Birmingham business elites also operated in cliques in which religious affiliation,

intermarriage, and involvement in municipal enterprise were key elements.[65]

One of these Birmingham cliques was a set of intermarrying Unitarian families, notably the Chamberlains, Kenricks, Martineaus, Oslers, Rylands, and Nettlefolds. They were industrialists and took an active part in Liberal politics in their city. The Chamberlains became national figures, producing three of the leading politicians of the Victorian age.

The first Joseph Chamberlain was a substantial businessman, an honored member of the Cordwainers' Company of London. He married a sister of another businessman, Joseph Strutt, and after her death he married his sister-in-law. (His marriage to his deceased wife's sister took place in 1792, a generation before Lord Lyndford's Act tightened up the prohibition on such unions.) He left a flourishing business to his son, also named Joseph Chamberlain, who made a fortune on his account, not least by financing a large and risky investment of his sister's husband, John Nettlefold.

Nettlefold was an ironmonger. In 1854 he bought an American patent for producing superior screws, and he needed £30,000 (nearly $3 million today) to finance a steam mill with which to produce them.[66] Joseph Chamberlain put up a third of the capital. He then dispatched his eighteen-year-old son, the third Joseph Chamberlain, to Birmingham to look after the investment. The partners prospered. After twenty years Joseph retired, a rich man. He then devoted himself to politics and was elected mayor of Birmingham in 1873. His energetic reform of the city's government made his name. In 1876 he was elected to Parliament. In time he held several cabinet posts, just missing out on the Prime Ministership.

Early in his Birmingham years Joseph Chamberlain had become friendly with the Kenrick brothers, Archibald and Timothy. The brothers were partners in the family iron foundry business, one of the two largest such firms in the country. The Kenricks were given to marrying Kenricks. Timothy was married to a Kenrick cousin. The family was also connected by marriages, often several marriages, to other families in their Birmingham milieu, notably the Martineaus.

In 1861 Joseph Chamberlain married Archibald Kenrick's daughter Harriet. She died giving birth to her second child, Austen, a future chancellor of the exchequer and foreign secretary. Joseph then married Harriet's cousin Florence, the daughter of Timothy Kenrick. By this marriage he had a son, Arthur Neville Chamberlain, who became Prime Minister. Joseph's sister Mary married William Kenrick, the brother of Joseph's first wife. Joseph's younger brother Arthur married Louisa Kenrick, the twin sister of Joseph's second

The Chamberlain-Kenrick marriages.

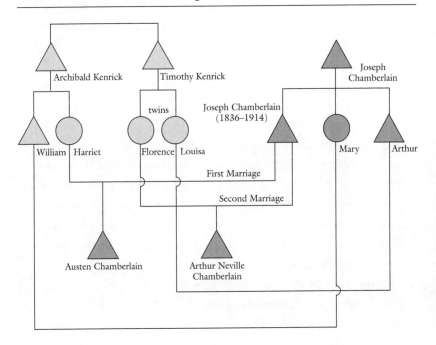

wife, Florence. Two of Arthur Chamberlain's daughters would marry Kenrick cousins.[67]

MY ARGUMENT in this book is that marriage within the family— between cousins, or between in-laws—was a characteristic strategy of the new bourgeoisie, and that it had a great deal to do with the success of some of the most important Victorian clans. And if those clans were growing in wealth, influence, and prestige, so was their country. In the course of the long nineteenth century it became an increasingly prosperous, secular, and democratic land. After the defeat of Napoleon, Great Britain was the leading power in the world. India was brought under the control of Parliament. Atlantic and Indian Ocean trade flourished, and this was a decisive factor in economic take-off.[68]

The leading bourgeois clans played a great role in the history of this industrial and imperial Britain. Their preference for marriages within the family circle was a crucial factor in their success. The marriage pattern of the English bourgeoisie therefore played a significant part in making the nineteenth-century world.

Historians have paid little attention to the public consequences of these private arrangements, but contemporaries were obsessed with them. If men and women persisted in marrying close relatives, they did not do so thoughtlessly. The bourgeoisie was remarkably educated, literate, historically conscious, scientifically minded, and reflective. Novelists dissected family dynamics, the pathologies of domestic authority, the dangerous intimacy of brother-sister relationships, and the love affairs between cousins. Anthropologists were fascinated by the incest taboo and its origins. The preference for marriage between in-laws ran up against the canon law prohibition on marriage with a deceased wife's sister, leading to one of the great Victorian public debates, which engaged politicians, lawyers, and clergymen. Cousin marriage troubled natural scientists and medical men; it became a personal obsession of Charles Darwin and his cousin Francis Galton, provoking revolutionary ideas about breeding and heredity. In short, the preference of the English bourgeoisie for marriage with relatives is one of the great neglected themes of nineteenth-century history.

PART I

a question
of incest

CHAPTER ONE

The Romance of Incest
and the Love of Cousins

*W*hen Emma Wedgwood's friend, Georgina Tollet, heard of her engagement to Charles Darwin, she remarked, "It is very like a marriage of Miss Austen's."[1] This was not altogether accurate. "The two had no obstacles to overcome," notes Darwin's biographer Janet Browne, "no delicate flirtations at picnics or dances, no misunderstandings wrenching the heartstrings."[2]

Yet it is true that romances between cousins feature prominently in Jane Austen's work, beginning with one of her engaging if badly spelled childhood stories, *Frederic and Elfrida:*

> The Uncle of Elfrida was the Father of Frederic; in other words, they were first cousins by the Father's side.
>
> Being both born in one day and both brought up at one school, it was not wonderfull that they should look on each other with something more than bare politeness. They loved with mutual sincerity but were both determined not to transgress the rules of Propriety by owning their attachment, either to the object beloved, or to any one else.

They were exceedingly handsome and so much alike, that it was not every one who knew them apart. Nay even their most intimate friends had nothing to distinguish them by, but the shape of the face, the colour of the Eye, the length of the Nose, and the difference of the complexion.[3]

In the end, "the parents of Frederic proposed to those of Elfrida, a union between them, which being accepted with pleasure, the wedding cloathes were brought and nothing remained to be settled but the naming of the Day."[4]

Austen's mature novels repeatedly probe and analyze alliances between cousins. In chapter 31 of *Sense and Sensibility* (1811), for example, Colonel Brandon tells Elinor the tragic story of his first love, who was his cousin. She was "an orphan from her infancy, and under the guardianship of my father. Our ages were nearly the same, and from our earliest years we were playfellows and friends." They loved each other. However, because she was rich, Colonel Brandon's father, her uncle, decided to marry her off to his eldest son. "My brother did not deserve her," Colonel Brandon tells Elinor, "he did not even love her." The young lovers arranged to elope, but were foiled. Pushed into a miserable marriage, the unfortunate young woman ran away, fell into the hands of bad men, and eventually died young of consumption. She left an illegitimate daughter, who was later seduced by the libertine Willoughby. Jane Austen compensates Colonel Brandon with a marriage to Elinor's sister, Marianne (who, according to the Colonel, resembled his lost love "as well in mind as person").

In *Pride and Prejudice* (1813), Mr. Bennett has four daughters but no sons. His heir is a relative, "my cousin, Mr. Collins," as Mr. Bennett explains to his family, "who, when I am dead, may turn you all out of this house as soon as he pleases."[5] Mrs. Bennett (but not the more sensible Mr. Bennett) hopes that Mr. Collins will marry one of her daughters. In the same novel, Lady Catherine de Bourgh expects her wealthy nephew Darcy to marry her daughter, in order to preserve "the noble line" and to keep the property in the family. (Darcy eventually marries Miss Bennett.)

In *Mansfield Park* (1814), Fanny and Edmund are the children of two sisters and, like Colonel Brandon and his cousin, they have been brought up in the same house almost as brother and sister. But they marry each other in the end. In *Persuasion* (1817), Elizabeth Elliot dreams of a marriage with her cousin and her father's heir, William Elliot (apparently her second cousin in the male line), although there are indications that he is more interested in her sister Anne. A minor character in the novel, the "country curate" Charles Hayter, marries his mother's sister's daughter, Henrietta Musgrave. "Charles's attentions to Henrietta had been observed by her father and mother without any disapprobation. 'It would not be a great match for her; but if Henrietta liked him,'—and Henrietta *did* seem to like him."[6]

COUSIN MARRIAGE was by no means an eccentric interest of Jane Austen. The novel began to flourish in England in the mid-eighteenth century, and readership was boosted by the new circulating libraries. An observer noted in the 1780s that novels "for half a century have made the chief entertainment of that middle class which subsists between the court and the people."[7] They were particularly popular among women. "Everywhere one looks in the literature of the period," Anna Barbauld remarked in 1820, "one sees women reading."[8]

And from the first, novels routinely featured romances and marriages between cousins. These were generally treated as unproblematic, in principle at least, although the plot was bound to introduce extraneous obstacles of character or fortune.[9] (I know, I know. They are not just stories, or even mainly stories, yet these novels did tell stories. There were tall tales, but there were also carefully realistic stories, the majority in fact. Writers and readers often believed in their characters and thought that the plots represented an approximation to the sorts of things that happened to their contemporaries, even to people like themselves, which was why the morals they drew could be so compelling.)

A generation after Jane Austen, the possibility of cousin marriages was a recurrent theme in the novels of the Brontë sisters (although Charlotte Brontë tended to be dismissive of Austen, and romances between cousins turn out less well in the novels of the Brontës than in Austen's). Jane Eyre rejects a proposal from her straitlaced cousin, St. John Rivers, preferring the fascinating but erratic Mr. Rochester (1847). In *Shirley* (1849), Caroline Helstone nearly dies for the love of her cousin. In Emily Brontë's *Wuthering Heights* (1847), Cathy Lindon marries two of her first cousins in succession, but the marriages are unhappy.

The cousins Richard and Ada marry in *Bleak House* (1852–53), but Charles Dickens generally drew his characters from the poorer urban classes, and such people rarely married cousins. In contrast, romances between cousins crop up regularly in the worldly novels of Anthony Trollope, which are set among the upper and upper-middle classes.[10] The disposition of estates is often a factor in these stories. In *Cousin Henry* (1879), Old Inofer Jones, a bachelor squire, is devoted to his niece Isobel, who is also popular with his tenants. He would like her to inherit his estate, Llanfeare Grange. However, convention dictates that he should make his nephew, Henry Jones, his heir. Inofer hopes that he can resolve his dilemma by persuading Isobel to marry her cousin Henry. She refuses because she cannot love him.

Land was not usually at issue in bourgeois families, but other financial interests might play a part. Margaret Oliphant's *Hester* (1883) begins with an account of two cousins, John and Catherine Vernon, who each inherit half-shares in the family bank. John's mother wants them to marry, and is outraged when the young people resist. "She asked her son how he could forget that if Catherine's money went out of the business it would make the most extraordinary difference? And she bade Catherine remember that it would be almost dishonest to enrich another family with money which the Vernons had toiled for."[11] In the end John nearly ruins the bank, and Catherine saves it. In the next generation her niece Hester takes over the management of the bank, and is wooed by no fewer than three (more distant) cousins.

But parents might have quite other motives for wanting cousins to marry. In Elizabeth Gaskell's *The Moorland Cottage* (1850), Mr. Buxton had disapproved of his sister's marriage. After her death "the only way he could devise to satisfy his reproachful conscience towards his neglected and unhappy sister, was to plan a marriage between his son and her child."[12] Mr. Buxton brings his niece up in his home alongside his son. However, his son falls in love with the daughter of a poor clergyman's widow, cheating him of his atonement.

And even between cousins love may be unrequited. In George Meredith's *Ordeal of Richard Feverel* (1859), Richard remains tragically unaware of the love of his cousin Clare, whom his late mother hoped he would marry. Mary Elizabeth Braddon (a great favorite of Tennyson) traces in *John Marchmont's Legacy* (1862) the hopeless passion of the cultivated Olivia Arundel for her indifferent cousin, who prefers a childlike young woman.

As ever, questions of status may complicate matters. Not all relatives are equal. In Thackeray's *The Newcomes* (1854), Ethel Newcome's family is horrified at the prospect that Ethel might marry her cousin Clive Newcome. Their branch of the family has risen far above those other Newcomes. Ethel must marry more grandly—though still to a relative. "You know that for a long time it was settled that she was to marry her cousin, Lord Kew. She was bred to that notion from her earliest youth."[13] But Ethel is an independent young woman, and she marries someone else entirely.

The theme was treated more lightheartedly in other genres. Wilde's *The Importance of Being Ernest* (1895) ends with the discovery that Ernest and Gwendolen are cousins. Ernest's mother was not a handbag, or Miss Prism. He is the long-lost son of Lady Bracknell's sister. Since Ernest and Gwendolen are the children of two sisters, even Lady Bracknell can have no objection to their marriage. This is a farcical reprise of a common plot. In "A Shocking Story" by Wilkie Collins (1878), for instance, a young woman falls in love with her aunt's groom, only to discover that he is her aunt's illegitimate son.

And even the coziest of childrens' stories featured cousin marriages. "When Benjamin Bunny grew up," Beatrix Potter wrote, "he married his Cousin Flopsy. They had a large family, and they were very improvident and cheerful."[14]

EMMA DARWIN used to read novels to Charles as he reclined on the settee between bouts of work. He insisted on happy endings, and a romantic interest. "A novel, according to my taste, does not come into the first class unless it contains some person whom one can thoroughly love, and if a pretty woman all the better."[15] Wholesome cousins were surely to his taste, and to Emma's. To be sure, the Wedgwoods had a particularly marked penchant for cousin marriages, but many members of the educated reading public came across cousin marriages in their own circles, probably in their own families.

This was certainly true of the authors themselves. Fanny Burney's eldest sister married her father's brother's son. Jane Austen's brother Henry married his glamorous widowed cousin, Eliza de Feuillide, his father's sister's daughter, who had earlier turned down an offer of marriage from Henry's brother, James.[16] (Eliza's husband, a

French officer, had been guillotined during the Terror.) Margaret Oliphant married her father's brother's son, the painter Frank Oliphant. (Her adored brother, also named Frank Oliphant, was put out by her marriage, and he immediately married a cousin himself.) Thackeray's elder daughter, Anny, married her cousin, Richmond Ritchie, who was, moreover, seventeen years younger than she was. Trollope's father's sister married her cousin, the Rev. Henry Trollope. The parents of both John Ruskin and Lewis Carroll were cousins, while the daughters of both Elizabeth Gaskell and Robert Southey married cousins.

Elizabeth Barrett Browning's "novel poem" *Aurora Leigh* (1857) —regarded in her lifetime as her masterpiece—describes an up-and-down romance between the cousins Aurora Leigh and Romney Leigh. Her own brother, Alfred, and her sister Henrietta both married cousins. (Their father, the notoriously jealous Edward Barrett, disinherited them, as he did Elizabeth when she married Robert Browning.) John Galsworthy had a secret ten-year-long affair with his cousin's wife, Ada, whom he eventually married in 1905. This relationship was fictionalized in the romance between young Jolyon and Irene in *The Forsyte Saga*. And H. G. Wells married his first cousin, Isabel Mary Wells, but the marriage lasted only three years.

This list is doubtless incomplete, but a catalogue of great writers of the period who fell in love with their cousins might be even longer. It would have to begin with Byron, whose first two boyhood passions were for cousins. It could fittingly end with another scandalous poet, the *fin de siècle* celebrity Algernon Charles Swinburne. Shortly after the premature death of his beloved sister Edith, Swinburne fell for his cousin Mary Gordon. "They were cousins many times over," Nancy Anderson points out. "Their mothers were sisters, their fathers first cousins, and the grandparents first cousins." They called each other "brother" and "sister."[17] Mary was probably the one great love of Swinburne's life. The love of two cousins, Redgie and Mabel, whose names echo Algernon and Mary, is at the heart of Swinburne's *The Sisters* (1892). ("I asked her if she thought it possible / That two such baby friends and playfellows, . . . / Could when grown up, be serious lovers." "Hardly. No. Certainly not," Mabel replies.)[18] When Mary was widowed, after twenty-five years of marriage, the cousins took up with each other and discovered a shared interest in flagellation.[19]

IN 1814 Jane Austen wrote in a letter to her niece, Anna Lefroy, "I like first Cousins to be first Cousins, & interested about each other. They are but one remove from Br & Sr—."[20] She was only encouraging her niece to keep up with her cousins, but some contemporaries did worry that a marriage between cousins might be a little too cozy—verging, even, on the incestuous.

In 1826 a brilliant young lawyer, Henry Nelson Coleridge, traveled to the West Indies, ostensibly for health reasons, but actually because his parents hoped that a foreign adventure would distract him from his infatuation with a cousin.[21] It did not work out that way. On his return Henry published, anonymously, *Six Months in the West Indies,* and he slipped in a defiant declaration: "I love a cousin; she is such an exquisite relation, just standing between me and the stranger to my name, drawing upon so many sources of love and tieing them all up with every cord of human affection—almost my sister ere my wife!"[22]

Henry's uncle, Samuel Taylor Coleridge, read this passage uneasily. He was then thoroughly dismayed to discover that Henry's beloved was his own daughter, Sara, and that they were secretly engaged to be married.

How much truth is there in this plea, Henry himself has let out, unawares, in the words "my Sister ere my Wife"—words which have given offence, I find, to three or four persons of our acquaintance and I own shocked my feelings . . . Surely, the best interests of Society render it expedient, that there should be some Outworks between the Citadel, that contains the very Palladium of the Human Race, and the Open Country.[23]

Henry's parents were also opposed to the marriage, but for a simpler reason: they thought that Samuel Taylor was unreliable, perhaps mad.[24] However, Coleridge himself came around in the end. "If the matter were quite open, I should incline to disapprove the marriage of first cousins; but the church has decided otherwise on the authority of Augustine, and that seems enough upon such a point."[25]

He was mistaken: Augustine strongly disapproved of cousin marriage.[26] But Henry and Sara married in 1829. Sara declared that he was her "cousin-husband, certainly nearer and dearer to me for being cousin, as well as husband."[27] The couple settled in Hampstead, near Sara's father's base in Highgate. After his death they devoted themselves to editing his manuscripts. When Henry died, Sara buried him in her father's vault.[28]

IN ENGLAND in the nineteenth century, perhaps most especially among the upper-middle classes, the brother-sister relationship was often infused with emotion, and siblings commonly remained close throughout their lives. A man starting out on a career might set up a household with one or more of his sisters.[29] A marriage would break up this comfortable arrangement, and quite often it was resented.

Influenced in part by Freudian theory, some writers argue that Victorian domestic arrangements actually fostered incestuous feelings between brothers and sisters.[30] The nuclear family was isolated; contacts between young men and women were restricted; sexual longings were repressed. Only brothers and sisters could freely show affection for one another.

Some recent commentators have taken a further and even bolder step: they argue that the incestuous passions of siblings—supposedly rife—motivated cousin marriages. "Love for a cousin was a convenient and fitting displacement of love toward a nuclear family member,"[31] according to Nancy Fix Anderson. Charles Darwin lost his mother while he was still a child, and his older sisters mothered him. Anderson suggests that he married Emma Wedgwood because he had an unresolved incestuous attachment to his sister Caroline, who had married Emma's brother. However, there is no indication that Charles was obsessed with any of his sisters. He was away for five years, at sea on the *Beagle,* and gave no signs of yearning for a return. Moreover, his marriage to Emma was remarkably successful, which suggests that its foundation was not particularly neurotic.[32]

In any case, English contemporaries did not generally regard such marriages as abnormal or as verging on the incestuous, and novelists typically represented them as calm, safe, rational arrangements. There were well-recognized, mundane reasons for the marriage of cousins, or of a brother- and sister-in-law, as there are in numerous other societies that favor marriages between close relations.

Incest nevertheless fascinated writers. One of the great themes of seventeenth-century drama, it was regularly treated by the early novelists. As Ellen Pollak remarks, "A striking number of English prose fiction narratives written between 1684 and 1814 predicate their plots on the tabooed possibility of incest."[33] Perhaps this tells us something about the dark imaginings of the English, but it has to be said that the treatment of the incest plots was as a rule anything but realistic.

In many eighteenth-century novels the story revolves around mistaken identity. Typically a brother and sister, separated as small children, often orphans, are brought together by accident as adults. They do not recognize each other, yet they experience a mysterious and immediate attraction.[34] They may even marry, as happens in

Daniel Defoe's *Moll Flanders* (1722), Sophia Lee's *The Recess* (1785), and Agnes Maria Bennett's *Agnes De-Courci* (1789). In Henry Fielding's *Joseph Andrews* (1742), the marriage of Fanny and Joseph is halted at the last moment by a false report that they are brother and sister. In Mary Robinson's *Vancenza* (1792), a woman discovers just before her marriage that her fiancé is her brother, and she falls ill and dies.[35] The hero of Fanny Burney's *Evelina* (1778) suffers through two misunderstandings: he nearly marries his own sister by mistake, and then finds himself falling for a woman whom he wrongly believes to be his sister. (Dr. Johnson's friend Mrs. Thrale was very impressed by *Evelina,* and when she fell in love with the Italian musician Gabriel Piozzi, in the autumn of 1780, she persuaded herself that he was her brother.)[36]

Treated by Fielding as farce, by Burney as romance, the love of brother and sister inspires fascination and horror in the Gothic novels of the late eighteenth and early nineteenth centuries. In Hugh Walpole's *The Mysterious Mother* (1768), the hero unwittingly sleeps with his own mother. They have a daughter, whom he eventually marries, again in ignorance of their real relationship. In Matthew Lewis's *The Monk* (1796), the heroine is ravished by an older brother whom she calls "Father" because he is a priest. Later he murders her. In Mary Shelley's *Frankenstein* (1818), Frankenstein's bride, Elizabeth Lavenza, is his adopted sister: "We called each other familiarly by the name of cousin. No word, no expression could body forth the kind of relation in which she stood to me—my more than sister, since till death she was to be mine only."[37]

The Romantic poets idealized the brother-sister relationship. Their incest stories are tempered by love, rooted in shared memories of an idyllic childhood, but they are distanced by remote, exotic settings. Brother and sister marry in Byron's *Cain* (1822), which is set in biblical times, and in the first version of *The Bride of Abydos* (1813), a Turkish story in which the hero is a pirate. The lovers themselves are doomed in Byron's *Manfred* (1817), set in "the Higher Alps," where incest leads to early death. In Shelley's visionary poem of the Islamic world, *Laon and Cythna*, published in the same year, the lovers end up in exile.

And it was not all fiction. Byron had a notorious affair with his half-sister, Augusta Leigh. To be sure, Byron was hardly typical. No more was William Wordsworth, who had a strange, obsessive relationship with his sister Dorothy. Separated for long periods in their childhood, they lived together throughout their adult lives. Their friend Thomas De Quincey heard rumors of Wordsworth "having been intimate with his own sister," but put these down to his eccentric habit of kissing female relatives.[38] F. W. Bateson has suggested that at some point William and Dorothy began to fear that they were falling in love, and that Wordsworth's marriage was a desperate attempt to deal with this crisis.[39] On the night before William's wedding, Dorothy slept with the wedding ring on her finger, and the next day she had some sort of breakdown.[40] Clearly William and Dorothy had a complicated emotional relationship, but according to Dorothy Wordsworth's biographer, Frances Wilson, it rested on a very particular romantic ideal: "The relationship between the Wordsworths was organised around a notion of perfect and exclusive brother-sister love which was imaginatively assimilated by them both to the point where it became the source of their creative energy, but its physical expression would have been of no interest to them."[41]

BYRON TRANSFORMED the brother and sister of *The Bride of Abydos* into cousins before publication, so making their romance respectable. (Shortly after the publication of the poem, the lovesick Captain Benwick reads it to Anne in Jane Austen's *Persuasion*.)[42] Characters in Victorian novels sometimes reversed Byron's maneuver: cousins are reclassified as siblings, and therefore they are not to be married. In a novel by Eliza Lynn Linton, *Lizzie Lorton of Grey-*

rigg (1866), a young man learns to respect, in a way to love, his rather plain cousin. "How I wish you were my sister instead of my cousin," he says, to excuse himself from wooing her. The narrator comments that for the sake of her sweet nature many men wanted Margaret as a sister, but that none of them "have yet loved her." But her cousin does marry her in the end. Jane Eyre, however, turns down her cousin St. John Rivers, in whose household she has been given sanctuary. "You have hitherto been my adopted brother—and I, your adopted sister: let us continue as such: you and I had better not marry." Evidently she rejects the moral of the classic nineteenth-century analysis of the difference—and similarities—between siblings and cousins, Jane Austen's *Mansfield Park* (1814).

Mansfield Park opens with an account of three middle-class sisters. The oldest marries Sir Thomas Bertram of Mansfield Park: "All Huntingdon exclaimed on the greatness of the match, and her uncle, the lawyer, himself, allowed her to be at least three thousand pounds short of any equitable claim to it" (that is, around $230,000 today).[43] The second sister marries the vicar of Mansfield, the Rev. Mr. Norris, "a friend of her brother-in-law, with scarcely any private fortune." The third sister makes an unfortunate marriage with a Lieutenant of Marines who becomes disabled from active service but lands her with a child every year for nine years.

Lady Bertram agrees to take in this sister's oldest daughter, Fanny, who is nine years old. Sir Thomas hesitates, but his other sister-in-law, Mrs. Norris, confronts his anxieties.

> You are thinking of your sons—but do not you know that of all things upon earth *that* is the least likely to happen; brought up, as they would be, always together like brothers and sisters? It is morally impossible. I never knew an instance of it. It is, in fact, the only sure way of providing against the connection. Suppose her a pretty girl, and seen by Tom or Edmund for the

first time seven years hence, and I dare say there would be mis-
chief . . . But breed her up with them from this time, and suppose her even to have the beauty of an angel, and she will
never be more to either than a sister.[44]

From the start, as a little girl, Fanny loves the younger Bertram son,
Edmund, but he becomes engaged to the wayward Mary Crawford.
Mary's brother, Henry, woos Fanny but he then runs off with a
married sister of Edmund. Mary Crawford makes light of the elopement. Another of Edmund's sisters forms a scandalous alliance.

Devastated by the disgrace of his sisters, Edmund turns to Fanny.
"She was ready to sink, as she entered the parlour. He was alone,
and met her instantly; and she found herself pressed to his heart with
only these words, just articulate, 'My Fanny—my only sister—my
only comfort now.'" But he realizes that he loves Fanny, and no
longer as a sister. He hopes that Fanny's "warm and sisterly regard
for him would be foundation enough for wedded love."[45]

There is no trouble about parental approval. Sir Thomas's har-
rowing experiences with his daughters have taught him not to be
swayed by position, wealth, and superficial charm, and he is delighted by the match: "Fanny was indeed the daughter that he
wanted."[46] Like Edmund, he has learned that marriage must be
based not on calculation or passionate impulse but on mutual understanding and respect.

The love of Fanny and Edmund is at the opposite pole from a
reckless, short-lived, and potentially destructive passion, exemplified
by the adventures of a Henry Crawford. Jane Austen editorializes
approvingly: "With so much true merit and true love, and no want
of fortune or friends, the happiness of the married cousins must appear as secure as earthly happiness can be."[47]

Fanny also has a real brother, William, from whom she was separated when Fanny was taken to Mansfield Park as a child. William

has since become a sailor. They correspond for seven years while he is at sea, and at last, as the drama begins at Mansfield Park, he comes for a visit. Sharing memories of early childhood, brother and sister are enchanted with each other.

> An advantage this, a strengthener of love, in which even the conjugal tie is beneath the fraternal. Children of the same family, the same blood, with the same first associations and habits, have some means of enjoyment in their power, which no subsequent connexions can supply; and it must be by a long and unnatural estrangement, by a divorce which no subsequent connexion can justify, if such precious remains of the earliest attachments are ever entirely outlived. Too often, alas! it is so. Fraternal love, sometimes almost everything, is at others worse than nothing. But with William and Fanny Price it was still a sentiment in all its prime and freshness, wounded by no opposition of interest, cooled by no separate attachment, and feeling the influence of time and absence only in its increase.[48]

The critic Glenda Hudson discerns an incestuous attraction between William and Fanny, and also between Fanny and Edmund, who had been brought up as brother and sister, and she links the two relationships: "Fanny falls in love with and later marries Edmund as a surrogate for her beloved brother William, for whom she feels an intense attachment. Throughout their long period of separation, Fanny and William relish their schemes to live their lives together in a comfortable little cottage. One critic has even gone so far as to say that William would make an ideal husband for Fanny."[49]

But this is speculation, surely anachronistic, and without any support from Jane Austen. The fraternal love of Fanny and William is explicitly contrasted to conjugal love. As for Fanny and Edmund, they are in a sense both cousins and siblings, and indeed Mary Crawford remarks that they resemble each other. Yet Jane Austen represents their love as natural and healthy, and never hints at any incestuous undertones. Describing the moment when Edmund realizes he is in love with Fanny, she comments, in her authorial voice: "With such a regard for her, indeed, as his had long been, a regard founded on the most endearing claims of innocence and helplessness, and completed by every recommendation of growing worth, what could be more natural than the change?"[50] The change is from a quasi-fraternal to a conjugal love. Edmund once treated Fanny as a young sister, but their mature love is not the same thing at all.

(Three weeks before her marriage, Emma Wedgwood wrote to Charles Darwin, "I am reading *Mansfield Park* which I find very suitable.")[51]

THE THEME of cousins raised together yet falling in love recurs in some of the classic Victorian novels. Indeed, in *Daniel Deronda* (1876), George Eliot replays the scene-setting conversation between Sir Thomas Bertram and his sister-in-law, Mrs. Norris. The Rev. Mr. Gascoigne has agreed to give a home to Gwendolen, the daughter of his wife's younger sister. ("The younger sister had been indiscreet, or at least unfortunate in her marriages.") Mrs. Gascoigne voices the familiar concern: "The boys. I hope they will not be falling in love with Gwendolen." But her husband reassures her.

> Don't presuppose anything of the kind, my dear, and there will be no danger. Rex will never be at home for long together, and Warham is going to India. It is the wiser plan to take it for granted that cousins will not fall in love. If you begin with precautions, the affair will come in spite of them . . . The boys will have nothing, and Gwendolen will have nothing. They can't marry. At the worst there would only be a little crying, and you can't save boys and girls from that.[52]

Reverend Gascoigne does not have any objection in principle to cousin marriage, but, a pragmatist, he "looked at Gwendolen as a

girl likely to make a brilliant marriage. Why should he be expected
to differ from his contemporaries in this matter, and wish his niece a
worse end of her charming maidenhood than they would approve as
the best possible?"[53] Gwendolen does eventually marry for the sake
of money and position, with disastrous consequences.

Cousins brought up in close proximity, even sharing the same wet
nurse, marry, if most unhappily, in *Wuthering Heights*. Yet despite
the classically uncertain origins of the foundling Heathcliff, and not-
withstanding its gothic overtones, the one horror that the novel
spares its readers is incest.

Thackeray's masterpiece, *The History of Henry Esmond*, published
in 1852 but set in the eighteenth century, borrows the classic eighteenth-century plot of the orphaned hero and the reconstituted family. Henry Esmond is the stereotypical mysterious orphan. The novel
ends with his marriage to his cousin's widow, who had been virtually
his foster mother.

Henry Esmond is apparently the illegitimate son of Colonel
Thomas, the second Lord Castlewood. The Colonel's heir is his
brother's son, Frank Esmond. (The Colonel hoped, in vain, that
Frank would marry his daughter.) When Frank succeeds to the title,
Henry is adopted into his cousin's household. On his deathbed,
Colonel Esmond reveals that he had once contracted a secret mar-
riage to Henry's mother. Henry is therefore the legitimate heir to
Castlewood. Henry decides to keep the secret, however, and when
Frank Castlewood dies Henry allows Frank's son to succeed to the
title and inherit the estate.

Relationships in the Castlewood household are now thoroughly
confused. Since Henry Esmond is apparently illegitimate he is "no
relative, though he bore the name and inherited the blood of the
house."[54] He accepts this position because of his love for Frank's
family. His deepest and most enduring attachment is to Frank's wife,
Lady Castlewood. While he is growing up, "'Twas difficult to say
with what a feeling he regarded her . . . a filial tenderness, a love

that was at once respect and protection filled his mind as he thought of her."[55] Henry falls in love with Lady Castlewood's daughter, his cousin Beatrix. Lady Castlewood, now a widow, is jealous, but she seems to support his suit. However, Beatrix turns Henry down. "Why you are old enough and grave enough to be our father," she tells him. "I feel as a sister to you, and can no more. Isn't that enough, sir?"[56] Beatrix grows up to be a cynical courtesan, while Lady Castlewood watches helplessly. "We are like sisters," she tells Henry, "and she the elder sister, somehow."[57] In a rather sudden climax to the novel, Henry and Lady Castlewood marry and emigrate to America, where they build an estate they call "Castlewood," on land in Virginia given to Henry's ancestors by Charles II.

A biographer of Thackeray, Ann Monsarrat, remarks that Thackeray had at first intended to pattern Henry Esmond's relationship with Lady Castlewood on his own tortured relationship with his mother. She judges that his "original intention still lurks in those early chapters, giving the book the lowering air of near-incest that so shocked Victorians, and which still nags uncomfortably at the mind today."[58] However, this "lowering air of near-incest" is not easy to pin down.

Since Lady Castlewood is the widow of Henry's cousin, her marriage to Henry is a sort of cousin marriage. This would not have been regarded as incestuous by the Victorians. On the other hand, Lady Castlewood initially behaved like a stepmother to Henry, and she refers to him several times as her son. When he is grown up, she calls him her brother. The *Edinburgh Review* did object that it was "neither natural nor pleasing" that "a man of forty falls in love with a woman of about fifty, who was the confidant and approver for many years of his love for her own daughter, whom he has always considered and wished to consider, as his mother."[59] But what most disturbed contemporary reviewers was the depiction of mother and daughter as rivals in love.

A critic in the *Westminster Review,* for instance, regretted that "the thoroughly loveable" Lady Castlewood, who was "adorned by so many gracious characteristics," should be placed by Thackeray "in a situation so repugnant to common feeling, as that of being the enamoured consoler of her daughter's lover."[60] Anthony Trollope, who considered *Henry Esmond* to be "the greatest novel in the English language," admitted that "fault has been found with the story, because of the unnatural rivalry,—because it has been felt that a mother's solicitude for her daughter should admit of no such juxtaposition."[61] Yet Trollope himself found nothing reprehensible in the love story, and he admired Thackeray's skill in conveying the "little touches of which the woman is herself altogether unconscious, that gradually turn a love for the boy into a love for the man."[62]

COUSIN MARRIAGE may seem remote and distinctly odd to the modern reader, but perhaps more troubling is the sense that children are exploited by older cousins. Edmund Bertram is a grown man when Fanny comes to Mansfield Park as a child and falls in love with him. "Loving, guiding, protecting her, as he had been doing ever since her being ten years old, her mind in so great a degree formed by his care, and her comfort depending on his kindness, an object to him of such close and peculiar interest, dearer by all his own importance with her than any one else at Mansfield."[63]

And yet the Victorians were not shocked even when adult men groomed girl cousins for marriage. In 1852, Edward White Benson came down from the university and found lodgings with his cousin, his mother's brother's daughter, Mary Sidgwick. He almost immediately began to woo Mary's daughter (also Mary, but known as Minnie), although she was only twelve years old.

> Let me try to recall each circumstance: the arm-chair in which
> I sat, how she sat as usual on my knee, a little fair girl of twelve

with her earnest look, and how I said that I wanted to speak to her of something serious, and then got quietly to the thing, and asked her if she thought it would ever come to pass that we should be married. Instantly, without a word, a rush of tears fell down her cheeks . . . She made no attempt to promise, and said nothing silly or childish, but affected me very much by quietly laying the ends of my handkerchief together and tying them in a knot, and quietly putting them into my hand.[64]

This is jarring to modern sensibilities, but for the Victorians the development from girlish adoration to adult love seemed natural enough. Benson's account is uncannily reminiscent of a scene in Charlotte Brontë's *Villette* (1853), which was published just at the moment when Benson began to flirt with Minnie. In the novel, Graham had known Polly as a child. Reunited as adults, they plan to marry. "He reminded her that she had once gathered his head in her arms, caressed his leonine graces, and cried out, 'Graham, I *do* like you!' He told her how she would set a foot-stool beside him, and climb by its aid to his knee. At this day he could recall the sensation of her little hands smoothing his cheek."[65]

Edward Benson continued to live alongside Minnie and her mother for the next five years. Their engagement was announced when Minnie was seventeen. They married in 1859, when he was twenty-nine and already headmaster of Wellington; Minnie was eighteen.

Benson himself went on to become Archbishop of Canterbury. He wrote emotional, even sensual letters to his wife,[66] but Mary Benson later confessed that she was bullied by her husband and never lost her fear of him.[67] Their son, the novelist A. C. Benson, wondered "if they ever *really* loved. Certainly I never remember them seeking each other's company or wanting to be alone together."[68] And after the death of her husband, Mary had a passionate affair with Lucy Tait, the daughter of Benson's predecessor as Archbishop of Canterbury. None of the six Benson children married, and several showed homosexual leanings—but whatever the reasons for this may have been, it was surely not because their parents were cousins.[69] That at least was nothing to worry about.

CHAPTER TWO

The Law of Incest

$\mathcal{U}$ntil the early nineteenth century, marriage law in England was in the hands of the church. "Adultery was not, bigamy was not, incest was not, a temporal crime," noted Frederic William Maitland, the eminent Victorian legal historian. By the law of England, "fornication, adultery, incest and bigamy were ecclesiastical offences, and the lay courts had nothing to say about them."[1]

But even in the eighteenth century, ecclesiastical regulation was feeble. The very process of marriage had become chaotic. In the first half of the eighteenth century, rogue clergymen operated an informal market in marriages from alehouses around the Fleet Prison, or even inside the prison itself.[2] Some 200,000 to 300,000 "Fleet marriages" were celebrated between 1694 and 1754.[3] A certain Parson Keith offered a comparable service to the upper classes from a base in Mayfair.[4] Similar operations sprang up in other cities. Generally offered at a bargain price, Fleet marriages did not require the publication of banns. Nor did they provide legal registration.

Nonetheless, the church recognized these unions, and also marriages that took place without clergy or witnesses, or against the wishes of parents, so long as both partners were of age and said that they were taking each other as husband and wife.[5] Even then the form of the words was not prescribed, except that bride and groom were particularly required to use the present tense.[6] A mere promise to marry someday was not sufficient. ("Of all the people in the world," Maitland commented, "lovers are the least likely to distinguish precisely between the present and future tenses.")[7] Although such homemade ceremonies might satisfy ecclesiastical requirements, civil courts required more formal proof of marriage when it came to settling questions of paternity or inheritance. Evidence from the Fleet industry was distrusted. The casualness of the procedures, the absence of witnesses, and the lack of proper records also made it difficult to prosecute cases of bigamy. Eventually, the authorities were prodded into action.

Lord Hardwicke's Clandestine Marriages Act of 1753 reaffirmed and codified clerical government of marriage and cracked down on irregular unions.[8] With the exception of Jews and Quakers, everyone now had to be married by the Church of England. This Act discriminated against Catholics and the large and growing constituency of Dissenters. As J. C. D. Clark noted, "Non-Anglicans grew from about ½ million out of 7 million in England and Wales in 1770 to slightly over half the churchgoing population at the 1851 religious census; and over half the population did not then attend church at all."[9] A majority no longer gave willing allegiance to "the confessional state."

Unitarians were given permission to perform their own marriages in 1827. In 1828–29, Dissenters and Catholics were granted full civil rights. Anglican control of marriage and divorce could no longer be sustained, and the Marriage Act of 1836, passed just as Victoria ascended the throne, recognized unions solemnized in Nonconformist or Catholic churches. The Act also made it compulsory to register marriages. Civil registrars were appointed. They could conduct civil marriages and had the power to prevent people from marrying unless they passed certain tests, one of which was a test of incest.[10] In 1857 the Matrimonial Causes Act introduced judicial divorce, and a secular Court for Divorce and Matrimonial Causes was established.

As the tide of secularism rose, there were serious concerns about the possible disestablishment of the Church of England. "The real question that now divides the country and which truly divides the House of Commons, is church or no church," the Duke of Wellington pronounced in 1838. "People talk of the war in Spain, and the Canada question. But all that is of little moment. The real question is church or no church."[11]

The question was never resolved. The upshot was a very English revolution—pragmatic, piecemeal, largely unacknowledged. As far as possible, direct confrontation was avoided and questions of principle left unresolved. The transfer of control of marriage from church to state was gradual. Parliament directed the new Court for Divorce and Matrimonial Causes to "proceed and act and give relief on principles and rules which . . . shall be as nearly as may be conformable to the principles and rules on which the Ecclesiastical Courts have heretofore acted and given relief."[12]

And yet there was no disguising the tectonic shift from religious to secular control of family law. Conflicts could not always be fudged. As Maitland pointed out, "Marriage is not a matter that can be left to judicial discretion or natural equity. It is preeminently a matter about which there must be hard and fast rules."[13] Secular canons had to be worked out, but this was not always easy. The establishment of a new doctrine proved to be most problematic when it came to incest.

FOR MOST of a very long period, stretching from the twelfth century until the early twentieth century, lay courts in England did not prosecute cases of incest. In Scotland incest had been a capital offense since the Reformation, and remained so until 1887.[14] In England, however, it was a matter for the ecclesiastical courts, and they treated incest simply as a form of fornication or adultery. By the sixteenth century prosecutions were rare,[15] and the penalties were light. In 1571 the authorities directed churchwardens faced with a case of incest to issue a "brotherly and friendly" warning. If the couple persisted, they were to be warned "sharply and vehemently." Only if that did not cause the sinners to mend their ways were they to be excluded from communion and required to perform a penance.[16]

Under Cromwell, the state took a censorious, obsessive interest in sexual matters. There was agitation to define incest more precisely, to extend the prohibitions, and to treat transgressors as criminals. In 1650 an act was passed "for suppressing the detestable sins of incest, adultery and fornication." Brothel keeping was severely punished. Incest and adultery now carried the death penalty.[17] There were only a handful of prosecutions for incest, however, and the death penalty was hardly ever actually imposed either for incest or for adultery.[18]

Official attitudes changed decisively after the collapse of the Republic and the coronation of Charles II. The Restoration court was anything but puritanical. Sir William Blackstone remarked in his monumental *Commentaries on the Laws of England* that "men from an abhorrence of the hypocrisy of the late times fell into a contrary extreme, of licentiousness, [and] it was not thought proper to renew a law of such unfashionable rigour. And these offences have been ever since left to the feeble coercion of the spiritual court, according to the rules of the canon law."[19]

By the late eighteenth century, when Blackstone was writing, the powers of the spiritual courts were indeed feeble, and their sanctions against fornication and even incest did not frighten most people. Fanny Burney's brother, James—who had sailed with Captain Cook—eloped with his half-sister in 1798 and lived with her for the next five years. People were scandalized, but the couple could not be punished by the courts.[20] Indeed, James eventually became an Admiral. Rather spookily, Fanny Burney's novel *Evelina*, published a decade before her brother's elopement, features a desperate man who finds himself in love with two women, both of whom he suspects to be his half-sisters. (One, fortunately, is not.)

In 1815–16 Lord Byron's estranged wife spread the story of his affair with his married half-sister, Augusta Leigh. Lady Byron also fed rumors that he had male lovers. Political opponents stoked the scandal—Byron once made a list of "the different worthies, ancient and modern" to whom he was compared in the press, a catalogue that included Henry VIII, George III, Caligula, Epicurus, and Nero.[21] Eventually he agreed to a separation, allowing his wife to keep their child, and he was effectively driven into exile.

His friend and biographer Thomas Moore noted that Byron's departure "had not even the dignity of appearing voluntary, as the excommunicating voice of society left him no other resource."[22] But Byron did not fear prosecution for incest.[23] The more dangerous charge against him was sodomy, which was a capital offense.[24] (Moore says that only his rank protected Byron from the law.)[25] Of course, Byron liked to flirt with disaster. It was at the height of his affair with Augusta that he wrote *The Bride of Abydos* (1813), which celebrated a love affair between a brother and sister. The heroine was based on Augusta. He did turn the lovers into cousins in the published version, however.

It was not only the upper classes who got away with incest. In the early nineteenth century a Somerset vicar railed in his diary: "That Villain Porter had the impudence to come [to church], it disconcerted me very much. His own daughter confesses herself to be with child by him. Oh Abominable Villain. I will punish him if there is any law to be had."[26] But there was not. As late as 1851 the House of Lords granted a man a divorce from his wife on the grounds of adultery, but did not remark on the fact—which came out at the trial—that her lover was her own full brother.[27]

An incestuous marriage was a more serious matter. Polly Morris found several instances of church marriages between step-brothers and sisters in Somerset in the eighteenth century, although the couple would generally take the precaution of marrying in a large parish where they were not known.[28] Nevertheless, a marriage within the prohibited degrees of relationship was always vulnerable. If challenged in the courts, it would be declared void. The wife would find herself unmarried, the children illegitimate.

When Moll Flanders, the heroine of Daniel Defoe's picaresque novel, discovers that her third husband is in fact her brother, she decides to keep it a secret from him. "I liv'd therefore in open avowed Incest and Whoredom, and all under the appearance of an honest Wife; and tho' I was not much touched with the Crime of it, yet the Action had something in it shocking to Nature, and made my Husband, as he thought himself even nauseous to me."[29] But Moll knows that she cannot be prosecuted for "the Crime of it." Her most urgent concern is that her husband might have the marriage annulled. If he "should take the Advantage the Law would give him, he might put me away with disdain, and leave me to Sue for the little Portion that I had, and perhaps waste it all in the Suit, and then be a Beggar; the Children would be ruin'd too, having no legal Claim to any of his Effects."[30]

NOT ONLY was there no crime of incest, but the English were uncertain as to what did, and what should, constitute incest. Incest was defined as an act of sexual intercourse between related persons whom the church prohibited from marrying. This might seem straightforward enough, but the doctrine was mired in centuries of theological argument, and the rules were occasionally stretched to accommodate the diplomatic needs of kings and princes. It was not always evident why a particular marriage was allowed or forbidden, or when the Pope might give dispensation for a marriage that was otherwise prohibited.

The English law on incest had been amended after the Reformation. However, the rationale of even the reformed code was difficult to grasp for anybody not versed in canon law. Why did Protestants allow the marriage of cousins, which was prohibited by the Catholic church? The rules with respect to relatives-in-law were particularly baffling. Two brothers could marry two sisters, yet if your wife died you could not marry her sister.

The doctrine on incest was based in the first instance on Leviticus 18:6–18. These verses prohibited sexual intercourse with certain close kin and with the wife of a father, a son, or a brother. But there was nothing against the marriage of cousins, and indeed the Bible was full of examples of cousin marriages, most famously the marriages of Jacob to his mother's brother's two daughters, Leah and Rachel. And while the Bible forbade the marriage of a woman to her nephew, it was silent on the marriage of a man to a niece. According to Josephus, such marriages were commonplace among Jewish aristocrats.[31]

Cousin marriage was also permitted in Athens in the fourth century B.C., and uncle-niece marriage was "relatively common."[32] But Church law was built in particular on Roman law, and the Romans kept changing their minds about marriage between kin. Marriage between cousins and also between uncles and nieces had once been banned in Rome. At some point, cousin marriages came to be tolerated. Then the emperor Claudius had the law altered so that he could marry his niece Agrippina, his brother's daughter. A supporter of Claudius urged the Senate to abandon their old prejudices: "Marriages to the daughters of our brothers are new to us. Yet in other countries they are regular and lawful. Here also, unions between cousins, long unknown, have become frequent in course of time. Customs change as utility requires, and this innovation too will take root."[33]

In fact, the opposite happened when the Roman emperors became Christians. According to Gibbon:

> Justinian's Code forbade marriage between blood relatives in the direct line of ascent and descent, between brothers and sisters, and between uncle and niece, nephew and aunt. The Trullan synod of 692 extended the prohibition to first cousins; the Ecloga went further and forbade the marriage of second cousins. These prohibitions were preserved by the Macedonian Emperors, and it was generally recognised that marriages within the 6th degree were illegal. It was even regarded as a question whether marriages in the 7th degree were permissible. They were forbidden by the Church in the 11th century, and this decision was confirmed by the Emperor Manuel.[34]

The Lateran Council of 1215 ruled that marriages between second cousins were null, but there was continuing uncertainty in the Roman church about marriages between more distant cousins. In the mid-sixteenth century the Council of Trent decreed that third cousins could be married, while first and second cousins could not.[35] Admittedly, this rule had no foundation in scripture. It was ecclesiastical, not divine or natural law. The Pope could accordingly grant dispensations for marriages between first or second cousins, or, where reasons of state made it advisable, even for a marriage between an uncle and a niece.

The rules were still more complicated where people related by marriage were concerned. In Leviticus, sexual relations were banned between a man and a woman who had been married to his father, son, or brother. Catholic doctrine extended the prohibition to the wives of more distant relatives. These more extensive prohibitions were derived from scriptural doctrines, but indirectly. Adam described Eve as "bone of my bones, and flesh of my flesh." Genesis 2:24 added a peremptory commentary: "Therefore shall a man leave his father and his mother, and shall cleave unto his wife; and they shall be one flesh." This text is referred to several times in the New Testament (in Matthew 19:6, Mark 10:8, and Ephesians 5:31). The verses underpinned the doctrine of "couverture," which became a cornerstone of the Catholic conception of marriage: the wife was part of the husband's body (he, however, was the head).

The Catholic church built on this doctrine to introduce restrictions on marriage with relatives-in-law beyond the range defined in Leviticus. It was reasoned that if your spouse was your flesh and bone, it followed that your wife's sister was your sister. Equally, your brother counted as the brother of your wife. For a man to have an affair with his wife's sister was as bad as having an affair with his own sister. Indeed, there was no difference between these offenses. Similarly, a woman who had sexual relations with a husband's brother was in principle committing incest with her own brother.

It was the act of sexual intercourse that made husband and wife "one flesh." According to Catholic doctrine, sexual intercourse created kinship even between the most casual of lovers.[36] This doctrine was accepted in English law until civil courts took over the divorce jurisdiction. In 1861, in *Wing v. Taylor*, a man sued for the annulment of his marriage because he had previously slept with his wife's mother. When the case came before the new probate and divorce court, which had been created in 1858, Judge Cresswell ruled that "marriage as well as carnal knowledge was necessary to create affinity so as to bring parties within the prohibited degrees."[37]

IT WAS the doctrine on incest that precipitated England's break with Rome. Henry VIII's first wife, Katherine of Aragon, bore him five children but only one, a daughter, Mary, survived. When it became clear that she could not have any more children, the king sought an annulment of the marriage on the grounds that Katherine had previously been engaged to his elder brother, Arthur, who had died at the age of fifteen. On some interpretations she was therefore his brother's widow—and so Henry's "sister"—and could not be married to him. The Pope had granted a dispensation for the marriage, but Henry argued that even the Pope could not waive the law of God.[38] This challenge to papal authority led to the separation of the Church of England from Rome. (One wit remarked that "the King divorced from lady *Katharine* and from the Pope, both at the same time.")[39]

After the divorce Henry married Anne Boleyn. She had a daughter, Elizabeth, but no sons, and Henry was impelled to move on once again. His first thought was to have his marriage to Anne annulled on the grounds that her sister Mary had been his mistress, but he eventually chose to have Anne executed on a charge of incestuous adultery with her own brother. Henry's third wife, Jane Seymour, bore a son, Edward, but she died within a fortnight of giving birth. Henry's fourth wife, Anne of Cleves, a German princess, was soon sent packing. The king claimed that the marriage had not been consummated.

Henry's fifth marriage, to Katherine Howard, posed a more troublesome legal problem. Katherine was a first cousin of one of his former wives, Anne Boleyn. (Katherine's father and Anne's mother were brother and sister. Their common grandfather was Thomas Howard, Duke of Norfolk.) Katherine therefore counted as a first cousin of Henry, on the principle that man and wife were "one flesh." As the law stood, he could not marry her. He duly set about having the law changed.

In 1540 the English parliament passed a statute which stipulated that "all persons be lawful that be not prohibited by God's law to marry; and that no reservation or prohibition, God's law except, shall trouble or impeach any marriage without the Levitical degrees."[40] Since marriages between first cousins were not prohibited in Leviticus, they were now to be permitted. This cleared the way for Henry's marriage to Katherine later that same year.

Henry's motives for the reform were obviously worldly, but Protestant authorities tended to agree that only those marriages prohibited in the Bible should be forbidden. Nowhere did the Bible indicate that cousin marriage was undesirable.[41] Indeed, some Puritans read the scriptures as showing that the parents of Jesus were first cousins.[42] The Catholic prohibition on marriage with a cousin was pilloried as a trick to extort cash for dispensations. To be sure, not all the reformers agreed on these questions, and some influential Calvinist writers disapproved of all close-kin marriages.[43]

In any case, the law remained uncertain for many years, as, indeed, did the fate of the Tudor dynasty. The youthful Edward VI briefly became king, closely supervised by regents. When he died in 1553 he was succeeded by Henry's oldest child, Mary, the daughter of Katherine of Aragon. A devout Catholic, Mary tried to bring about an English counter-reformation in partnership with her husband, Philip II of Spain. She lost no time in revoking the statutes that Henry had passed in order to divorce her mother and, later, to allow himself to marry his "cousin" Katherine Howard.

Mary died in 1558 and was succeeded by Elizabeth, Henry's daughter by Anne Boleyn. Elizabeth restored Henry's statutes. However, they were ad hoc measures that had been passed to resolve particular problems raised by the king's marriages, and the law of incest remained confused. The church courts struggled with some high-profile cases—notably the marriage of the Earl of Westmorland to the sister of his deceased wife.[44] Complaining of "a sea of perplexities,"[45] Archbishop Parker compiled a "Table of Kindred and Affinity." Published in the *Book of Common Prayer* from 1563, and displayed in every church, the Table listed sixty categories of relatives with whom marriage was prohibited: thirty for a man and a matching thirty for a woman. Marriage with a wife's sister or husband's brother was forbidden. Nor could a man marry his niece or his aunt.[46] But cousin marriage was permitted.

This was fortunate, since James I, who succeeded Elizabeth, was the son of first cousins. But not everyone was satisfied by the new laws, not even all Protestants. Under Cromwell, there were moves to broaden the incest prohibitions. Even after the Restoration, a desultory debate about the prohibited degrees continued in theological circles. In 1669, however, Chief Justice Vaughan ruled that Henry's statute allowed first cousins to marry.[47] This judgment was nicely timed: in 1677 William, Prince of Orange, married Mary, the daughter of his mother's brother, James, Duke of York (later James II). In 1689, William and Mary ascended the English throne together.

HENRY'S REFORMS left untouched the Catholic restrictions on marriage with relatives-in-law. Indeed, the Tudors found these prohibitions rather convenient. After all, this was the doctrine on which Henry relied in order to have his marriage to Katherine of Aragon annulled. When Anne Boleyn's daughter, Elizabeth, became Queen, she very naturally endorsed the ban of marriage with the sister of a deceased wife, or indeed the brother of a deceased husband. She later excused herself from marrying Philip II of Spain because he had been married to her sister Mary.

Nevertheless, the theological basis for these prohibitions was shaky. Some authorities fell back on the doctrine that husband and wife were one flesh. A man's wife's sister, or his brother's wife, was therefore no different from his own sister. But had this principle been applied in biblical times? A key text was Leviticus 18:18: "Neither shalt thou take a wife to her sister, to vex her, to uncover her nakedness, beside the other in her life time." This reads as if it was addressed to a polygamist, warning him not to marry two sisters. On the other hand, the Bible offered the confusing example of Jacob, who was polygamously married to two sisters, his cousins Leah and Rachel. Moreover, the phrase "in her life time" suggested that the prohibition on marrying a wife's sister fell away after the death of the wife. Everything hinged on the correct translation of the Hebrew—a matter of some dispute, particularly before the Authorized translation of the Old Testament was issued in 1611.

The ban on a marriage with a brother's wife was even more difficult to justify on biblical grounds, since Deuteronomy 25:5–6 made it the duty of a younger brother to "raise up seed" with the widow of an older brother, at least in certain circumstances.[48] Theologians debated the correct doctrine, but warily. After all, the legitimacy of the royal succession rested upon it.

These taboos became a common theme in Tudor and Jacobean drama; Hamlet's denunciation of his mother for marrying her deceased husband's brother is only the most famous example.[49] Incestuous adultery was especially piquant. According to gossip, Henry VIII had slept with Anne Boleyn's sister, and perhaps even with her mother. In an early English best-seller, Aphra Behn's *Love Letters Between a Nobleman and His Sister* (1684), a married aristocrat has an affair with his sister-in-law, the "sister" of the title. (The novel was based on the trial of Lord Grey of Werke in 1683. He eloped with the sister of his wife. The charge was seduction, but the incest added spice to the scandal.)[50] Elizabeth Haywood's *The Mercenary Lover* (1726) depicts a man who marries an heiress for her money. He then seduces her sister and makes her pregnant. He tells her that "the Ties of Blood or Affinity were but imaginary Bars to Love," revealing what a villain he is. He finally persuades the unfortunate young woman to rewrite her will in his favor. Then he poisons her.[51]

And yet there were perfectly respectable reasons for a man to marry his sister-in-law. When a wife died, leaving young children, an unmarried sister might move in to look after the family. A marriage then often suited all concerned. As the law stood, however, such a marriage was forbidden.

This prohibition began to be questioned in the eighteenth century. A tract published in 1774 blamed the prohibition on marriage with a deceased wife's sister on "the absurdities of crafty and designing priests." Its author complained that the issue had been little discussed,[52] but *The Gentleman's Magazine* had published a series of letters on the topic between 1746 and 1750, reflecting a growing public interest.[53] A century later, a full-blooded national debate erupted. It was one of the most divisive and long-running controversies in Victorian England.

THE IDEA that a brother-in-law or a sister-in-law was very like a brother or a sister had some purchase in England. At least among the gentry, brothers-in-law were called "brother" and sisters-in-law "sister"—Jane Austen's novels give ample instances of this usage.[54] Nevertheless, everyday experience suggested that sisters-in-law were very different from real flesh-and-blood sisters. And the Common Law reflected this. For instance, a wife's sister had no claim when it came to inheritance.

"Men will not regard their sisters-in-law as their sisters, let the Statute book and the Prayer-book together affirm it ever so strenuously," an MP remarked during the debate on the Deceased Wife's Sister Bill in 1873.[55] Lord Gage pressed the point when the House of Lords debated the measure. "Are sisters-in-law sisters?" he inquired. "This is just what they are not." Cousins were surely more closely related, yet they could marry. "It is a curious idea of incest," Gage concluded, "to call it incest to marry an alien in blood when it is not incest to marry with a first cousin."[56] A member of Parliament demanded "what argument applied against contracting marriage with a wife's sister which would not equally operate against marriages with first cousins?"[57] The radical John Bright suggested that if anything, it was the marriage of cousins that constituted a problem. "Was there any man of common-sense who would not say that on every natural ground the marriage of first cousins was more objectionable than the marriage of a man with his deceased wife's sister?"[58]

Opinion was divided even within the church. Some clergymen were ready to marry a man to his dead wife's sister. If necessary, a couple could usually find a city church where their relationship was unknown. And yet a marriage within the prohibited degrees was "voidable": an ecclesiastical court could declare that no marriage had been contracted, and order the couple to separate and to perform penance. Anyone could challenge such marriages at any stage. Since the legal status of a voidable marriage was never secure, the legitimacy of the children could be impugned, in order to exclude them from inheritance of property or succession to a title. Blackmail was a real risk. Nevertheless, Parliament took up the matter only when a very influential man found himself in difficulties.

After the death of his wife, the seventh Duke of Beaufort married her half-sister. This second marriage produced his only son. As the law stood, anybody could challenge the legitimacy of the son and so block his succession to the title. In 1835 Lord Lyndhurst, a former Lord Chancellor, set about finding a way to help the Beauforts. He drafted a Marriage Act which had the sole purpose of relieving the Duke's concern. "Lord Lyndhurst's Act" granted recognition to any marriage within the prohibited degrees that was extant before August 31, 1835.

The deadline was crucial. According to one MP, the bill was "passed with little discussion, and in the last hours of a session protracted into the month of August."[59] In the course of the desultory debate, conservatives insisted that the law should be effective only retrospectively. They also tacked on an extra clause which provided that in the future, any marriage contracted within the prohibited degrees was to be void from the very start.

Evidently a deal was made: Lord Lyndhurst got his client off the hook, but the church hardened its stance. Some members apparently went along with the Act on the understanding that a new law would be passed to permit marriage with a deceased wife's sister.[60] However, the Archdeacon of London told the Royal Commission in 1848 that Parliament's intention had been "to strengthen not alter the old law."[61] That was indeed the paradoxical effect of Lord Lyndhurst's Act. For the following six decades, marriage with a deceased wife's sister was not recognized by the English courts.

The consequences were disastrous. Half a century later, a Home Office memo gloomily reviewed the long-term effects of the Act:

> What had before been a somewhat loose and uncertain prohibition became part of the regular law of the land. The English law became at once the most rigid in respect of such prohibitions in force in any civilized country. At a time when many churches relaxed their rule by dispensations, and most countries had allowed wide liberty in this matter, the Canon Law of the English Church was made of binding force even over members of persuasions which tolerated these connections, or approved them.[62]

It was not only "members of other persuasions" who tolerated such marriages. Even after the passage of Lord Lyndhurst's Act, unions with a deceased wife's sister were far and away the most common marriages within the prohibited degrees. A Royal Commission found that there were 1,364 unions within the prohibited degrees in five districts in England between 1835 and 1848, and 90 percent of these were with the deceased wife's sister. The investigators were certain that they had undercounted irregular marriages because of the stigma associated with them.[63] And they found that very respectable men—lawyers, officers, even clergymen—had contracted such marriages.[64]

Matthew Boulton and Richard Lovell Edgeworth, friends of Erasmus Darwin and Josiah Wedgwood, and fellow members of the Lunar Society, both married their deceased wife's sisters.[65] Matthew Boulton's capital came largely from his two wives. The first Mrs. Boulton was a distant cousin. After her death, in about 1767, he married her younger sister. His brother-in-law opposed the marriage because his sisters stood to inherit a substantial sum from the family estate. The younger sister would now get the first Mrs. Boulton's share as well, and it too would pass under Boulton's control. In the end, Boulton was able to marry her with the approval of his mother-in-law.[66]

When Edgeworth's wife was dying in childbirth in 1773, she had urged her husband to marry her younger sister. There was, however, a public fuss about the propriety of the marriage. Edgeworth took on the Bishop of Lichfield in a series of ill-tempered exchanges in a Birmingham newspaper. Wedgwood heard a rumor that they had gone to Scotland to marry, but on Matthew Boulton's advice they went to London, where there was nobody to oppose the banns.[67]

The matching restriction on marriage with a brother's widow was apparently less troublesome, or at least less commonly breached,[68] but the public followed with glee the Regency comedy of the Waldegrave brothers. In 1839 Frances Braham, the enchanting daughter of a celebrated Jewish tenor, married John Waldegrave, illegitimate son of the sixth Earl Waldegrave. John was extremely handsome, but dissolute. Within a year he died from drink, leaving a substantial fortune to his widow.

Almost immediately John's elder brother, the seventh earl, proposed to Frances. She agreed that she would marry him unless it was forbidden in the Bible, and was reported to be making an assiduous study of the Book of Leviticus. For his part,

Lord Waldegrave was almost daily with his lawyer, and had the wording of the Marriage Act of 1835 as word perfect as Frances had her Bible. John's marriage had not been consummated in view of his health. The disastrous Act of '35 excluded Scotland. John had no legal status. The lawyer . . . found every proof that this marriage would be valid.[69]

Every part of this advice was unreliable. It might also have been objected that Frances was still a minor, and that she did not have her father's consent to this marriage. Nevertheless, five months after John's death, Frances married Lord Waldegrave in Edinburgh. The couple passed the next six months in prison, where Lord Waldegrave served a sentence for assaulting a policeman during celebrations following the Derby. After six years of marriage Lord Waldgrave died, and Frances inherited his estates. Only twenty-six years old, and now thanks to the legacies from her two husbands a substantial landowner with an income of around £20,000,[70] Frances married a sixty-year-old Member of Parliament, Granville Harcourt, and became a notable political hostess.

AFFLUENT PEOPLE regularly traveled abroad to marry in order to evade the English restrictions; a favored venue was Altona in Schleswig Holstein (then part of Denmark). Such marriages became problematic after the passage of Lord Lyndhurst's Act, and for many years their legal status was uncertain, but in 1861 the House of Lords ruled that even if a marriage with a deceased wife's sister was legally contracted abroad, it was invalid in England *(Brook v. Brook)*. In 1888 a distinguished émigré artist, Sir Hubert von Herkomer, married his deceased wife's sister in Germany, but he had to renounce his British citizenship in order to protect the marriage.[71] British citizens, however, still took their chances with the law, the Huxleys among others. Thomas Henry Huxley accompanied his daughter, Ethel Gladys, to Norway in 1889, where she married the portrait painter John Collier. He had been married previously to her sister Marian, who had died two years earlier.

Lord Lyndhurst's Act created so many problems that Parliament soon found itself bombarded with petitions demanding reform.[72] In 1847, a Royal Commission was set up to investigate "the state and operation of the Law of Marriage as relating to the prohibited degrees of affinity." Its conclusions favored the legalization of marriage with a deceased wife's sister, and the arguments it put forward would be repeated again and again for the six decades that intervened before the law was reformed.

First, the commissioners pointed out that marriage with a deceased wife's sister was legal in many British colonies, in most European countries, and in the United States. After the American Revolution, the northern states had dropped the most irksome prohibitions on affinal marriage. Most of the states that joined the Union in the nineteenth century relaxed prohibitions on marriages with relatives-in-law, or got rid of them altogether; Kansas even allowed a marriage between a step-parent and child.[73] Judge Story of the United States Supreme Court described marriages with the deceased wife's sister as "the very best sort of marriages," and added that "nothing is more common in almost all of the States of America than second marriages of this sort."[74]

Moreover, such marriages might offer an efficient solution to a very real crisis. If a woman died in childbirth, or when her children were young, a widowed or unmarried female relative had to be drafted to help out. When Edward Austen's wife died suddenly in 1808, his mother and his sisters, Jane and Cassandra Austen, moved to live close to him so that they could assist with the children. After the Rev. Patrick Brontë lost his wife in 1821, her sister joined the household to look after the family, which included the young Charlotte, Emily, Branwell, and Anne.

There was an abundant supply of unmarried sisters and sisters-in-law. In 1851, 32 percent of women over the age of thirty had never married. The proportion rose through the rest of the century; by 1891, 44 percent of the cohort had never married.[75] Many spinsters lived with their brothers or brothers-in-law, particularly if the head of the household was unmarried—in half of the upper-middle-class households that included an unmarried sister or sister-in-law, the male head of the household was a bachelor or a widower.[76] The spinster found a home, the widower someone to manage the household and to care for any children.

And it often suited all concerned if the widower then married his sister-in-law. "Many conveniences may result from it," John Alleyne had urged in 1774. "Experience teaches us that the aunt, however kind as such, becomes the most affectionate mother-in-law [i.e., stepmother]; the severe loss of the husband is in some degree mitigated; and the hope of her children being tenderly bred, comforts, in the moment of departure, the expiring mother."[77] The commissioners agreed: "In all cases where there are children of a tender age, there is a vacancy made by the death of the wife which her sister appears, above all persons, qualified to supply."[78]

A dying woman might even urge her husband to take this step, as did the first Mrs. Edgeworth. Thomas Hardy presents a macabre and melodramatic instance in the climactic act of *Tess of the d'Urbervilles* (1891). As Tess awaits execution, she begs her husband to marry her younger sister. He is horrified. "If I lose you I lose all! And she is my sister-in-law." "That's nothing, dearest. People marry their sisters-in-law continually around Marlott."[79]

Such a marriage could be represented as an act of fidelity on the part of the sister: she was taking on her late sister's duties and honoring her memory. The husband, for his part, was perpetuating his marriage. "It would be repugnant to my feeling to displace old associations, and to seek marriage elsewhere," a solicitor who had himself married his dead wife's sister remarked to the commissioners. "I could not do it. My wife's sister disturbs nothing; she is already in the place of my wife."[80] Reformers pointed out that the widower and his wife's sister would typically be of mature years, motivated by duty rather than passion.[81]

Still, it was not an altogether respectable option. Another brother of Jane Austen, Charles, who rose in the navy to become an Admiral, took in his wife's sister to look after the children when he was widowed. He married her in 1820. The lady was not popular with his brothers and sisters, but their mother, Mrs. Austen, was more charitable. "Charles has certainly secured a careful and attentive mother to his children for such she has proved herself during the almost six years she has had the charge of them." She admitted to relief that the couple were living some distance away for the time being, but she was confident that "by and bye wonder and censure will subside and in a year or two he may be willing to change his station for one nearer his family and friends. I hope they will be happy."[82]

BUT POWERFUL voices were raised against reform. Gladstone warned the House of Commons in 1849 that "the purity of sisterly love itself . . . was threatened to be tainted by the invasion of possible jealousies."[83] This fear was widely shared. Harriet Martineau's novel *Deerbrook* (1839) dramatized the hidden rivalry between two sisters. Margaret lives with her cash-strapped sister and her husband, sharing the household expenses. Her sister's husband falls in love with her and struggles with his feelings, of which Margaret remains unaware.

Henry James tells the story of an English gentleman, a Mr. Lloyd, who comes to New England. Two sisters compete jealously for him. He marries the younger sister, Perdita. She dies in childbirth. The elder sister, Rosalind, moves in—ostensibly to help with the child—and they marry. There was nothing against it in the law of Massachusetts. Nevertheless, it wasn't quite right. "They were married, as was becoming, with great privacy—almost with secrecy—in the hope perhaps, as was waggishly remarked at the time, that the late Mrs. Lloyd wouldn't hear of it." When Rosalind opens the trunk in which Perdita's jewels and clothes were locked, she is strangled by her sister's ghost.[84]

In *The Battle of Life* (1846), Charles Dickens described a woman who was in love with her sister's husband. There may have been an element of autobiography: gossip suggested that Dickens himself was risking his marriage for an affair with his sister-in-law, Georgina Hogarth. (Thackeray stoutly denied it. "No says I no such thing— its with an actress.")[85] A similar triangle features in Geraldine Jewsbury's *The Half-Sisters* (1848), and in Elizabeth Gaskell's *Wives and Daughters* (1866).[86]

The most unyielding opponents of reform, however, appealed to doctrine. Dr. Pusey, professor of theology at Oxford and a leader of the Oxford Movement, warned that a change in the law would put the very sacrament of marriage in danger. "Those who deny that the sister is akin to the husband, must deny that the husband and wife are really one, and so at once strike at the very root of the holiness and mysteriousness of marriage."[87] As late as 1903, Winston Churchill would tell the House of Commons that it was bound to defend "the principle . . . that when a man and a woman were married they became as one," and that in consequence "any person the man could not marry by reason of consanguinity to himself he could also not marry if similarly related to his wife."[88]

A NUMBER of Victorian novels dramatized the arguments concerning marriage with a deceased wife's sister.[89] They often made ironic play of the fact that while marriage was banned with a sister-in-law, marriage with a first cousin was permitted, even favored.

Felicia Skene, an associate of the Oxford Movement, published

The Inheritance of Evil in 1849, just after the Royal Commission recommended to Parliament that the law be changed to allow marriage with the deceased wife's sister. *The Inheritance of Evil* is a tract in the form of a novella. Two sisters are orphaned. The elder, Elizabeth, is engaged to Richard Clayton, the weak and idle son of an upstanding clergyman. Elizabeth's younger sister, Agnes, comes to visit. She has become a beauty, and "an indescribable pang shot through [Elizabeth's] heart;—her future husband was standing with his eyes fixed on Agnes, gazing at her with a look of the most warm and unqualified admiration, a look such as had never been bestowed on herself!"

> But in another instant she repelled this unworthy feeling almost with horror, for she remembered how, in a very few days, Richard Clayton would hold for Agnes Maynard the sacred name of **brother.** They twain were about to be made by a most holy ordinance **ONE FLESH,** and from that hour **her** sister must be **his** sister also, in the sight of God and man. Her cheek burned with a flush of shame, to think that she should have harboured for one moment what was in truth an unholy thought; and taking Richard by the hand, she drew him towards Agnes, and prayed him to love their sister dearly for her sake.[90]

Elizabeth soon dies, leaving a daughter. Richard marries Agnes, but finds that the whole village has turned against him and his wife. They have a son, but he dies. "And from that hour Richard and his wife repented them of the **deed** which they had done, because the world had visited them heavily for it; but they repented not yet of the **crime,** for the judgment of God was still to come."[91] That is, the sin of the parents is visited upon the children. Richard's daughter by Elizabeth becomes engaged to an aristocrat. When his parents find out the shocking truth about her father's ménage, they refuse to allow the marriage. The unfortunate girl drowns herself, and Richard perishes in an unsuccessful attempt to save her.

On the whole, better writers took the side of reform. Dinah Mulock Craik was a successful novelist whose *John Halifax, Gentleman,* published in 1856, was one of the great Victorian best-sellers. She published a propagandist serial in *Macmillan's Magazine* in 1869–70 in support of the Married Women's Property Act. In 1871, she tackled the topic of marriage with the deceased wife's sister in an ambitious three-volume novel, *Hannah.*

Hannah is described as "middle-aged" (she is thirty years old). She has been in love only once, with an invalid cousin, "who, from his extreme gentleness and delicacy of health, was less like a brother than a sister—ay, even after he changed into a lover."[92] (He dies young.) Hannah's sister is married to a respectable clergyman, Rivers. (These novels are full of cross-references: Jane Eyre's cousin, whom she nearly marries, is a puritanical Christian, St. John Rivers.) Hannah meets her brother-in-law for the first time only after her sister's death: there can be no suspicion of a prior flirtation. She is deeply attached to her sister's child, cherishes her sister's memory, and sees no moral barrier to marriage with Rivers. "Now what was he? Not her brother—except by a legal fiction, which he had himself recognised as a fiction."[93]

Subplots explore variations on the theme. A sister of Rivers is married to a Mr. Melville. Melville's parentage is relevant: his mother was his father's deceased wife's sister. They were married in 1834 and so benefited from Lord Lyndhurst's amnesty. "Then what was right one year was wrong the next?" Hannah asks, ironically.[94] But Melville's own marriage provides a cautionary tale. His wife is an invalid, and he flirts with her three younger sisters. Another subplot tells the story of a working-class man who persuades his dead wife's sister to marry him. Later he deserts her, telling her that it was never a legal marriage.

In the end Hannah and Rivers emigrate to France, where they can marry and live together legally. Soon after *Hannah* was published, a close friend of Dinah Craik traveled to Switzerland to marry her late sister's widower. Dinah Craik accompanied her. This was a brave act, for the marriage aroused strong feelings. The widower in question was the pre-Raphaelite artist Holman Hunt. He and his friend, the sculptor Thomas Woolner, had married two sisters. When Hunt married the third sister (Dinah Craik's friend), the men quarreled and never spoke again. Hunt was also shunned by a shocked Christina Rossetti.

Hannah's thesis was nicely parodied by Matthew Arnold: "The place of poor Mrs. Bottles will be taken by her sister Hannah, whom you have just seen. Nothing could be more proper; Mrs. Bottles wishes it, Miss Hannah wishes it, this reverend friend of the family [a Baptist minister], who has made a marriage of the same kind, wishes it, everybody wishes it."[95] Other novelists followed Dinah Craik, however, dramatizing the private anguish that the law had caused.

William Russell Clark, best known for his novels on the merchant navy, published a novel actually entitled *The Deceased Wife's Sister* in 1874. Despite the title, this is no tract; the moral is ambiguous. Again, the protagonists are two orphaned sisters. They live with a difficult and overbearing aunt. Her son wants to marry his cousin Maggie, the younger of the two sisters. Maggie believes that he is merely sorry for her and turns him down. The older sister, Kate, marries a Major Rivers. (His name is—hardly by chance—the same as Hannah's husband in Craik's novel.) They invite Maggie to live with them, but she refuses. Kate dies, and Maggie and her aunt take in the baby. Maggie is attracted to Rivers and eventually marries him. She is happy at first, but then Kate's son dies. Rivers and Maggie have a daughter, but she is born blind and deformed (precisely the sort of consequence popularly expected of an incestuous union). Rivers abandons Maggie for another woman. Maggie is reunited with her cousin. Rivers is killed in a duel. The cousins marry.

It is a final irony that Maggie's marriage with a cousin is completely acceptable to the society that had hounded her for marrying her brother-in-law. The point is made again and again in these novels. Hannah's innocent romance with her cousin is another example. Elsewhere in that novel, a woman is warned against going to live with her deceased sister's husband: it might lead to marriage. However, her employer, Lady Dunsmore, remarks, rather eccentrically, "it is not nearly so bad as marrying your cousin."[96]

In Joseph Middleton's *Love vs Law: Or Marriage with a Deceased Wife's Sister* (1855), the central character, Walter, is the son of a second marriage to a deceased wife's sister. His mother reflects on her feelings for her dead sister: "Jealous—jealous, indeed, and of what? Of the kind thoughts which were associated with my sister's name —of the gentle memories which clung around her grave? Not so— not so." However, this virtuous marriage is not recognized in law. Walter loses his inheritance—but he happily marries his first cousin, Marian. "There was the old, familiar, sisterly smile upon her cheek; the same old, familiar sisterly confidence in her manner and address."[97]

By the 1870s, sophisticated writers were treating the issues more lightly. In *The Way We Live Now* (1875), Trollope describes a gentry family, the Longestaffes, whose daughter, Georgina, is having little success in the marriage market. Her mother, Lady Pomona, hopes she may marry a cousin. To her mother's horror, Georgina becomes engaged to a respectable Jewish businessman, much older than herself. "It seems to me that it can't be possible," says Lady Pomona. "It's unnatural. It's worse than your wife's sister. I'm sure there's something in the Bible against it."[98]

THE DECEASED Wife's Sister's Marriage Act of 1907 was the outcome of one of the most protracted struggles in British parliamentary history.[99] First mooted in 1842, the debate on reform raged for 65 years. *The Times* published annual leading articles. There was also a great pamphlet war.[100] Associations were set up to promote the arguments for and against reform and to lobby Parliament. The House of Commons held forty-six sessions of debate, and eighteen times it passed the law only for the House of Lords to knock it back.

The parliamentary stalemate became a national joke. In Gilbert and Sullivan's *Iolanthe* (1882), the Queen of the Fairies threatens that her agent Strephon will magically drive a whole list of unlikely measures through the House of Lords. To top it all:

> He shall prick that annual blister,
> Marriage with deceased wife's sister.

But it was no laughing matter, certainly not for those who believed that divine law was at stake. Was this reform the thin edge of the wedge? Bills introduced in the 1840s to legalize marriage with the deceased wife's sister would also have allowed the marriage of a man to a niece, his late wife's sister's daughter.[101] The sacrament of marriage was threatened. The very primacy of the Church of England might be at risk. Even as the Marriage Act was finally passed, in 1907, one member warned Parliament that it would be an "installment of disestablishment . . . a bit of the Church will be broken off from the State and left with jagged edges."[102]

For their part, however, members of Parliament had to reckon with influential and vocal constituents who had been frustrated by the law. There was also the matter of the British colonies: most of the colonial countries had altered the law. In consequence, an Australian could make a perfectly legal marriage to his deccased wife's sister only to find that his marriage was invalid in England, his children illegitimate. Lord Henage reported to the House of Lords that at a dinner for visiting colonial Prime Ministers, he had met three Premiers who were married to a deceased wife's sister. One joked that he could now ditch his wife in England and marry someone else without risking any difficulty with the law.[103]

In 1905, this anomaly provided the crux of Shaw's play *Major Barbara*. Undershaft, a millionaire armaments manufacturer, is tempted to hand over his business to a young Australian, Adolphus Cusins. However, Undershaft was a foundling and he has sworn that he must be succeeded by a foundling. Then suddenly Cusins explains that his parents were not legally married.

> LADY BRITOMART: Now Adolphus, don't dare to make up a
> wicked story for the sake of these wretched cannons.
> Remember: I have seen photographs of your parents; and
> the Agent General for South Western Australia knows them
> personally and has assured me that they are most
> respectable married people.
>
> CUSINS: So they are in Australia; but here they are outcasts.
> Their marriage is legal in Australia, but not in England. My
> mother is my father's deceased wife's sister; and in this
> island I am consequently a foundling. [Sensation].

In 1906, a bill was passed recognizing these colonial marriages. This made it more difficult to resist a change in the law as it applied to British citizens. The following year the bill permitting marriages with the deceased wife's sister was driven through Parliament in a rare all-night sitting by a Liberal government backed by a large majority. The House of Lords, facing its own threat of reform, caved in.

Yet the passage of the statute in 1907 did not finally settle the arguments. It was only in 1921 that a companion law was passed to allow marriage with a deceased husband's brother. And even after that date, adultery with a wife's sister in the wife's lifetime continued to be defined in law as "incestuous adultery." This had always been treated as a particularly heinous form of adultery. The first woman in England to secure a divorce—a Mrs. Addison, in 1801—proved that her husband had committed adultery with her sister. The court found that if she now had intercourse with her husband, it would constitute incest.[104] Incestuous adultery was one of the few grounds on which a woman could be granted a divorce until 1923, when a law was passed allowing a woman to divorce her husband for any adultery. The Church of England changed its own doctrine only in 1946, but the 1949 Marriage Act still prohibited marriage between a man and his *divorced* wife's sister.

PUBLIC CONCEPTIONS of incest changed decisively in the last decades of the nineteenth century. Incest came to mean sexual relations between close kin, particularly between father and daughter, uncle and niece, or brother and sister. Moreover, it was now thought of as a crime, an offense committed by an adult man against a young girl. To put it in modern terms, incest came to be conceived of more and more as a form of child abuse. And child abuse had become a major public issue.

In the 1870s, campaigners began to target child prostitution.[105] They had official support. In 1881 the director of prosecutions for the Metropolitan Police told a Select Committee of the House of Lords that there were "children of 14, 15 and 16 years of age, going about openly soliciting prostitution" around the Haymarket and Piccadilly.[106] In 1885 W. T. Stead, a strict non-conformist who became a crusading journalist, wrote a series of reports in the *Pall Mall Gazette* under the title "The maiden tribute of modern Babylon." He described visiting a shelter run by the National Society for the Prevention of Cruelty to Children, where he met girls between the ages of five and seven who had been sexually assaulted. Most dramatically, he told of buying the thirteen-year-old daughter of a chimney sweep from her own mother for a little more than five pounds.[107] The age of consent at the time was twelve, but Stead was tried and convicted at the Old Bailey for abduction and indecent assault because he had the girl examined by a midwife to check her virginity.

He was sentenced to three months in Holloway Gaol. The publicity triggered a moral panic.[108] The National Vigilance Association was founded; Parliament was petitioned. Sexual intercourse with children under thirteen was made a felony and the age of consent raised to sixteen.

Yet experienced magistrates believed that child prostitution was uncommon.[109] A more general and sensitive problem was the sexual abuse of girls in the congested family quarters of the large cities. When Beatrice Webb worked in a sweatshop in 1888, she was shocked to find talk of incest commonplace (perhaps taking her fellow workers too literally). In her diary she describes a seamstress muttering to her that the girls at the next table were a bad lot. "Why bless you, that young woman just behind us has had three babies by her father, and another here has had one by her brother."[110] Webb went further in a published memoir: "And the younger workers, young girls, who were in no way mentally defective, who were, on the contrary, just as keen-witted and generous-hearted as my own circle of friends—could chaff each other about having babies by their fathers and brothers . . . The violation of little children was another not infrequent result. To put it bluntly, sexual promiscuity, and even sexual perversion, are almost unavoidable among men and women of average character and intelligence crowded into the one-room tenement of slum areas."[111]

Expert witnesses who gave evidence to the Royal Commission on the Housing of the Working Classes (1884–1885) testified that incest between young girls and their close male relatives was prevalent.[112] Home Office studies of cases of carnal knowledge and rape that came up for review led to the same conclusion.[113] It was also obvious that many cases were unreported. Others were dismissed because of the difficulty of producing evidence, although the Prevention of Cruelty to Children Act, passed in 1889, permitted wives to testify against their husbands, which made successful prosecution easier. Opponents of legislation argued that incest (in this sense) was rare, but Home Office statistics told a different story. In 1906 an internal Home Office memo summed up the official view in blunt terms: "Incest is very common among the working classes in the big towns."[114] Legislation could not be avoided. A law was drafted in 1903, but it was rejected because it included stepdaughters and sisters-in-law. Incest could not be criminalized until the problem of marriage with the deceased wife's sister was resolved.

The Punishment of Incest Act was passed in 1908—just one year after the law was at last reformed to permit marriage with a deceased wife's sister. The new incest law referred only to sexual acts between close blood relatives. Sex with relatives by marriage or adoptive relatives, even a stepdaughter, did not constitute incest.[115] If convicted of incest, the male partner was liable to imprisonment for between three and seven years.

Not only was the range of the incest prohibition redefined, and transgressions criminalized. There was a sea change in thinking about incest. Until the end of the nineteenth century, restrictions on the marriage of some close kin were justified by theological arguments. But a secular perspective gradually displaced the religious discourse. Social reformers insisted that incest was a sexual pathology, children the victims. And influential scientists, Darwin among them, worried about health risks to the offspring of children of blood relatives.

CHAPTER THREE

The Science of
Incest and Heredity

*E*ven many contemporaries thought it decidedly odd that Parliament should devote so much time to debating the rights and wrongs of marriage with a deceased wife's sister. In the middle of the nineteenth century, just as the long controversy over marriage with the deceased wife's sister took off, another debate began, this one about cousin marriage. It had a very different tone, however. The protagonists appealed to science, not theology.

Marriage between first cousins was legalized in France and Italy by the Code Napoléon (1804), and first-cousin marriages soon became much more common in these countries.[1] A generation further on, scientists began to argue that inbreeding might be a cause of deafness, blindness, insanity, and infertility.[2] Some medical men suggested that cousin marriages should be discouraged, perhaps even forbidden, together with the marriage of alcoholics or the mentally ill.

"I'm not quite sure that it's a good thing for cousins to marry," remarks Dr. Crofts in Trollope's *The Small House of Allington*, published in 1863. "They do, you know, very often," he is reminded, "and it suits some family arrangements."[3] To be sure, the doctor had a personal interest in the matter: a young woman whom he hoped to marry had just become engaged to her cousin. But he might have had a less selfish concern. The British medical press was raising questions about the risks to offspring.[4] A bright young doctor would have been familiar with the professional debates. Dr. Crofts was perhaps talking as a responsible medical man. (And, in the end, he gets his girl.)

Charles Darwin picked up on these concerns very early. He had personal worries about heredity in general and about the consequences of cousin marriage in particular. Shortly before his own marriage he consulted a new book, Alexander Walker's *Intermarriage: Or the Mode in Which, and the Causes Why, Beauty, Health, and Intellect Result from Certain Unions, and Deformity, Disease and Insanity from Others* (1838). It touched a sensitive nerve. His Darwin grandmother, the wife of Erasmus Darwin, was addicted to gin and suffered from bouts of madness. Married at seventeen, she bore Erasmus five children before dying of cirrhosis of the liver at the age of thirty. Her son, Dr. Robert Darwin, worried that insanity might be inherited. If so, he would not want to have children. He would even consider it unfair to marry.[5]

In 1792 Robert wrote to consult his father, and Erasmus Darwin responded frankly.[6] Mrs. Darwin had suffered from "violent convulsions" and temporary bouts of delirium brought on by opium and wine. "This disease is called hysteria by some people. I think it allied to epilepsy." She had probably inherited her alcoholism from her father, and Erasmus was convinced that her indulgence in alcohol caused her other ailments. "All the drunken diseases are hereditary in some degree and I believe epilepsy and insanity are produced originally by drinking."

Yet while Mrs. Darwin had inherited her alcohol addiction from her father, Dr. Darwin did not believe that her madness was heredi-tary. Her father "was never to my knowledge in the least insane, he was a drunkard both in public and private—and when he went to London he became connected with a woman and lived a debauched life in respect to drink, hence he had always the Gout of which he died but without any the least symptom of either insanity or epi-lepsy, but from debility of digestion and Gout as other drunkards die." On balance, Erasmus offered his son qualified reassurance. Alcoholism brings on the dropsy, gout, epilepsy, and madness, but "one sober generation cures these drunkards frequently, which one drunken one has created. I know many families, who had insanity in one side and the children now old people have no symptom of it. *If it was otherwise, there would not be a family in the kingdom without epileptic gouty or insane people in it.*"

Ten years later, in a note to his poem *The Temple of Nature* (1803), Erasmus Darwin restated his thesis. "A tendency to these diseases is certainly hereditary, though perhaps not the diseases themselves; thus a less quantity of ale, cyder, wine, or spirit, will induce the gout and dropsy in those constitutions, whose parents have been intem-perate in the use of those liquors."[7]

Rounding off his letter to his son, Erasmus confessed that "I have lately taken to drink two glasses of home-made wine with water at my dinner, instead of water alone, as I found myself growing weak about two months ago." Robert Darwin himself was "vehement against drinking," his son Charles remembered. "He himself never drank a drop of any alcoholic fluid."[8]

VICTORIAN MEDICAL men insisted upon the power of inheritance and the dangers of familial "taints." In the 1860s the pioneer psy-chiatrist Henry Maudsley laid it down that drunkenness in the first generation led to a frenzied need for drink in the second, to hypo-chondria in the third, and to idiocy in the fourth.[9] But the mechanisms of heredity remained frustratingly uncertain.[10] Even the scientific terminology was unsettled, and the educated public found it alien. Erasmus Darwin had written of "hereditary diseases," but his grandson Francis Galton recalled that when he published *Hereditary Genius* in 1869, the very term *hereditary* "was then considered fanciful and unusual . . . I was chafed by a cultured friend for adopting it from the French."[11] Yet whatever it was called, his contemporaries were obsessed with it. Doctors warned that "taints" passed from generation to generation within the same family. On the other hand, desirable qualities were also inherited, not to mention property and status. Indeed, pedigree and breeding were the mantra of the upper classes.

The family line could become an obsession, parodied by Jane Austen in the person of Sir Walter Elliott, "a man who, for his own amusement, never took up any book but the Baronetage," and who passed contented evenings contemplating the history of his lineage.[12] And it was not only aristocrats and gentry who went in for genealogy; the fashion also spread to the bourgeoisie. Even the Darwins and the Wedgwoods became fascinated by family trees.

Robert Darwin had once been caught up in a controversy about inheritance. He interviewed elderly relatives and chased down documents. Charles Darwin began to study his father's cache of records when his first child was born. His cousin, brother-in-law, and friend, Hensleigh Wedgwood, was looking into Wedgwood family history at the same time, and the two men exchanged discoveries. Charles's son George inherited this hobby and made himself an expert on the Darwin lineage, eventually commissioning a pedigree from a professional genealogist, Colonel Chester. His father teased him, and called him "the Herald." "Oh good Lord that we should be descended from a Steward of the Peverel, but what in the name of heaven does this mean?"[13] Yet Charles really was fascinated, at least by the Darwin line.

Emma Darwin was less interested. She wrote to a daughter, "The Darwin pedigree raged more than ever last night, as [her sons] Leonard and George had found out some more things and also [Charles's sister, Caroline, married to Emma's brother] asked me a multitude of questions, so I curse the old D's in my heart." And to another daughter she complained, "F[ather] has received the MS. from Col. Chester carrying the Darwins back 200 years. I don't know how it is, I should care *a little* if it related to Wedgwoods. F[ather] is intensively interested and the old wills are curious."[14]

Emma had reason to complain. Even in the manuscript of his *Autobiography*, which he wrote for his children, Charles paid hardly any attention to his Wedgwood mother, who had died when he was eight years old. He merely noted the date of her death and added "it is odd that I can remember hardly anything about her except her death-bed, her black velvet gown, and her curiously constructed work-table"[15]—so inviting the later speculations of Freudians. However, he went on at some length about his father, Dr. Robert Darwin.[16]

Charles Darwin was no snob. His interest in pedigree was a private, personal aspect of his scientific project. "Descent with modification" was the central theme of *The Origin of Species* (1859). Hensleigh Wedgwood's hobby of genealogy also had a parallel in his philological research: his *Dictionary of English Etymology*, which appeared in 1857, traced the descent of words. This book influenced Darwin, who found parallels between the descent—with modification—of words and natural organisms.

Yet crucially, maddeningly, the mechanism of heredity remained mysterious. In the late 1860s Darwin hesitantly advanced his theory of "pangenesis." This allowed for discrete elements—"gemmules," he called them—to be inherited from each parent. These gemmules circulated in the blood. They could pick up fresh characteristics in a person's lifetime, and these could be passed on to children—so, for instance, the child of a tubercular mother might be born with tuber-culosis. But even loyal Darwinians were skeptical. "Genesis is diffi-cult to believe," the faithful Huxley complained, "but Pangenesis is a deuced deal more difficult."[17] Galton experimented with blood transfusions between white and black rabbits.[18] These did not breed the mottled rabbits which he had been expecting, and he decided that traits acquired in a parent's lifetime were not, after all, inher-ited by the children. Darwin fretted, sometimes almost despairing. "I shall never work on inheritance again," he wrote to Galton in February 1877, toward the end of his life.[19]

It was clear at least that a child inherited some qualities from its father, others from its mother. However, Darwin believed that a mechanism operated alongside natural selection, "sexual selection," which acted only on the male of the species. In *The Descent of Man and Selection in Relation to Sex* (1871), he argued that males had al-ways competed with one another for mates. That is why men were larger, more muscular, and more aggressive than women, and also, Darwin insisted, more intelligent.

> The chief distinction in the intellectual powers of the two sexes is shewn by man attaining to a higher eminence in what-ever he takes up, than woman can attain—whether requiring deep thought, reason, or imagination, or merely the use of the senses and hands. If two lists were made of the most eminent men and women in poetry, painting, sculpture, music (inclu-sive both of composition and performance), history, science, and philosophy, with half-a-dozen names under each subject, the two lists would not bear comparison. We may also infer . . . that if men are capable of decided eminence over women in many subjects, the average standard of mental power in man must be above that of woman.[20]

Darwin nevertheless conceded that the raw material was similar in both sexes. "It is, indeed, fortunate that the law of the equal transmission of characters to both sexes prevails with mammals; otherwise it is probable that man would have become as superior in mental endowment to woman, as the peacock is in ornamental plumage to the peahen."[21]

Crucially, in Darwin's view, native intelligence was not developed in girls. "In order that woman should reach the same standard as man, she ought, when nearly adult, to be trained to energy and perseverance, and to have her reason and imagination exercised to the highest point," Darwin wrote, "and then she would probably transmit these qualities chiefly to her adult daughters."[22]

And yet a man should be prudent in his choice of a wife. A mother was responsible for the moral development of her young children, particularly her daughters. Above all, she should be fertile and free of the dreaded hereditary taint. Alas! "Man scans with scrupulous care the character and pedigree of his horses, cattle, and dogs before he matches them," Darwin complained, "but when he comes to his own marriage he rarely, or never, takes such care. He is impelled by nearly the same motives as the lower animals."[23] Darwin feared that the aristocracy was ruining itself because noblemen chose wives simply for their looks or money, preferably both. Their children might be the most handsome in England.[24] But since they took no account of health or fertility in selecting their brides, many aristocrats failed to produce heirs.

Erasmus Darwin had pinpointed another problem: "It is often hazardous to marry an heiress, as she is not unfrequently the last of a diseased family."[25] Charles Darwin added that the insistence on primogeniture hastened the decline of aristocratic lineages, since just one poor specimen might bring ruin to a noble house.[26] "The feeble births acquired diseases chase / Till Death extinguish the degenerate race," Erasmus Darwin had intoned.[27] Charles Darwin thought that aristocrats would do better to mimic animal breeders and concentrate resources on the best specimens in a brood.

Another grandson of Erasmus Darwin, Francis Galton, despaired

entirely. "I look upon the peerage as a disastrous institution, owing to its destructive effects on our valuable races," he wrote. "The
most highly-gifted men are ennobled; their elder sons are tempted
to marry heiresses, and their younger ones not to marry at all, for
these have not enough fortune to support both a family and an aris-
tocratical position. So the side-shoots of the genealogical tree are
hacked off, and the leading shoot is blighted, and the breed is lost
for ever."[28]

ALL THE more reason, Galton concluded, to take care of Thomas
Carlyle's "unclassed Aristocracy by nature,"[29] the men of genius
who constituted the nation's true elite. Galton's *Hereditary Genius,*
which appeared in 1869, was designed to demonstrate that certain
intellectual accomplishments ran in families. *Men of the Time,* a catalogue published in 1865, listed the most eminent Victorians. Not all
were geniuses, Galton conceded, but having risen so high in their
professions, these men must have been blessed with outstanding native qualities. He reconstructed their genealogies, in some cases with
the assistance of George Darwin. With its page upon page of family
trees, *Hereditary Genius* is an extraordinary testament to the Victorian obsession with pedigrees. Tabulating the clusters of male relatives, Galton calculated that the son of an eminent man had one
chance in four of becoming eminent, and so of making it himself
into *Men of the Time.*

Heredity was all, in Galton's view. Nurture did not affect the
shape of the nose or the color of the eyes; nor did it affect intelligence or talent. But as H. G. Wells (the son of a professional crick-
eter) pointed out, Galton ignored "the consideration of social advantage, of what Americans call the 'pull' that follows any striking
success. The fact that the sons and nephews of a distinguished judge
or great scientific man are themselves eminent judges or successful
scientific men, may after all be far more due to a special knowledge

of the channels of professional advancement than to any distinctive family gift."[30]

But Galton had no doubts. And he not only calculated the odds of the relatives of a famous man achieving eminence; he also discovered that exceptional qualities were diluted with every step of genealogical distance. "Speaking roughly, the percentages are quartered at each successive remove, whether by descent or collaterally."[31] This tendency of the descendants of great men to revert to mediocrity was an example of a more general principle that he called the "regression to the mean."

What explained this finding? An obvious surmise was that brilliant men often married less gifted women. Just as aristocrats notoriously chose their wives for money or looks, perhaps men of genius tended to marry attractive, or wealthy, women who might lack any intellectual distinction. Galton thought this was unlikely:

> First, the lady whom a man marries is very commonly one whom he has often met in the society of his own friends, and therefore not likely to be a silly woman. She is also usually related to some of them, and therefore has a probability of being hereditarily gifted. Secondly as a matter of fact, a large number of eminent men marry eminent women . . . the great fact remains that able men take pleasure in the society of intelligent women, and, if they can find such as would in other respects be suitable, they will marry them in preference to mediocrities.[32]

The real problem was that relatively few clever women married. Galton observed that they valued their independence, and coming as they very probably did from gifted families, they found most men tedious in comparison with their own fathers and brothers. Or perhaps, accustomed to free intellectual discussion, they were often of a "dogmatic and self-asserting type . . . unattractive to men."[33] He was, at least, right that educated women tended to remain unmarried. A study published in 1895 showed that of 1,486 women with a university education, only 208 had married.[34]

In any case, Galton agreed with Darwin that mothers influenced the moral development of their sons rather than their intelligence. The only eminent men who owed a great deal to their mothers, Galton believed, were the bishops, for whom a highly developed sense of morality might be more important than brains. He accordingly paid little attention to the marriages of the intellectual elite, with one exception. Childless himself, he was obsessed with fertility.

Galton anxiously scoured his records of eminent men, and was reassured to find that they generally had large families—all except judges, but there was a special reason for that: "There is a peculiarity in their domestic relations that interferes with a large average of legitimate families. Lord Campbell states . . . that [in the early nineteenth century] when he was first acquainted with the English Bar, one half of the judges had married their mistresses. He says it was then the understanding that when a barrister was elevated to the Bench, he should either marry his mistress, or put her away."[35] But by that time she would be too old to bear him many legitimate children. Galton concluded that a man should marry a young wife, and avoid a woman from a small family. He should also beware of women from families with a hereditary weakness.

This was Charles Darwin's personal nightmare. His mother, unwell throughout his childhood, died from an agonizing stomach ailment, probably peritonitis, at the age of fifty-two. Charles was eight years old when she died, and as an adult he was obsessively concerned with his own ill health, particularly the recurrent stomach complaints that recalled his mother's fatal illness. Both his mother and Emma were Wedgwoods, and the Wedgwoods were notorious for their ill-health.[36] Whenever one of his children fell ill, Charles was inclined to see the same symptoms in himself, and to worry that it revealed a family propensity.

Or were the frequent illnesses of his children, and the health problems of the Wedgwoods, perhaps the consequence of cousin marriages?[37] This was a growing concern in scientific circles in Britain in the 1860s. "In many families, marriages between cousins are discouraged and checked," Francis Galton noted in 1865.[38] Charles Darwin's son George actually published a note recommending that cousin marriage should be avoided.[39]

THE FIRST thorough study of the subject in the United Kingdom was published in 1865, by Arthur Mitchell, Deputy Commissioner in Lunacy for Scotland. Scotland was an obvious choice. It was widely believed that marriage between close relatives was rampant in remote Scottish regions, particularly the Highlands and Islands. Mitchell noted that popular opinion in Scotland condemned "blood-alliances" as "productive of evil."[40] And indeed, national statistics showed that nearly 14 percent of "idiots" in Scotland were children of kin. In 44 percent of families with more than one mentally handicapped child, the parents were blood relatives. Six percent of the parents of deaf mutes were close relatives.

Nonetheless, Mitchell was not convinced that this was the whole story. Fewer than 2 percent of marriages in Scotland were between first or second cousins. The rate was indeed higher in some isolated regions, but the evidence for bad effects was uncertain. In one small town on the northeast coast of Scotland, 9 percent of marriages were with first cousins and 13 percent with second cousins. Mitchell acknowledged that the children of these cousin marriages were often unprepossessing, but then many fishing families in the region were "below par in intellect."[41] A more telling case was the island of Berneray-Lewis (now Great Bernera, off the Isle of Lewis). Here 11 percent of marriages were with first and second cousins, yet Mitchell remarked that "instead of finding the island [Berneray-Lewis] peopled with idiots, madmen, cripples, and mutes, not one such person is said to exist in it."[42]

Perhaps environmental factors—"occupation, social habits, etc." —influenced the outcome. One "shrewd old woman" remarked to Mitchell: "But I'll tell ye what, Doctor, bairns that's hungert i' their youth aye gang wrang. That's far waur nor sib marriages."[43] Mitchell concluded that close-kin marriage tended to reinforce "evil influences."

Darwin was fascinated by the consequences of in-breeding. Between 1868 and 1877 he published three monographs on cross-fertilization in animals and plants.[44] In the first of these books, *The Variation of Animals and Plants under Domestication,* he proposed that "the existence of a great law of nature is almost proved; namely, that the crossing of animals and plants which are not closely related to each other is highly beneficial or even necessary, and that interbreeding [i.e., inbreeding] prolonged during many generations is highly injurious."[45]

Darwin thought this was probably true of human beings as well, although he was reluctant at first to press the issue. ("Before turning on to Birds, I ought to refer to man, though I am unwilling to enter on this subject, as it is surrounded by natural prejudices.")[46] In any case, he was bound to consider the implications for his own family. His scientific project and his personal concerns could hardly be separated. "The philosophical difficulties and practical consequences of cousin marriages troubled him for years afterwards," Janet Browne observes. "There was no other theme in Darwin's science that more clearly reflected the personal origins of his intellectual achievement. He could scarcely have arrived at pangenesis without this attention to his marriage, his children's ill health, and his own sickness."[47]

He began to canvass his correspondents. William Farr, the senior statistician in the Registrar General's office, suggested to him that the 1871 census should include a question on cousin marriage.[48] Darwin began to lobby for it. His neighbor and ally, John Lubbock, had just been elected to Parliament. In the summer of 1870, Darwin asked him to put Farr's proposal to the House. He even drafted arguments for Lubbock to use.

> In England and many parts of Europe the marriages of cousins are objected to from their supposed injurious consequences; but this belief rests on no direct evidence. It is therefore manifestly desirable that the belief should either be proved false, or should be confirmed, so that in this latter case the marriages of cousins might be discouraged. If the census recorded cousin marriages it could be established whether they were less fertile than the average. Later it might also be possible to find out whether or not consanguineous marriages lead to deafness, and dumbness, blindness, &c.[49]

Lubbock put it to the House that "consanguineous marriages were injurious throughout the whole vegetable and animal kingdoms." It was obviously "desirable to ascertain whether that was . . . the case with the whole human race."[50] The response was unenthusiastic. One member remarked that Parliament was already busy every year debating marriage with the deceased wife's sister: "If there were to be legislation about the marriage of first cousins also, the whole time of the House would be taken up in deciding who was to be allowed to marry anybody else."[51] According to George Darwin, the proposition was rejected, "amidst the scornful laughter of the House, on the ground that the idle curiosity of philosophers was not to be satisfied."[52] Yet forty-five members voted for Lubbock's motion in committee. Ninety-two voted against, but Lubbock remarked in his summing up that virtually everyone who spoke shared his concern.[53]

Farr now proposed to Darwin that an "inquiry might be under-taken through private channels."[54] Darwin agreed and entrusted the study to his eldest son, George. George Darwin was not only an amateur genealogist; he was also an accomplished mathematician. Influenced by the eugenic theories of his cousin Francis Galton, he had advocated controls on marriage between unsuitable partners. The ban on marriage with a deceased wife's sister was absurd, he suggested, but there might be good scientific reasons to prevent the marriage of first cousins, and certainly the mentally ill should be kept from marrying.[55] Clearly he was primed for his father's commission.

Darwin laid out the research design. George was to compare the incidence of close-kin marriage in the general population with that among the parents of patients in asylums. If it turned out that mar-riages between close relatives produced a disproportionate number of "diseased" children, this would "settle the question as to the inju-riousness of such marriages."[56]

The first step was to find out how common it was in England for first cousins to marry. Apparently, nobody knew the answer. George Darwin was given estimates that ranged from 10 percent to one in a thousand. "Every observer," he concluded, "is biassed by the fre-quency or rarity of such marriages amongst his immediate surround-ings."[57] He would have to discover the facts for himself. Expert in the new statistical techniques that were being developed by Farr and by Francis Galton, George decided to attempt a scientific survey. It was to be one of the very first statistical studies of a social problem.

Marriage announcements in the *Pall Mall Gazette* seemed a good starting point. Looking through them, George noticed one mar-riage between a man and a woman with the same surname. This led him to consult the Registrar-General's annual reports. (Since the of-fice was created by the Marriage Act of 1836, Darwin's friend Farr had organized the Registrar-General's statistics on family and mar-riage.) These reports were full of valuable and often surprising information. One table gave the proportions of persons who had various surnames. Smith was the most common: one in 73 of the population was a Smith. Most surnames, of course, were much rarer. Of a total number of 275,405 people whose names were registered, there were an average of 8.4 per surname. The chance that two unrelated people with the same surname would marry was slight—one in a thousand, George Darwin calculated.[58] Returning to the *Pall Mall Gazette*, he and an assistant checked through 18,528 marriage announcements published between 1869 and 1873, and found that 1.25 percent of the couples had the same surname. Very nearly all of these marriages must have been between close relatives on the father's side of the family.

George Darwin now sent out a barrage of questionnaires "to members of the upper middle and upper classes."[59] He also studied the genealogies in Burke's volumes on the peerage and the landed gentry. In this upper-class sample, 4.2 percent of marriages were with first cousins. Marriages between first cousins with the same surname accounted for about a quarter of all first-cousin marriages. There appeared to be no preference for one form of cousin marriage over another. Referring back to his data from the *Pall Mall Gazette*, he concluded that 3.5 percent of marriages in "the middle classes" were between first cousins.[60] He then collected a large sample of marriages from the General Registry of Marriages at Somerset House. About 4.5 percent of marriages in the aristocracy were with first cousins; 3.5 percent in the landed gentry and the upper-middle classes; about 2.25 percent in the rural population; and among all classes in London, about 1.15 percent.

The level of cousin marriage in country districts seemed surprisingly low. George Darwin's cousin, Clement Wedgwood, made an inquiry on his behalf among skilled artisans in the Potteries. In a sample of 149, he did not find a single case of first-cousin marriage. "He was further assured that such marriages never take place amongst them," George Darwin noted.[61] Both men must have been familiar with the cousin marriages in the earlier, humbler generations of Wedgwood potters, but they were evidently unusual. (Perhaps their cousin marriages helped to make them so successful.) Except in very isolated districts, like those investigated by Arthur Mitchell, rural people were not inclined to marry cousins. This conclusion is supported by the findings of Alan Macfarlane, who studied the marriage records of 800 people in East Colne, Essex, for the sixteenth to the eighteenth century and found only one first-cousin marriage and two marriages with more distant cousins.[62]

THE NEXT step was to gather statistics from mental asylums. Charles Darwin wrote on George's behalf to the heads of the leading institutions, and several provided detailed responses. These indicated that only 3 to 4 percent of patients were the offspring of marriages between first cousins. "For Heavens sake," Charles urged his son, "put a sentence in some conspicuous place that your results seem to indicate that consanguineous marriage, as far as insanity is concerned, cannot be injurious in any very high degree."[63] George complied. "It will be seen [he concluded] that the percentage of offspring of first-cousin marriages [in mental asylums] is so nearly that of such marriages in the general population, that one can only draw the negative conclusion that, as far as insanity and idiocy go, no evil has been shown to accrue from consanguineous marriages."[64]

Other studies suggested that the offspring of cousin marriages were more likely to suffer from blindness, deafness, or infertility. George Darwin accepted that these conditions were highly hereditary, but saw no convincing evidence that they were a result of cousin marriage. In fact, first-cousin marriages were, if anything, more fertile than others. Presumably a man was more likely to marry a cousin if he had many to choose from. First-cousin marriage would therefore be more common among people who came from large—and so presumably fertile—families.[65]

Only one small piece of evidence gave George pause. Among men who had rowed for Oxford or Cambridge, men who were obviously the fittest of the fit, sons of first-cousin parents appeared slightly less frequently than might have been expected (2.4 percent as opposed to 3 to 3.5 percent among their peers).[66]

George Darwin was well aware that his conclusions flew in the face of a common and ancient prejudice. He conceded that marriages between cousins might be quite all right for the rich but bad for the poor.

> I may mention that Dr Arthur Mitchell, of Edinburgh, conducted an extensive inquiry, and came to the conclusion that, under favourable conditions of life, the apparent ill-effects were frequently almost nil, whilst if the children were ill fed, badly housed and clothed, the evil might become very marked. This is in striking accordance with some unpublished experiments of my father, Mr Charles Darwin, on the in-and in-breeding [i.e., repeated inbreeding] of plants; for he has found that in-bred plants, when allowed enough space and good soil, frequently show little or no deterioration, whilst when placed in competition with another plant, they frequently perish or are much stunted.[67]

In short, cousin marriage caused no harm in the best families. Charles Darwin endorsed these conclusions.[68] In later editions of *Variation* he modified his original rule, weakening the claim: "It is a great law of nature, that all organic beings profit from an *occasional* cross with individuals not closely related to them in blood" (emphasis added).[69] On the other hand, the experience of animal breeders indicated that "the advantage of close interbreeding [i.e., inbreeding], as far as the retention of character is concerned, is indisputable, and often outweighs the evil of a slight loss of constitutional vigour."[70]

The densely intermarried Wedgwoods liked to joke that any hint of laziness or illness was an infallible sign of familial degeneracy.[71] The Darwinian establishment, however, was now convinced that the risks of cousin marriage were slight, at least within prosperous families. Francis Galton wrote enthusiastically to George Darwin that he had "exploded most effectually a popular scare." He added that his cousin could make a fortune from his discovery:

> Thus: there are, say, 200,000 annual marriages in the kingdom, of which 2,000 and more are between first cousins. You have only to print in proportion, and in various appropriate scales of cheapness or luxury: WORDS of Scientific COMFORT and ENCOURAGEMENT To COUSINS who are LOVERS then each lover and each of the two sets of parents would be sure to buy a copy; i.e. an annual sale of 8,000 copies!! (Cousins who fall in love and don't marry would also buy copies, as well as those who think that they might fall in love.)[72]

Galton's protégé, Karl Pearson, made a follow-up study in 1908. He was less systematic than George Darwin, relying on correspondence from readers of the *British Medical Journal*. These select respondents reported a very high incidence of first-cousin marriages in their families. A smaller proportion of marriages were with more distant cousins, but Pearson remarked that second and third cousins in these families were also often related in more than one line. He lumped them all together and concluded that "consanguineous marriages in the professional classes probably occur in less than 8 per cent. and more than 5 per cent. of cases." Yet only 1.3 percent of patients in the Great Ormond Street Hospital for Children were the children of cousins. Pearson concluded that "the diseases of children are not largely due to any consanguinity between their parents."[73]

Endorsed by the Darwinian establishment, George Darwin's conclusions reassured many people whose family trees featured marriages between cousins. Englishmen could also rest easier when they considered that Queen Victoria was married to a first cousin, and that several of her descendants had married cousins. And Darwin's conclusions seemed only common sense to landowners in the House of Lords, who knew that the inbreeding of good stock was sound policy.

THERE WAS another way of looking at incest and cousin marriage, one that also appealed to Darwin. Was the incest taboo a law of nature? Or were marriage restrictions rather the fruit of civilization, as Matthew Arnold believed? These questions had been picked over by leading philosophers in the Scottish Enlightenment.[74] Now they were taken up by a new set of specialists, the anthropologists. Incest became a particular obsession among Darwin's allies in the Ethnological Society.

The Victorian anthropologists took it for granted that the earliest human societies were essentially kinship groups. Henry Maine set out a general law: "The history of political ideas begins, in fact, with the assumption that kinship in blood is the sole possible ground of community in political functions."[75]

As Maine saw it, the original primitive society must have been simply the family writ large. He had in mind something like the household of the patriarch Abraham, which included several wives, sons and their wives and children, and servants and hangers-on. Other anthropologists imagined a promiscuous horde of kin, without families, without marriage, without even a taboo on incest. J. F. McLennan speculated that the most successful bands were made up of marauding warriors. They killed their daughters in order to be able to move more freely, and they captured women from other bands to be their wives.[76] But if they practiced infanticide and rape, at least they avoided incest. Edward Burnett Tylor, a Quaker, revolted against this violent scenario. The whole purpose of exogamy, he felt, was to prevent war by setting up diplomatic alliances between groups.[77]

Henry Maine (who was married to his father's brother's daughter) thought that the prohibition of incest was a public health measure. People who had the brains to make fire and to domesticate animals would eventually have recognized that "children of unsound constitutions were born of nearly related parents."[78] The fastidious James George Frazer wondered whether finer feelings had not simply prevailed.[79]

Darwin dismissed these speculations. "The licentiousness of many savages is no doubt astonishing," he conceded. Yet even the lowest savages were not genuinely promiscuous.[80] Among the apes, adult males tended to be jealous. Primitive men had probably been equally reluctant to share their females. And incest was abhorred even among "savages such as those of Australia and South America" with "no fine moral feelings to confuse, and who are not likely to reflect on distant evils to their progeny." Darwin thought that primitive men simply found foreign women alluring, "in the same manner as . . . male deerhounds are inclined towards strange females, while the females prefer dogs with whom they have associated."[81] But whatever the original reason might have been for the incest taboo, Darwin was sure that out-breeding groups would be more successful than their rivals. He concluded that avoidance of incest had spread by natural selection.[82]

There was, however, a difficulty with the argument from natural selection. Tylor pointed out that not all primitive peoples banned marriages between close relatives; in fact cousins, or at least some cousins, were often preferred marriage partners. Did this indicate that cousin marriage was a primitive custom—that its persistence in Victorian society was a throwback? The Catholic Church prohibited marriage between cousins, up to third cousins. Protestants, however, allowed first-cousin marriage. Which rule was more civilized?

McLennan speculated that early civilizations had the most extensive restrictions.[83] Frazer concurred: "Among many savages the sexual prohibitions are far more numerous, the horror excited by breaches of them far deeper, and the punishment inflicted on the offenders far sterner than with us."[84] Contemporaries would have recognized the implication: the Protestant code was more progressive than that of the Catholics. It was quite right—in fact, more civilized—to do away with the superstitious old law against marriage to a sister-in-law. On the other hand, cousin marriage was thoroughly civilized. No new law was required after all.

This was fortunate, since there was resistance to government interference in such private matters. In the same year as George Darwin's paper was published, a gentleman scholar of liberal opinions, Alfred Henry Huth, noting that "the subject has been exciting increased attention from all quarters," published a book entitled (with characteristic Victorian amplitude) *The Marriage of Near Kin: Considered with Respect to the Laws of Nations, the Results of Experience, and the Teachings of Biology.* Yet another Victorian intellectual who had married his first cousin, Huth argued that legal restrictions on marriage could not be justified even if it was proved that the children of close relatives were liable to have various defects. After all, he noted, marriage was permitted in the case of people suffering from hereditary illnesses.[85]

family concerns

CHAPTER FOUR

The Family Business

$\mathcal{F}$amily businesses in England began to issue
shares after the passage of the Joint Stock Act of 1844. Regional
stock exchanges sprang up. The number of joint stock companies
grew from under a thousand in 1844 to nearly three thousand in
1868, and over ten thousand in 1887.[1] The Company Acts of 1855–1865
allowed for limited liability, which made company shares more attractive.

Nevertheless, the typical nineteenth-century firm was a private
partnership. The owners shared unlimited liability: each and every
partner was liable to personal bankruptcy if the business failed. Trust
was therefore essential, and so family businesses were the norm. If a
man set up a successful enterprise, it would usually be carried on by
his sons. Brotherhood provided the model of partnership, almost its
very definition. "Partnerships were in some senses *brothers* who represented each other," explained W. S. Holdsworth, a Victorian historian of English law.[2] Since brothers-in-law were ideally treated
(and addressed) as brothers, they might well go into business together. Whether the partners were brothers or brothers-in-law, they

had an incentive to encourage marriages between their children, which would be first-cousin marriages.

Yet while the financial side of a marriage was obviously of special importance in business families, even businessmen could seldom dictate the marriage choices of their children. And kinship counted for something in itself. Fathers might emphasize economic considerations. Mothers and sisters were more susceptible to the claims of family. Yet although material and emotional considerations might sometimes pull in different directions, quite often they reinforced each other. As David Sabean remarks, "the flows of sentiment and money operated in much the same channels."[3]

Membership of the same minority religious community was another source of solidarity and trust. Such communities were also highly endogamous. Quakers and Jews had particularly strong feelings against marrying out. Moreover, the richer families in these communities tended to marry among themselves, within what was a very restricted circle. Jews and Quakers were also disproportionately represented in banking circles, and before the advent of joint stock companies and limited liability, partners in a bank simply had to trust one another, and also their major creditors. Bankers were therefore particularly likely to team up with close relatives, or to forge marriage links among themselves or with the merchants and industrialists who were risking their capital, and with whom they were probably already connected by religious affiliation or common membership in some civic association.

For all these reasons, wealthy Jewish and Quaker men were very likely to marry relatives. They were allowed to marry in their own fashion. Lord Hardwicke's marriage act of 1753 permitted Jews and Quakers to perform their own marriage ceremonies, unless one of the partners was of a different faith. ("We marry none; it is the Lord's work," George Fox had explained. A Quaker couple simply exchanged vows at a Meeting in the presence of witnesses.) Nevertheless, they were bound by the national laws on incest. A man was not permitted to marry a deceased wife's sister, although neither Jews nor Quakers had a religious objection to such marriages.

On the other hand, first-cousin marriage, legal in England, had been frowned upon by the Quakers since the middle of the seventeenth century. These marriages were nevertheless "curiously attractive," the Quaker author Verily Anderson remarks,[4] and in the eighteenth century they seem sometimes to have been tolerated. There were local variations, since the different congregations were largely autonomous, but in the nineteenth century the influential London Meeting would not permit marriages between first cousins.

The great Quaker physician Thomas Hodgkin—after whom Hodgkin's disease is named—fell in love with his mother's sister's daughter, Sarah Godlee, but their families would not allow them to marry. Sarah married a second cousin, the architect John Rickman, who was also the second cousin of Thomas. (Marriage between second cousins was permitted by Quakers.) Rickman died in 1836. Sarah then nursed Hodgkin through an illness and became his devoted assistant. The couple wished to marry, but Thomas's father insisted that they first had to get the approval of the London Meeting.

In 1840 Hodgkin addressed a pamphlet to his fellow Quakers, *On the Rule which Forbids the Marriage of First Cousins*, which pointed out that the Bible endorsed the marriage of cousins. Drawing on his medical authority, he also downplayed any risk to the health of the children of such a marriage. However, the Meeting was not to be persuaded, and the couple reluctantly separated. In 1849 Hodgkin married the widow of one of his patients. In the 1850s the Meeting decided not to expel several first-cousin couples who had been married by a "hireling priest," but it was only from 1883 that such marriages were permitted in Quaker Meetings.[5]

Yet while upper-class Quakers were not supposed to marry first cousins, they were very likely to marry into families with whom they did business. Quite commonly, several marriages between brothers-and sisters-in-law knitted the same families together. These tight clusters of intermarried families formed further alliances with other, similar sets. In the course of the nineteenth century, a great network of Quaker banks was fostered by a series of carefully judged marriage alliances.

IN THE early eighteenth century two Quakers, John Freame and Thomas Gould, set up a banking partnership in London and married each other's sisters. Gould's son set up on his own after his father's death, but he soon went bankrupt. John Freame went on to become the leading Quaker banker. The Society of Friends deposited their central funds with him, and Freame financed various Quaker ventures, including the Pennsylvania Land Company. In time, his son Joseph became his partner.

A client of the Freames was David Barclay. Barclay had been apprenticed to a London merchant, whose daughter he married. In 1723, following the death of his wife, he married John Freame's daughter, Priscilla, who stood to inherit a quarter interest in the bank. Ten years later the Freames took him into partnership.

James Barclay, David's son by his first wife, married a sister of Joseph Freame, so becoming his father's brother-in-law. Even more oddly, his wife was his step-aunt. In any case, he too became a partner in the bank. David Barclay had two sons by Priscilla Freame, David Barclay the younger and John Barclay. They also were taken into partnership. The Barclays and Freames now extended their connections in tandem. A daughter of Joseph Freame married the Birmingham industrialist James Farmer, while a niece of David Barclay married Farmer's partner, Samuel Galton. (Francis Galton was her grandson.)

All went well for a while, but the Freame-Barclay partnership faced a crisis in 1766 when the two senior partners, James Barclay and Joseph Freame, died within a week of each other. James Barclay left daughters but no sons. The younger David Barclay, now the largest shareholder, had only a daughter. Another Barclay-Freame marriage was hurriedly arranged. Christiana, a sister of the younger David Barclay, had married into another Quaker banking family, the Gurneys. Widowed in 1761, she was free to marry Joseph Freame's son, John Freame. Her new husband was her first cousin, the son of her mother's brother. And in consequence of this marriage, her half-brother James became her uncle.

John Freame and Christiana settled in the Freame family house at 54 Lombard Street, the seat of the bank. Christiana's brother John Barclay lived there as well with his wife and five children. John

The Barclays and the Freames.

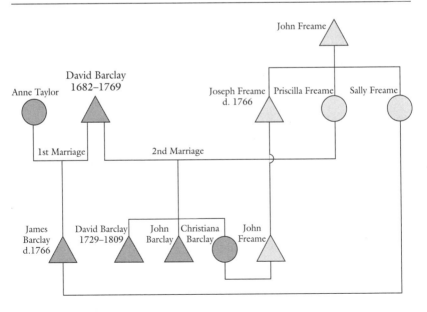

Freame's widowed mother ruled the roost. The partnership was secured. However, Christiana had no children, and on the death of John Freame the younger David Barclay found himself in control of the bank.

He extended the family interests, buying the Anchor Brewery in Southwark from Dr. Johnson's friend Mrs. Hester Thrale, and he took several of his Barclay cousins and nephews into partnership. As ever, marriages reinforced business connections. David's sister Lucy

Robert Barclay's marriages.

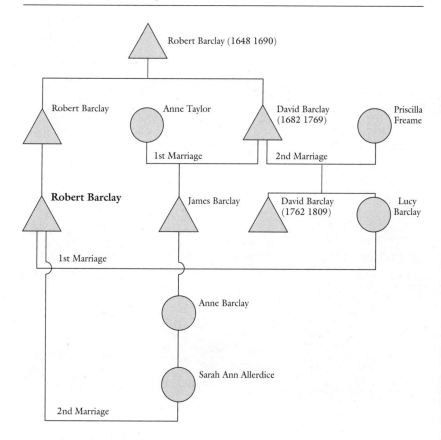

married the most enterprising of his cousins, Robert Barclay. After Lucy's death Robert married the granddaughter and heir of James Barclay and Sarah Freame, Sarah Ann Allerdice, changing his name to Barclay-Allerdice.

The Barclays also found partners among their brothers-in-law. Timothy Bevan was married to David's half-sister Elizabeth. John Tritton was the husband of the daughter—and heir—of John Barclay, and the Trittons' daughter married a nephew of the Barclay brothers. Both Bevan and Tritton became partners in the bank, which now traded as Barclays, Bevan & Tritton.

As always, relationships became overlaid with others. When Bevan's wife Elizabeth Barclay died, he remarried. His second wife, Hannah, née Gurney, was the widow of a business associate of David Barclay named Nathaniel Springall. Springall himself had previously been married to David Barclay's sister Richenda. After his second

David Barclay's brothers-in-law.

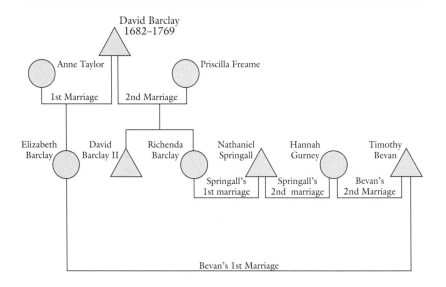

marriage Bevan was described as his "wife's husband's wife's sister's widower,"[6]—a lighthearted testimony to the involuted quality of Barclay alliances.

The Barclays were also connected by marriage—indeed, by several marriages—with the Gurneys of Norwich, another Quaker banking family. Joseph Gurney was the first husband of the younger David Barclay's sister Christiana. David's only child, Agatha, married Joseph's nephew, Richard Gurney, who became the chief partner in Gurney's Bank. Another of David's nephews and partners, "Black Bob" Barclay, married Richard Gurney's sister, Rachel. Kitty Bell,

The Barclays and the Gurneys.

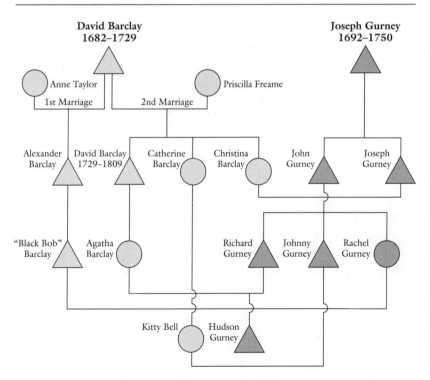

the daughter of another of David's sisters, Catherine, married Johnny, the brother of Richard and Rachel Gurney.

The two families were now intricately intertwined. Agatha's son, Hudson Gurney, inherited a major share in Gurney's Bank and in another family venture, the London bill-broking business Overend, Gurney and Company, which became the greatest discounting house in the world in the first half of the nineteenth century. Through his mother, Hudson also became the principal heir of David Barclay. Moreover, he married the daughter of Robert Barclay-Allerdice.

The Gurneys themselves were given to endogamy. The two principal lines of descent, from the brothers Richard Gurney of Keswick and John Gurney of Ealham, intermarried for three genera-

Selected marriages within the Gurney family.

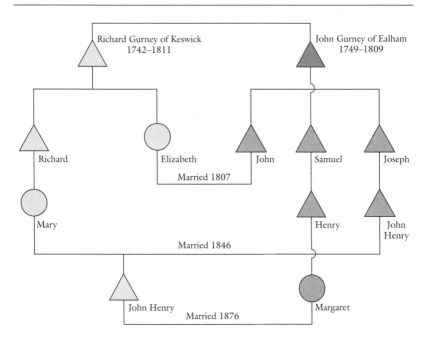

tions. In the first generation, children of the brothers married; in the second generation, grandchildren; in the third generation, great-grandchildren.

The Gurneys were further allied by repeated marriages to other prominent Quaker families. These cross-cutting ties could generate rather complicated relationships. Richard Gurney's first marriage was to Agatha Barclay, daughter and heir of the second David Barclay. After her death he married Rachel Hanbury. Rachel's brother, Sampson Hanbury, married Richard's daughter by Agatha Barclay. Sampson's brother-in-law, Richard Gurney, now became his father-in-law. His sister Rachel was his stepmother-in-law.

The marriage alliances between the Barclays and Gurneys were extended to encompass other elite Quaker families up and down the country. There was a particular tendency for Quaker banking

Marriages between three elite Quaker families.

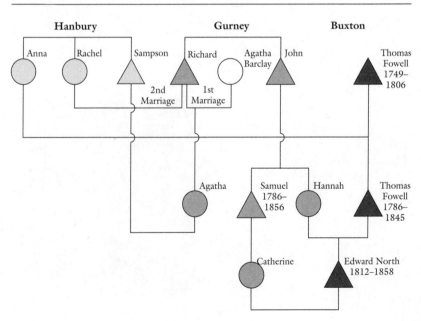

families to intermarry—notably the Barclays, Gurneys, Lloyds, Birkbecks, and Backhouses. Eventually, in 1896, twenty of these intertwined largely Quaker provincial banks, including Gurney & Co. of Norwich, merged under the name of Barclay & Co. Limited. The merger was the logical culmination of more than a century of marriage alliances.

JEWISH BANKERS had a similar preference for marriage between close relations, but they were in no way averse to cousin marriage. The greatest of these families, the Rothschilds, were indeed determined that cousins should marry.

Mayer Amschel Rothschild began his career as a financier in Frankfurt, in partnership with his brother Kalman. After Kalman's death in 1782, Mayer Amschel continued on his own until his sons were old enough to join him. At first they were merely his assistants. Officially in 1810, but probably earlier in fact, Amschel, Salomon, and Carl became partners of their father in Frankfurt, and established branches in Vienna (under Salomon) and Naples (under Carl). Another brother, Nathan, set himself up in London. He may have become a partner at an early stage, but his legal relationship to the Frankfurt Rothschilds was kept secret during the Napoleonic wars. James, the youngest of the five, became a partner on attaining his majority and established the bank in Paris.

The House of Rothschild was far and away the largest bank in the world between the end of the Napoleonic wars and the beginning of the First World War. A unique, pioneering multinational, it commanded Europe's financial markets and held the fate of governments in its hands. And yet it remained a family firm, and until the 1870s its main concern was the management of the family's own capital.[7] Most of the business of each branch was conducted with other branches. In the heyday of the family firm, the fortunes of the partners were inextricably linked. Profits were shared, but losses were also borne collectively. Mutual trust therefore had to be absolute—so much so that, for instance, Salomon would sometimes forge Nathan's signature to bills that he had neglected to endorse.[8]

The unitary structure of the bank survived until the 1870s, when the political and financial environment was transformed by the rise of Prussia, the weakening of the Austro-Hungarian empire, the defeat of France, and the rise of the joint-stock banks. The Rothschilds then had to adapt to a more nationalist and competitive world. In consequence, according to Niall Ferguson, "by the end of the 1870s co-operation between the four [surviving] houses was not much greater than co-operation between each house and its local allies."[9]

Until the 1870s, however, the unity of the five branches was carefully nurtured. "If there was a single 'secret' of Rothschild success," Ferguson emphasizes again and again in his magisterial study of the Rothschild phenomenon, "it was the system of co-operation between the five houses which made them, when considered as a whole, the largest bank in the world, while at the same time dis-

The Rothschild brothers.

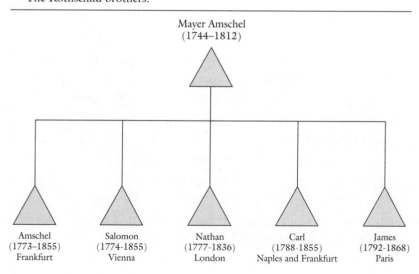

Mayer Amschel
(1744–1812)

Amschel
(1773–1855)
Frankfurt

Salomon
(1774-1855)
Vienna

Nathan
(1777-1836)
London

Carl
(1788-1855)
Naples and Frankfurt

James
(1792-1868)
Paris

persing their financial influence in five major financial centres spread across Europe."[10]

The unity of the branches rested on the rock of family solidarity. "The prosperity of the Rothschilds," Disraeli remarked, "was as much owing to the unity of feeling which alike pervaded all branches of that numerous family as in their capital and abilities. They were like an Arabian tribe."[11] But the Rothschilds did not rely on traditional kinship values and institutions to hold the branches together. They forged new mechanisms of alliance, inheritance, and succession, honed to the specific requirements of their very unusual multinational enterprise. Indeed, they were as creative and entrepreneurial in the field of kinship as in more technical aspects of banking; and their kinship strategies yielded a competitive advantage that may have been decisive.

THE FIRST principle on which the unity of the House of Rothschild depended was fraternity. "In the end," Ferguson comments, "there were authentic bonds of brotherly love, forged in the Judengasse, which no other ties could rival. 'Did anyone promise us more when we all slept in one little attic room?' asked Salomon when Nathan was grumbling at having sold some consols too soon."[12] The brothers corresponded constantly, often visited each other, and held regular conclaves. Holidays were arranged jointly, and there were obligatory pilgrimages to Frankfurt, where Mayer Amschel's widow, Gutle, lived in the old family home. (She died in 1849 at the age of 96.)

Mayer Amschel had ruled his sons in classic patriarchal style, keeping the largest share of the capital in his own hands. After their father's death the brothers were legally equals, but in fact there was always a *primus inter pares*. The eldest brother, Amschel, was his father's successor in Frankfurt, but the leadership of the business passed to the third son, Nathan. He was the head of the London house, which had emerged as the most successful of the Rothschild banks at the end of the Napoleonic wars, but Nathan dominated his brothers largely because of his imperious personality. His brothers referred to him as the commanding general, or the *Finanz-bonaparte.*

Nathan's tendency to boss his brothers around caused tensions, particularly in the dangerous years 1814–1815, when it seemed as though the failure of one of the continental branches might sink the whole bank. Salomon showed a sample of Nathan's correspondence to an Amsterdam-based associate. Shocked, he wrote to remonstrate with Nathan. "I have to confess sincerely, dear Mr Rothschild, that I was embarrassed for your own brother, when I found these big insults in your letters. Really, you call your brothers nothing but asses and stupid boys . . . Now God gave you the good fortune to carry out large-scale transactions, such as, I think, no Jew has ever done. So you should be happy about it together with your brothers."[13]

Nevertheless the structure survived, partly because the other brothers ceded extra capital shares (and so income) to the London branch. (This allocation of shares was made somewhat more palatable by the brotherly observation that Nathan "has a big family, he needs more.")[14] The capital shares were regularly reallocated to reflect the relative success of the branches, and the earlier system of equal shares was restored in 1825, when the other branches had recovered.[15] Similar adjustments had to be made in the aftermath of the European upheavals in 1830.

Following Nathan's death in 1836, the youngest brother, James, exercised a degree of leadership. Although he never enjoyed the power that Nathan had held, and was forced to concede considerable autonomy to the London house, he steered the bank through the turbulence that followed in the wake of the 1848 revolutions, when the Paris and Vienna houses nearly went under and had to be bailed out by London with some help from Naples and Frankfurt.

Next to the spirit of fraternity, or perhaps logically following from it, came the strict rule that only Rothschild men were eligible to be partners. This was in sharp contrast to the custom of the Quaker bankers. Mayer Amschel's will excluded Rothschild women and their husbands, indeed all relatives-in-law, from active participation in the bank.[16] On the other hand, all sons were treated equally. Primogeniture was not a Rothschild principle.[17]

In the next generation, the bank had to accommodate sons of the original partners. Nepotism represented a dilution of fraternity, and young men required careful grooming. On coming of age, they were posted to other branches of the bank to learn the trade. But the partners required further reassurance. They instituted a radical new marriage policy: Rothschilds should marry Rothschilds. Effectively binding on their sons and, in due course, on their grandsons, this was the third principle on which the family operated, and it came to be their main kinship strategy.

IN 1824 the youngest of Mayer Amschel's five sons, James, married his niece, the daughter of his elder brother, Salomon. This marriage inaugurated the new strategy. Between 1824 and 1877, thirty-six male patrilineal descendants of Mayer Amschel married. Thirty of them married cousins, and of these, twenty-eight married first or second cousins to whom they were related in the male line. During this half-century of sustained intermarriage, only two Rothschild men and four women married people to whom they were not related.

More specifically, the preference was for a marriage between cousins whose fathers were partners in different branches of the bank. "The first and most important reason for the strategy of intermarriage," Ferguson writes, "was precisely to prevent the five houses drifting apart."[18] Marriages were systematically arranged in order to maintain the cross-cutting links between these houses.

The founder of the London bank, Nathan Rothschild, married Hannah Barent Cohen, the daughter of a merchant who had come

to London from the Netherlands. Her sister Judith married the
Jewish statesman and philanthropist Moses Montefiore, and Montefiore's brother, Abraham, married Nathan's sister, Henrietta. (Marriage into the Anglo-Sephardi elite was, from an English perspective,
marrying up.)

In the next generation the new policy of Rothschild endogamy
came into play. Nathan's first son, Lionel, married the eldest daughter of Carl Rothschild in 1836. In 1842, his younger daughter married
Carl's older son. In the same year Nathan's third son, Nat, married
the eldest daughter of the youngest of his Rothschild uncles, James
(and reluctantly resigned himself to living permanently in Paris).

Nathan's two other sons also married cousins, but not Rothschilds. Anthony married Louisa Montefiore, his father's sister's

Marriages between the branches of the House of Rothschild: (A)
descendants of Nathan (London); (B) descendants of Carl (Frankfurt and
Naples); (C) descendants of Salomon (Vienna); (D) descendants of James
(Paris). *Note:* The oldest of the five brothers, Amschel, was childless. When
he died, Carl took over the Frankfurt house.

	A	B	C	D
A	–	2	2	2
B	2	–	4	2
C	2	4	–	2
D	2	2	2	–

daughter. Mayer married Juliana Cohen, his mother's brother's daughter. That was satisfactory, but three years after Nathan's death his daughter Hannah Mayer contracted a scandalous marriage with Henry FitzRoy. He was the younger brother of Lord Southampton, had aristocratic connections that included the Duke of Wellington, and was a member of Parliament. He was altogether most respectable, but he was a Christian and, of course, not a relation. The Rothschilds were upset on both counts, but Henry's mother, the Duchess of Cleveland, was also far from happy. "I feel it is a sore trouble that my son should choose as his wife, and the mother of his children, a woman who is not a Christian," she confessed. "My only comfort is that he seems very happy."[19] Hannah's mother accepted the marriage in the end for the same reason.

Nathan's first son, Lionel, succeeded him as head of the London bank. Lionel had five children, the first three of whom mar-

Cousin marriages of the children of Nathan Rothschild.

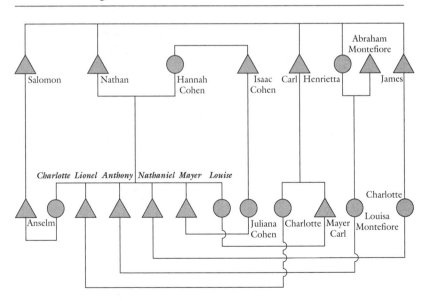

ried Rothschild cousins. His oldest son, who was to succeed him as head of the London Rothschild bank, married Carl's oldest son's daughter. (They were both, of course, direct descendants of Mayer Amschel in the male line, but she was also his father's sister's daughter.) Lionel's oldest daughter married James's son's son. His second daughter married Anselm's son's son. The son of Lionel's brother Nat married another granddaughter of Carl.

When Hannah Mayer made her shocking marriage in 1839, her uncle James wrote a letter to her brothers, his London nephews, which smoothly elided the tradition of Jewish endogamy with the new Rothschild doctrine that Rothschilds should marry Rothschilds. The "main point," he insisted, was "religion," but he then immediately passed on to the constraints imposed by the Rothschild destiny:

> I and the rest of our family have . . . always brought our offspring up from their early childhood with the sense that their love is to be confined to members of the family, that their attachment for one another would prevent them from getting any ideas of marrying anyone other than one of the family so that the fortune would stay inside the family . . . Do you really think that all the nicely conceived projects [will come to fruition]—that is, that Mayer will marry Anselm's daughter, that Lionel's daughter will marry the child of another member of the family so that the great fortune and the Rothschild name will continue to be honoured and transmitted [to future generations]—if one doesn't put a stop to this?[20]

James took it for granted that the structure of the bank depended on Rothschild men marrying Rothschild women. He also insisted that the wealth should be kept in the family.[21] That was a different matter, however. It is true that Rothschild brides brought with them considerable dowries, but only the sons of partners held the precious shares in the bank. In any case, whatever the financial attraction of unions between Rothschilds, it was not sufficient to motivate further cousin marriages beyond the 1870s, when the structure of the bank changed. The last of the traditional cousin marriages was contracted in 1877. Some Rothschild matriarchs were of the opinion that hardly any other Jewish families were of equivalent standing,[22] although they accepted occasional marriages into elite Jewish families such as the Montefiores. But once the unified structure of the House of Rothschild had been abandoned, it turned out that there were in fact perfectly adequate husbands and wives to be found in other families.

It is sometimes suggested that the Rothschilds were following an established model. One notion is that they were behaving like a European royal family, but no European royal family particularly favored marriage between cousins related in the male line only. Disraeli compared the family to an Arabian tribe, yet it is equally implausible that the Rothschilds were faithfully reproducing an ancient Middle Eastern preference for marriages of this type. It is true that there is a long-standing preference in many Arab communities for marriage with the father's brother's daughter, but no other modern European Jews showed the same specific preference for marriages between cousins related exclusively in the male line.

The fact is that the distinctive Rothschild system of marriage alliance was not shared by European royalty, European Jews, or indeed by other European banking dynasties. It was a creative adaptation to the unique structure of the multinational family bank.

THE ROTHSCHILDS were, of course, exceptional, in all sorts of ways. And banking was a very particular sort of business. Nevertheless, many Victorian enterprises were family concerns, if on a much smaller scale, and prosperous Victorian merchants and industrialists did quite frequently marry cousins, although by no means at the rate achieved by the Rothschilds.

The Wedgwood patriarch, Josiah Wedgwood, started work at the age of fourteen as an apprentice to his brother Thomas. He wanted to marry a cousin, but his uncle, a particularly successful potter, thought that his daughter could do better for herself. Josiah was made to wait for years until he could match "guinea for guinea" the £4,000 that that his uncle planned to settle on his daughter.[23] (This would be equivalent to $645,000 today.)

Josiah eventually accumulated this steep brideprice, and married his cousin in 1764. He went on to become the most successful of all the potters in Staffordshire. He began his career with a legacy of £10. At the end of his life, he was worth half a million pounds (about $56 million today).[24] His fortune was well earned. He innovated, experimented with new processes and materials, organized his production along modern lines, and introduced fresh designs. His factory at Etruria made Wedgwood pottery world-famous. And it was very much a family business. Josiah's brother John became his London representative. The son of a widowed sister was taken on as bookkeeper and was made a partner alongside Josiah's three sons. As supervisor of the works, Josiah hired a cousin. When the business began to stretch his resources he leased one of his pottery works to another cousin, young Joseph Wedgwood, who married the daughter of another sister of Josiah.

Yet Josiah's children did not marry cousins. The youngest, Tom —a bohemian, a dabbler in drugs, an associate of the Lake Poets— died young, unmarried. Josiah's older sons, John and "Jos," married two sisters. Their father-in-law was a wealthy and tyrannical country gentleman, John Bartlett Allen, "domineering and possessed of a vile disposition, quarrelling with his neighbours and making life practically intolerable for his two sons and nine daughters."[25] The

Allen sisters, however, were spirited and charming, and very fond of one another.

An alliance with a county family like the Allens was a step up socially for the Wedgwoods. Jos cared about this, and disregarded the fact that his wife was five years his senior. But Josiah Wedgwood himself was happier when his favorite daughter, Susannah, married Robert Darwin, the son of his close friend Erasmus Darwin.

Erasmus Darwin was a doctor, a natural philosopher, and a poet. An expansive and unconventional eighteenth-century figure, he was suspected of being an atheist, and after the death of his wife he lived openly with a mistress who was also his servant. He and Josiah Wedgwood were members of the famous Lunar Society of Birmingham. Their families lived 25 miles apart and visited each other often.

The Wedgwoods, Darwins, and Allens.

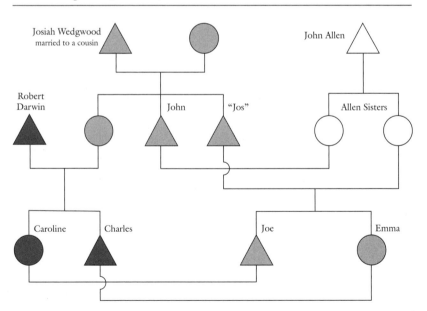

The two friends exchanged precious gifts. Erasmus Darwin sent Josiah Wedgwood an advance copy of his poem, *The Botanic Garden,* which would become a literary sensation. Six months later Josiah presented Erasmus with the first perfect copy of the Portland Vase, which initiated the fashion for Wedgwood china. (Erasmus included a description of the vase in the published edition of his poem, illustrated with an engraving by William Blake.) They were delighted that their children decided to marry.

In the next generation, Erasmus Darwin's son Robert was a particular friend of his brother-in-law, Jos, the eldest son of Josiah. The two men had an understanding that Jos's own eldest son, yet another Josiah Wedgwood, known as Joe, would marry Robert Darwin's daughter, Caroline, who was, of course, his cousin. Joe was in no hurry to get married, but he went along with his father's wishes, eventually. His marriage to Caroline Darwin was celebrated in 1837, when Joe was 42 years old and Caroline was 37. Obviously they were not slaves to passion. Nor were they simply being pushed around by their fathers. But their marriage did make excellent financial sense. Dr. Robert Darwin was not only a prosperous physician, like his father Erasmus; he also operated as a private banker, and he had lent a lot of money to Jos. The two men were involved in joint speculations in canals and later in railways. And Robert Darwin advised Jos on most of his financial arrangements, including those within the family. Since Joe was in line to take over the Etruria pottery works, his marriage to Caroline Darwin would ensure that important debts and obligations were kept within the family, and this may have been a consideration for their fathers.

Jos was also perfectly happy when, two years later, his daughter Emma reinforced the alliance with the Robert Darwins by marrying Charles Darwin. Charles had always been a favorite with his uncle, with whom he used to go shooting at Maer, where he was particularly welcome because his Wedgwood cousins were rather sedentary.

(Charles called Maer "Bliss Castle.")[26] And it was Jos who had persuaded a reluctant Robert Darwin to allow Charles to sail on the *Beagle*.[27] Like their fathers, they were friends, united by exchanges. When the engagement was announced, Jos told Robert Darwin: "You lately gave up a daughter—it is my turn now."[28]

The two fathers made a settlement that allowed the young couple to live independently. "I propose to do for Emma what I did for Charlotte and for three of my sons," Jos Wedgwood wrote to Robert Darwin. He planned to "give a bond for £5,000, and to allow her £400 a year, as long as my income will supply it, which I have no reason for thinking will not be as long as I live."[29] Robert Darwin contributed shares worth £10,000 that provided an income of some £600 a year.[30] (Multiply by 100 to get the approximate current dollar value.) Charles's brother Erasmus and Emma's brother Joe were appointed executors of the trust set up for the couple.[31] The fact that Emma was marrying her cousin made no difference to the marriage settlement. Jos made similar provisions for all his married children, some of whom married cousins while others did not.

Six of Jos's nine children married, four of them to first cousins. At least two of these cousin marriages were poor financial risks, and they were resisted by prudent fathers. John Wedgwood had been Jos's partner in the pottery, but he was a hopeless businessman and Jos eased him out. John then went into banking, failed, and had to be bailed out by Jos. Jos was not best pleased when Henry, the least promising of his own sons, married John's daughter, Jessie Wedgwood, the beauty of her generation, although Jessie was his niece twice over (she was his brother's daughter, and moreover his wife and Jessie's mother were sisters). Jessie herself had her doubts about the match, but her mother and her Allen aunts were in favor, and she eventually capitulated.[32]

Hensleigh, another of Jos's sons, fell in love with his mother's sister's daughter, Fanny Mackintosh. Fanny's mother, a third Allen

The children of "Jos" Wedgwood and Elizabeth Allen.

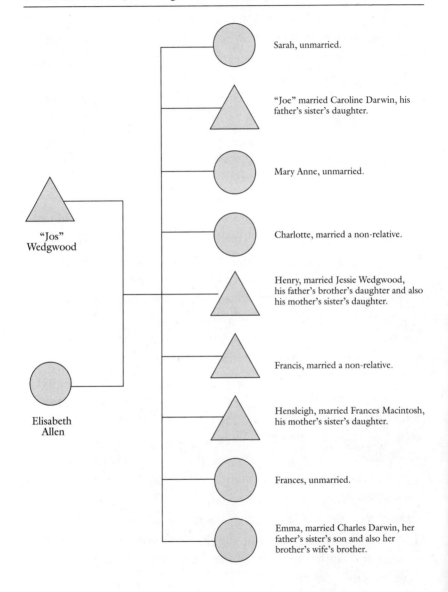

Sarah, unmarried.

"Joe" married Caroline Darwin, his father's sister's daughter.

Mary Anne, unmarried.

Charlotte, married a non-relative.

Henry, married Jessie Wedgwood, his father's brother's daughter and also his mother's sister's daughter.

Francis, married a non-relative.

Hensleigh, married Frances Macintosh, his mother's sister's daughter.

Frances, unmarried.

Emma, married Charles Darwin, her father's sister's son and also her brother's wife's brother.

sister and yet another of Jos's sisters-in-law, had married the rising statesman James Mackintosh. Mackintosh opposed the marriage. He was reluctant to see his daughter leave home, and he thought—rightly, as it turned out—that Hensleigh's worldy prospects were poor. Once again the Allen sisters caballed, and Mackintosh eventually gave in. (A generation later, Hensleigh's daughter's stepdaughter married Charles Darwin's unpromising son Horace, again despite the objections of her father.)

So fathers generally paid close attention to financial considerations when their children married, but this was not a necessary reason for cousin marriage, certainly not in the Darwin-Wedgwood clan. Nor was it a sufficient reason, even within the Wedgwood family concern. When Josiah grew old, his cousin Thomas Byerley effectively

The Wedgwoods and the Allens: the third generation.

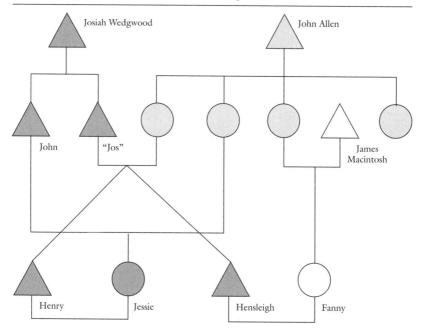

became the manager of the Etruria works. On Thomas's death, the Wedgwoods took on his son Josiah Byerley as manager. This was at least partly because the young Byerley was the executor of his father's will, and the Wedgwoods would have to deal with him over Byerley's share in the firm and his debts to it.[33] Yet no marriage was mooted between the Byerleys and their (much grander) Wedgwood cousins.

Finally, in families like the Wedgwoods, fathers might not have the last word on the marriages of their daughters, let alone their sons. A determined alliance like the Allen sisters often carried the day. Family sentiment counted for a great deal—certainly to the ladies.

Families that intermarried over the generations virtually fused together. "You've none of you ever seen a Darwin who wasn't mostly Wedgwood," one of Charles Darwin's sons told his daughter, "rather sadly," she thought, "as of a dying strain."[34] Outsiders who married into these close-knit clans were immediately enveloped in a web of emotional relationships. When his wife died, James Mackintosh very nearly married yet a fourth Allen sister, Francis, although she was, of course, his deceased wife's sister. She was very much in love with him, and acted as his hostess for the rest of his life.[35]

Jos Wedgwood's daughter Charlotte married a clergyman, Charles Langton. After her death he remarried—to one of Charles Darwin's sisters. To put it another way, his two wives were sisters-in-law to each other: indeed, doubly so, since two of the Wedgwood siblings had married two of the Darwin siblings. They were also, of course, first cousins.

In the inner circles of the clan, relationships could become extremely complicated. Charles Darwin's older brother, Erasmus, never married. His closest friend was his cousin Hensleigh Wedgwood, who had finally overcome James Mackintosh's resistance and married Fanny. Erasmus took to seeing Fanny and her children several times a week. They sometimes went on holidays or trips alone together, and Fanny came to stay at his house to nurse him when he fell ill. He started referring to her as "Missis" and "the wife," and spoke of "our daughters." Fanny's marriage nevertheless survived, and Hensleigh and Erasmus remained friends.[36]

In the next generation, Godfrey Wedgwood, son of Hensleigh's brother Francis, fell in love with Hensleigh's daughter, Effie. She rejected him and Godfrey married someone else, but he pined for Effie, and even confided to his pregnant wife that he remained in love with his cousin. When his wife died in childbirth, he proposed to Effie again. Now a spinster in her mid-forties, she turned him down once more, and almost immediately married Lord Farrer of Abington. But she urged Godfrey to marry her younger sister, Hope, who

Godfrey Wedgwood, Effie, and Hope.

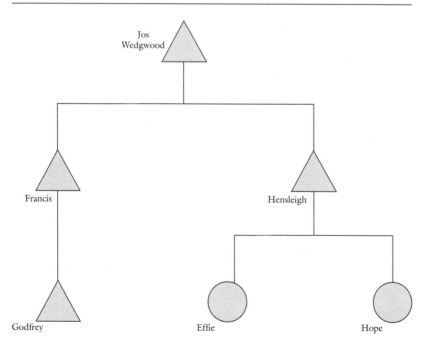

was in her mid-thirties. Despite family worries that the relationship between the sisters would be ruined, they remained very close to each other. Hope had a child whom she insisted on sharing with Effie, who was childless, saying that she would have two mothers. Effie always spoke of "our child."[37]

CLEARLY THE nineteenth-century bourgeois family was not a closed circle of parents and children huddled together before a single hearth. Uncles, aunts, cousins, and brothers- and sisters-in-law often settled within visiting distance of one another. They congregated for Sunday lunches or teas, holidayed together, attended the same churches. The extended family was the main arena in which women were active, while the men shared interests in business enterprises or in intellectual or religious or political projects that might be yet more absorbing.

This emotionally charged family circle was regularly reinforced by the marriage of cousins or in-laws. And the most successful clans persisted for generations, producing many of the leading politicians and bureaucrats, the titans of finance and industry, the scientists and engineers, and the great writers of Victorian England.

CHAPTER FIVE

Wilberforce and the Clapham Sect

*M*arriages to each other's sisters bound business partners together. Cousins might well be encouraged to marry if they stood to inherit shares in a family concern. But would a bourgeois marry—or be pushed into a marriage—simply in order to keep the wealth in the family? The cliché was current, and it was sometimes true enough. Yet material considerations were not necessarily decisive, even in commercial families, as the fortunes of three generations of Wedgwoods indicate. And marriages between cousins or brothers- and sisters-in-law were just as common in families of doctors, lawyers, and clergymen, or in the Anglo-Indian dynasties of high civil servants, judges, and engineers.

To be sure, more diffuse expectations influenced the choice of husbands and wives. Interests of other kinds were involved. Relatives could usually be counted on also to help one another in their careers and to offer companionship, understanding, and trust. The yield of each marriage was multiplied as whole families were drawn into a new set of relationships. These effects spread beyond the members of the nuclear family, for uncles and aunts were rather like parents, and cousins were very like brothers and sisters (except, of course, that they could marry).

Family networks—islands of intimacy, confidence, and mutual aid —provided the model for other close associations. Trusted friends stood as godparents to one another's children. They might be treated—perhaps addressed—as brothers and sisters. It was common for a man to marry the sister of a friend, while a woman might encourage her brother to marry her own best friend. Associates who consecrated themselves to a common project evolved quite naturally into a kinship network—metaphorical at first, then in reality. This was the elite Quaker model, but it was adopted by other sets of idealists, activists, or entrepreneurs who shared a common vision, an absorbing project, a sense that they were different from the rest of the world.

Three of the Lake Poets—Samuel Taylor Coleridge, Robert Lovell, and Robert Southey—married three Fricker sisters. Coleridge hoped to make this fraternity the core of a utopian movement, the Pantisocracy, which he planned to transport to America in 1795, to the banks of the Susquehanna. When he began to collaborate with Wordsworth, Coleridge fell in love with Sara Hutchinson, the sister of Wordsworth's wife, Mary. (Wordsworth's younger brother, John, had been in love with Mary Hutchinson. He was devastated by her marriage to William.) As Kathleen Jones points out, the Wordsworths, the Hutchinson sisters, Southey, Coleridge, and the Fricker sisters had something in common: all of them were orphans who had suffered poverty and loss of status after the death of their fathers. "This shared experience was one of the things that bound them together as they sought—in their friendships—to recreate the loving, secure family relationships they had lost."[1]

A LARGER and more enduring network of metaphorical brothers, and real brothers-in-law, was constructed by the Clapham Sect. At the end of the eighteenth century a set of earnest, upper-middle-class Christians, adherents of the new evangelical movement, several of them members of Parliament, came to live in Clapham, near London, in order to be close to their leader, William Wilberforce.[2] They were dedicated to the reform of manners, the revival of Christian belief, and the spread of Christian ideas throughout the Empire. Their greatest crusade was the abolition of slavery.

And they were to be remarkably successful. "The truth is that from that little knot of men emanated all the Bible Societies, and almost all the Missionary Societies, in the world," the historian Thomas Babington Macaulay, a son of Clapham, assured his sister. "The whole organisation of the Evangelical party was their work. The share which they had in providing means for the education of the people was great. They were really the destroyers of the slave-trade, and of slavery."[3]

Yet they were not universally admired. Their members of Parliament were mockingly called the Saints. They were also charged with hypocrisy: the high churchman Sydney Smith suggested that their Society for the Suppression of Vice should really be named "The Society for the Suppression of Vice among those with less than £500 [say, $40,000] a year."[4] Worse still, conservative Anglicans detected a whiff of sectarianism.[5] "Is not Mr. Wilberforce at the head of the church of Clapham?" Smith inquired, with feline malice.[6]

The term "Clapham Sect" was probably applied for the first time by a loyal son of Clapham, James Stephen, in an essay published in the *Edinburgh Review* in 1844, after the founding fathers had passed away. He intended it ironically. (It was the editor of the *Edinburgh Review* who—to Stephen's chagrin—actually entitled his piece "The Clapham Sect.")[7] It was, of course, the term "sect" that caused problems, and it touched a sensitive nerve.

The parents of several of the Clapham circle had been influenced by John Wesley, and might loosely have been described as Methodists. The Claphamites retained some of the stricter doctrines of the older generation: God's will was revealed uniquely in the Bible; conversion should be a transformative experience; private prayer and self-examination were required. But they rejected imputations of sectarianism and always insisted that they were Anglicans. As James Stephen explained, they felt that orthodox believers differed from them not in the substance of their beliefs but "as solemn triflers differ from the profoundly serious."[8]

They were, moreover, very different from their puritanical fathers in their style. "Absolute as was the faith of Mr. Wilberforce and his associates," James Stephen remarked, "it was not possible that the system called 'Evangelical' should be asserted by them in the blunt and uncompromising tone of their immediate predecessors."[9] They were also more ecumenical. Communion and saints' days were regularly celebrated at the Clapham church.[10]

Nevertheless, the "Clapham Sect" tag fitted well enough. The men saw themselves as forming a select, perhaps a saved, brotherhood. They looked to one another for support and inspiration. "It is not permitted to any Coterie altogether to escape the spirit of Coterie," James Stephen admitted. "The commoners admired in each other the reflection of their own looks, and the echo of their own voices. A critical race, they drew many of their canons of criticism from books and talk of their own parentage; and for those on the outside of the pale, there might be, now and then, some failure of charity. Their festivals were not exhilarating."[11] Isaac Milner, the doyen of evangelical dons, was relieved when Wilberforce left Clapham for Kensington. Milner sensed in Clapham "the danger of conceit and spiritual pride, and a cold, critical spirit."[12]

THE FORERUNNERS of the Clapham Sect were a clergyman, Henry Venn, and a very wealthy businessman, John Thornton. The Thornton family came originally from Hull, which was the hub of the Baltic and Russian trade. It was also an important center of the new evangelical movement. An evangelical, a merchant in the Russian trade, and a director of the Bank of England, John Thornton had inherited a fortune from his father, who was also in the Russian trade and also a director of the Bank of England. But the son prospered on his own account. When he died, the *Gentleman's Magazine* described him as "the greatest merchant in Europe, except Mr. Hope of Amsterdam."[13] John's son Henry remarked that his father was "rough, vehement and eager," and complained that when he got older he would only attend at his business two days a week, and that he lost money in various speculations. "But he noted approvingly that John would not remain in a room when an improper toast was sung, and that he spent between £2000 and £3000 a year [roughly $300,000–$450,000] on the extension of gospel knowledge."[14]

John Thornton bought up livings and supported promising evangelical clergymen.[15] He helped the famous preacher John Newton to a pulpit in London. And he appointed a young Cambridge evangelical, Henry Venn, as curate of Clapham's Holy Trinity Church in 1754. Venn called Thornton his first friend in Christ,[16] and named his son John after him. Thornton named his youngest son, Henry, after Venn.

John Thornton's first two sons, Samuel and Robert, both members of Parliament, inherited his two mansions in Clapham. Samuel moved up in the world, and drifted away from the evangelicals.[17] His brother Robert speculated, was bankrupted, deserted his wife and children, and ended up as a fugitive in America.

The third of the Thornton brothers, Henry, followed Samuel and Robert into Parliament, where he distinguished himself as an authority on monetary theory.[18] (According to John Hicks, Henry Thornton's *Enquiry into the Nature and Effects of the Paper Credit of Great Britain* contained all but one of the key elements of the theory later developed by Keynes.)[19] However, Henry declined to take the family route into the Russian trade. Instead he became a banker. And unlike his older brothers, he remained devoted to the evangelical cause. His principles as a banker, he confided to his diary, "connect themselves . . . with still higher principles."[20] His philanthropy was certainly impressive. In 1794, when he was still unmarried, Thornton spent £3,750 on charities and £3,400 on himself (roughly half a million dollars on each, by today's values).[21] After his marriage he gave a third of his income each year to charity.[22]

THE CLAPHAM Sect began to take shape when Henry Thornton was brought together with William Wilberforce. Wilberforce was one of the great men of the age. The son of a rich merchant in Hull, he had been a contemporary at Cambridge of William Pitt (Pitt the Younger), who had been born in the same year. Both men were elected to Parliament in 1780, at the age of twenty-one, and they became allies. Two years later Pitt was Chancellor of the Exchequer. A year and a half further on, he was Prime Minister. "Pitt does not make friends," Wilberforce himself remarked,[23] but the new leader soon put him on the government front bench as an advocate of official policy. The two men belonged to the same clubs in London and took holidays together. When Wilberforce bought a house in Wimbledon, Pitt moved in with him for extended periods.[24] "In the early days of their political life Pitt and Wilberforce were 'exactly like brothers,'" Wilberforce's sons commented, quoting their father's own phrase.[25]

In 1785 Wilberforce experienced a conversion and became a devout evangelical Christian. He now reconsidered his political priorities. Pitt encouraged him to take up the Abolitionist cause. As Wilberforce began to make contact with the anti-slavery lobby, the charismatic preacher John Newton pressed him to approach a sympathetic young member of Parliament.[26] This was Henry Thornton.

In fact, the Wilberforces and Thorntons had long-standing connections. Their wealth came from the same source, the Baltic and Russian trade centered on the port of Hull. The families had been business associates. And they were related by marriage. Wilberforce's grandfather, also William Wilberforce, twice mayor of Hull, had served an apprenticeship to Henry Thornton's great-grandfather, John Thornton. He married John's daughter, Sarah Thornton. Their second son, another William Wilberforce, married Hannah Thornton, his mother's brother's daughter, and was employed in the Thornton family firm. This couple made a temporary home for the young William Wilberforce after the death of his father.

William Wilberforce and Henry Thornton formed a close partnership. Thornton's house in King's Arms Yard became Wilber-

Intermarriages between the Wilberforce and Thornton families.

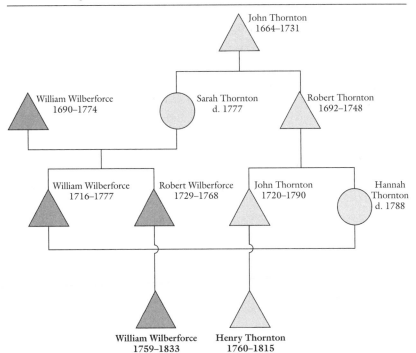

force's informal political home. In 1792, two years after his father's death, Henry Thornton bought a Queen Anne house, Battersea Rise, in the Thornton family neighborhood (described by James Stephen as "the villa-cinctured common of Clapham").[27] William moved to Clapham to live with him, and they shared accommodation and expenses in what Wilberforce called their "chummery" for four years.

While Wilberforce was the magnetic center of Clapham and its unchallenged leader, Henry Thornton was its organizing genius. His house, Battersea Rise, doubled as a headquarters for the Sect. Thornton installed thirty-four bedrooms and persuaded Wilberforce's friend William Pitt, the Prime Minister, to design a library, which became the regular meeting place for what the inner circle of Claphamites called their "Cabinet Councils." (And it soon became the custom to lend out books from the library to family and friends for a fee of a penny per book.)[28]

From the first, Thornton planned to build a community around Wilberforce:

> On the whole [he wrote to another early Claphamite, in 1793], I am in hopes some good may come out of our Clapham system. Wilberforce is a candle that should not be hid under a bushel. The influence of his conversation is, I think, great and striking. I am surprised to find how much religion everybody seems to have when they get into our house. They seem all to submit, and to acknowledge the advantage of a religious life, and we are not at all queer or guilty of carrying things too far.[29]

Thornton built two new houses in the large grounds of Battersea Rise and set out to attract new settlers. His first catch was Charles Grant, freshly returned from a successful career in India, where he had become an evangelical. Grant had been instrumental in securing Henry Thornton's election to Parliament for Southwark in 1782, rallying the clerks in the India Office to support him.[30] In 1794 he bought one of Thornton's houses and named it Glenelg, after his estate in Scotland.

In India, Grant had become a close friend of another evangelical convert, John Shore. They both prospered in the reformed East India Company, which now governed India under the direct responsibility of Parliament, thanks largely to the efforts of Pitt and Wilberforce. Charles Grant became Director of the Directors of the Court of the Company. John Shore, Lord Teignmouth, served as governor-general of India from 1793 to 1798. (Spelling out the influence of Clapham for the benefit of his sister, Macaulay commented that "Lord Teignmouth governed India at Calcutta. Grant governed India in Leadenhall Street.")[31] When Teignmouth returned to England he bought the Clapham house of Henry's brother, Samuel Thornton, who had acquired a country estate. ("Seek a neighbour before you seek a house," he said.)[32]

The other new house that Thornton built, Broomfield, was rented by Edward Eliot, Pitt's brother-in-law and an intimate friend of Wilberforce. Eliot's wife had died suddenly in childbirth after a year of marriage, leaving him almost inconsolable. He turned to Wilberforce for support, and was converted to his faith. Wilberforce described Eliot as "a bond of connexion, which was sure never to fail" between himself and Pitt.[33]

A few months after Thornton and Wilberforce moved to Clapham, John Venn took occupation of the rectory. The son of Henry Venn, John had been appointed rector of Clapham by trustees nominated by John Thornton. Henry Thornton furnished the rectory with a full wine cellar.[34] Venn became a regular visitor at Battersea Rise, and the Thornton children came to treat the rectory as a second home.

Venn now made friends with Wilberforce, and he told his father that "he had not received so much benefit from any man as he had done from Mr. Wilberforce."[35]

One by one, the young men married. Venn was the first: he married a well-to-do young woman from a good evangelical family in Hull. When she died, in 1803, Venn's sister moved in with him and looked after the children. In 1812 he married again; his second wife was the daughter of another Clapham family, the Turtons. His sister was devastated. "Undoubtedly the shock which she received from parting from my house was very great," John confessed, "and had I known how great it could have been, I should, I think have sacrificed every prospect of my happiness to hers."[36] He died the following year.

Henry Thornton had asked Venn to check up on another young woman in Hull, Marianne Sykes, the daughter of Joseph Sykes of West Ella, a well-known merchant. William Wilberforce may have had a hand in arranging the match. He regarded Marianne Sykes as a sister. Her father, Joseph Sykes, was a former business partner of Wilberforce's father. Wilberforce's father died when William was a boy of nine, and he had been virtually adopted into the Sykes household, where he had become "as intimate as a brother with my mother and her brothers," Marianne's daughter later wrote. "His delight at her marriage afterwards with 'the dearest friend he had in the world' he expressed most warmly, and up to the day of her death his affection for her never varied."[37] In effect, Thornton became Wilberforce's brother-in-law.

Thornton married in 1796. A few months later Wilberforce found a wife and bought Broomfield, one of the two houses Thornton had built on the land of Battersea Rise. Neighbors now, the Thorntons in Battersea Rise, the Wilberforces in Broomfield, and the Grants in Glenelg operated almost as a single commune.[38] Wilberforce was in and out of Battersea Rise, a Pied Piper to the children. "Mr. Wilberforce seemed so entirely one of our family," Henry Thornton's daughter recalled, "that I can remember having a game of play with him earlier than with any one."[39] He would turn up for meals with the Thorntons whenever it suited him. "He dines with us naturally at any hour but mine," Mrs. Thornton complained.[40]

Mrs. Thornton did not care for Mrs. Wilberforce, but she and Mrs. Grant were the best of friends. Her daughter recalled that "in nearly every confinement Mrs. Grant came to nurse my mother, and she generally brought over some of her daughters . . . our houses and grounds were almost common property."[41]

WILBERFORCE WAS the focal point of the Clapham network. He was the candle, in Thornton's phrase, or more fulsomely, in Stephen's, "the Agamemnon of the host we celebrate—the very sun of the Claphamic system."[42] It was through him that most members of the sect were recruited. Henry Thornton acknowledged this in a note in his diary:

> Few men have been blessed with worthier and better friends than it has been my lot to be. Mr Wilberforce stands at the head of these, for he was the friend of my youth. It is chiefly through him that I have been introduced to a variety of other most valuable associates, to my friends Babington and Gisborne and their worthy families, to Lord Teignmouth and his family, to Mrs Hannah More and her sisters: to Mr Stephen and to not a few respectable Members of Parliament. Second only to Mr Wilberforce in my esteem is now the family of Mr Grant.[43]

In fact, Wilberforce was the central figure in several networks. He now drew his friends together. They were generally prosperous and influential men, well known in Westminster and the City. Several were members of Parliament, where they formed the core of Wilberforce's following in the House, the "Saints." And they began to marry into each other's families, or recruited their brothers-in-law to the sect.

Thomas Babington, a member of Parliament and the squire of Rothley Temple in Leicestershire, and Thomas Gisborne, curate of Yaxall in Staffordshire, had been friends of Wilberforce while they were all undergraduates at St. John's College, Cambridge. After Wilberforce went down from university, he and Pitt were known to gamble. The two country puritans kept their distance, but the three men became warm friends once again after Wilberforce's conversion. It was Babington who introduced Wilberforce to the woman he married.

Babington and Gisborne were by now brothers-in-law: Gisborne married Babington's sister, Mary Babington. Thomas Babington himself made a more adventurous match. He was friendly with Aulay Macaulay, a young Scotsman of his own age, who was curate at Claybrooke, in Leicestershire. In 1787 the two young men were holidaying in the Scottish Highlands and paid a visit to Aulay's father, a Presbyterian minister. Babington fell in love with one of the daughters of the manse, Jean Macaulay. They married without delay, but before bringing Jean home to Rothley Temple, his country estate in Leicestershire, Babington took her to stay for half a year at Gisborne's rectory. The plan was that Babington's sister, Mrs. Gisborne, would instruct his new wife in the duties of her new, rather grand position. "It speaks well for the temper and sense of all concerned that this extraordinary plan thoroughly answered," remarked Jean's great-niece, Lady Knutsford, "and that the most cordial relations grew up and subsisted always between Mrs. Babington and her husband's family. At the end of a probation of six months she was pronounced capable of taking the head of her own house."[44] (And when the living at Rothley fell vacant, Babington gave it to Jean's brother, his old friend Aulay Macaulay, now his brother-in-law.)

Jean's younger brother, Zachary Macaulay, was soon recruited by the Clapham network. He had left the manse at sixteen and spent two dissipated years in Glasgow, "draining the midnight bowl," he later sorrowfully recorded, reading the atheistic works of David Hume, and "poring over such abominable, but fascinating works as are to be found under the head of novels in the catalogue of every circulating library."[45] Through the recommendation of a distant relative, he found a position as bookkeeper on a sugar plantation in Jamaica. In 1789, just twenty-one years old, he returned to England, an uncle having promised him a better job. This never materialized. At a loose end, Zachary went to stay for a while with his sister, now Jean Babington, at Rothley Temple. Here he experienced a conversion. At the same time, he became convinced of the iniquity of slavery.

Visiting Rothley Temple, Wilberforce and Thornton were impressed by the young man. On Babington's recommendation they sent him out to West Africa, to report on the progress of their new settlement for freed slaves in Sierra Leone. Two years later, Macaulay was sent back to Sierra Leone as a member of the council of the colony. In 1794 the Clapham cabinet appointed him governor. He was then twenty-six years old.

The one woman who became a member of Clapham's inner councils, Hannah More, had made a name for herself as a playwright and poet. She was a member of the Bluestocking circle in London, a brilliant set of intellectual women that included the artist Angelica Kauffman, the novelist Fanny Burney, the political and social commentators Maria Edgeworth and Mary Wollstonecraft, and the poet Anna Seward, who wrote a controversial memoir of her friend Erasmus Darwin which infuriated his grandson, Charles Darwin. Hannah More was also a friend of Joshua Reynolds, Dr. Johnson, and David Garrick, who produced her plays. However, she had a conversion experience, precipitated by a sermon of John Newton, and returned to live in Cheddar in the west country with her four sisters. ("What! Five women live happily together!" teased Dr. Johnson. "God for ever bless you; you live lives to shame duchesses.")[46] Wilberforce encouraged her to set up schools for local women and children, and Thornton financed them. The Mendip schools were soon flourishing.

When Zachary Macaulay returned to England on leave from Sierra Leone in 1795, Thornton urged him to visit the More sisters in Cheddar. He duly went, and fell in love with a teacher at one of the Mendip schools, Selina Mills. The daughter of a prosperous Quaker bookseller in Bristol, she had been virtually adopted by the More sisterhood and lived in their household. Selina gave signs of returning Zachary's feelings, but when he joined the Mores for Christmas in Bath, Hannah More took him aside and confided that Selina was not in love with him. Leaving the house in despair, Zachary heard the sounds of sobbing from the drawing room. Opening the door, he saw Selina in tears. He went to comfort her, and they declared their feelings for each other.

Hannah More may perhaps have been deceiving herself about Selina's feelings, but in any case the More sisters were set against Selina's marriage. Indeed, they seem to have had a principled objection to marriage itself, which they saw as the enemy of sisterhood. Hannah More's youngest sister, Patty, had recently turned down an offer of marriage. Macaulay complained to Selina that "Miss Patty's dislike to marriage appears whimsical."[47] Lady Knutsford believed that Patty was in love with Selina.[48] A recent biographer of Hannah More suggests that Selina had become "the Mores' surrogate sister, and had replaced Patty as the baby of the family," and she discerns "the possessive closing of the ranks against marriage, seen as the mortal enemy of their special relationship. It was a breaking of the fellowship, a rift in the warm solidarity they had built up against a world all too ready to mock and despise single women. To desert the sisterhood for the sexual and emotional demands of a man and the constrained lifestyle of a married woman was the ultimate betrayal."[49]

Hannah More was eventually persuaded to countenance an engagement, but she would not permit Selina to travel to Sierra Leone. Zachary Macaulay spent a further three years in Africa while Selina remained with the Mores, dependent on his letters. These letters, which he described as a journal, are intensely frank and intimate, though couched in the evangelical idiom. "You shall be my tutelary Saint," he wrote in a characteristic letter to Selina. "Your smile shall cheer me, your counsel shall guide me, your example shall animate me, your love shall lighten my labours, and your intercessions shall bring down on me the blessing of heaven."[50]

Macaulay resigned as governor of the colony in 1799 and returned to London as secretary of the Sierra Leone company, on a salary of £500 a year (or $50,000 in 2009).[51] He and Selina married shortly afterwards. They lived for three years on the premises of the Thornton family bank in Birchin Lane, which also housed the offices of the Sierra Leone company. In 1802, they moved to Clapham. But it was some time before the More sisters forgave them. Patty More had even refused an invitation to the wedding. "After the wedding party left Bristol, the More sisters collapsed into collective grief, sobbing themselves into an exhausted acquiescence."[52] Selina eventually managed to effect a reconciliation, and in 1810 Hannah More stood as godmother to Selina's daughter, who was named Hannah More Macaulay.

A final recruit to Clapham was another man who, like Zachary Macaulay, had emerged from poverty. James Stephen was the son of a bankrupt. After a rough-and-ready schooling he married Anne Stent, the sister of a school friend, although he had other affairs, one of which produced an illegitimate son. ("I have been told, that no man can love two women at once; but I am confident that this is an error," he remarked in an autobiographical essay written for his children.)[53] His brother, who was working for a rich uncle in the West Indies, subsidized his law studies and then helped to set him up in practice in the Caribbean. This exposure to a slave society turned Stephen into an Abolitionist.

On a visit to England in the winter of 1788–89, Stephen made the acquaintance of Wilberforce. In 1794 he returned to England, a wealthy man, and moved to Clapham to be near Wilberforce, who had become his guiding light. Two years later, his wife died. Wilberforce comforted him, and in 1800 he married Wilberforce's widowed sister, Sarah Clarke, a woman of extreme and apparently almost crazed piety, who gave all her money to the poor and walked around in rags.[54]

"The marriage probably marked Stephen's final adhesion to the Evangelical party," his grandson remarked. "He maintained till his death the closest and most affectionate alliance with his brother-in-law Wilberforce."[55] Stephen became a central figure in Clapham, but, he wrote to Wilberforce, "in this new system I am a satellite, not a primary planet, placed in it more for your sakes than my own, though for my own, too, in a subordinate degree."[56]

Stephen was the most fiery and uncompromising partisan in the Abolitionist Party, and he quickly caught the eye of a political ally of Pitt and Wilberforce, Spencer Perceval. Something of an honorary Claphamite, Perceval had bought Lord Teignmouth's house in Clapham in 1808. He became Prime Minister in the following year, and Wilberforce persuaded him to abandon Monday sittings of the House, since it forced some members to travel on a Sunday.[57] In 1811 Perceval engineered Stephen's appointment as a Master in Chancery, despite his shaky knowledge of the law, and in the following year he found Stephen a seat in Parliament.[58] When Perceval was shot and killed in Parliament in 1812, Stephen "was made ill by the shock, but visited the wretched criminal to pray for his salvation."[59]

James Stephen died in 1832. He was buried at Stoke Newington by the side of his mother. Wilberforce had promised to be buried near to him,[60] but when he died in the following year, as Parliament finally abolished slavery in the British Empire, he was interred in Westminster Abbey.

"IT WAS the custom of the circle," Lady Knutsford wrote in her biography of her grandfather, Zachary Macaulay, "to consider every member of that coterie as forming part of a large united family, who should behave to each other with the same simplicity and absence of formality, which, in the usual way, characterizes intercourse only among the nearest relatives."[61] The men regarded one another as brothers and quite commonly roomed together as bachelors. When they married, often to sisters of their close associates, they bought houses near each other. They stood as godparents to one another's children, who took their names. And their children in turn cherished these relationships, and quite often found their husbands and wives within the Clapham circle.

Battersea Rise, Glenelg, and Broomfield were virtually common property to the Wilberforces, Thorntons, and Grants. The Claphamites came together at every opportunity. "They were in the habit of either assembling at the same watering places during what may ironically be called their holidays, or else spending them at one another's houses, taking with them as a matter of course their wives and children," Lady Knutsford wrote.[62] On holiday in 1809, Wilberforce reported "halting for five or six days with Henry Thornton, where I carried Mrs. Wilberforce and my six children to the same house in which were now contained his own wife and eight."[63] Babington's country house, Rothley Temple, was a favorite refuge. Marianne Thornton, Henry's daughter, recalled turning up there with her eldest brother, who remarked to Babington that their arrival might be inconvenient, since his house was full. "'I do not deny,' said Mr.

Babington, 'that your coming has put us to considerable inconvenience, but the pleasure of your society quite outweighs it,' and so satisfied were we with his sincerity that we stayed."[64]

At home in Clapham, working in London, journeying to visit Gisborne at Yoxall Lodge, or Babington at Rothley Temple, or the More sisters in Cheddar, they lodged together, talked, planned, exchanged confidences, and threw joint parties for their children. When they were apart, the Claphamites sent each other long and frequent letters.

An evidence of their intimacy was their readiness to criticize each other, in the frank and tactless evangelical fashion. Wilberforce reproved his own parents. Thomas Babington and his brother-in-law Macaulay were supposed to act as "Censor" to each other.[65] Even their pastor was not exempt. One night Venn came to Thornton's house with a problem. Wilberforce was present. "We discussed and told Venn his faults," Henry Thornton noted in his diary.[66]

And yet there appear to have been no hard feelings. Mrs. Wilberforce may have been unpopular, and Mrs. Thornton and Hannah More were at first rather jealous of each other, but the men remained lifelong friends. A typical entry in Venn's diary reads: "Called at Mr Stephen's and Lord Teignmouth's, supped at Mr Macaulay's, visited sick, dined at Mr Wilberforce's."[67] And in a characteristic letter to his wife, in 1799, Henry Thornton describes his weekend:

> I wrote several letters to Gisborne among the rest. Then talked with Macaulay . . . The next morning [Sunday] I rode to Clapham Church and heard an excellent sermon from Venn . . . Called on Grant after dinner . . . Drank tea with Sam [his brother, Samuel Thornton] who looks ill, and we went to church together.[68]

The Sect survived Wilberforce's reluctant move back to London in 1808, as parliamentary pressures increased. "I dread the separation which my leaving Broomfield would make from my chief friends, the

Thorntons, Teignmouths, Stephens, Venn, Macaulay, with whom I now live like a brother," he noted in his diary in 1805.[69] Hannah More wrote to Mrs. Thornton blaming his wife, Barbara Wilberforce, for the desertion. She had shown "want of decency . . . in not concealing her satisfaction at quitting a place so pleasant, so advantageous, so congenial to her husband."[70] But Clapham adjusted. When Wilberforce moved to Kensington Gore, James Stephen followed him, buying a house in Ormond Street. In 1829 he moved next door to Wilberforce. Thornton and Teignmouth also bought houses nearby.

Later in life, they nursed each other in illness. Henry Thornton died in Wilberforce's house, and Wilberforce's daughter died in Stephen's house. And they firmly expected to be reunited in the afterlife. The death of Henry Thornton in 1815 represented the greatest personal loss in the experience of Zachary Macaulay.[71] To comfort himself, and the widow, he wrote to Mrs. Thornton: "I have been pleasing myself with figuring to my mind our dear friend Venn [who had died in 1813] welcoming his former associate in the heavenly course to a participation of the joys with a foretaste of which they had been blessed on earth. A few short years over, and if we are followers of their faith and patience we shall join them . . . We know what the delights of their society were on earth, what must it be in heaven?"[72]

WITH THE exception of Zachary Macaulay, who was ten years their junior, the inner members of the circle were of much the same age. With the exception again of Macaulay and of the rector, Venn, the Claphamites were also well-to-do. And they were gentlemen. A code of conduct drawn up by a country member of the Sect, Thomas Gisborne, was entitled *An Enquiry into the Duties of Men in the Higher and Middle Classes* (1794). (Gisborne wrote a companion volume on the duties of ladies, which Jane Austen read with pleasure.)[73]

Yet they were resolutely not fashionable. Wilberforce moved easily in the highest circles, but his father was a businessman in Hull, and he himself married into a family of merchants, bankers, and ironmasters in Birmingham. And Henry Thornton, according to his daughter, felt alienated from his oldest brother, Samuel, also a member of Parliament, because Samuel "was anxious to connect himself with fashionable people."

> [Samuel Thornton] quitted his house on Clapham Common and bought Albury Park, became M.P. for Surrey and certainly looked down on my father whose society consisted of people who were his associates in his works of benevolence and charity, and who were his companions in political affairs. [Henry] often smiled at his brother's ideas of the importance of the Thornton family. "We are all City people and connected with merchants, and nothing but merchants on every side," he used to say and if we reminded him of the Levens, he did not scruple to tell us that the only thing that his father had ever done that he much lamented was allowing his daughter to marry Lord Leven.[74]

Samuel Thornton might be his brother, but Henry placed more value on the new ties that were forged in Clapham, ties that mimicked kinship bonds but were more compelling.

It was not only Wilberforce who held Clapham together, nor only their shared faith, nor even their establishment of a sacred family circle. The Claphamites agreed with the evangelical theologian Charles Simeon that salvation required good works and not faith alone. There was one drawback of going to heaven, John Venn reflected in a sermon at Clapham; the saved would have no opportunity to visit the sick, clothe the naked, relieve the afflicted, or rebuke and reclaim the profligate.[75] The Sect's good works were not confined to charity, but included public service and political activity. Shortly after the crisis of his conversion, Wilberforce wrote in a letter to a friend, "My business is in the world; and I must mix in assemblies of men, or quit the post which Providence seems to have assigned to me."[76] And Providence was very specific. "God Almighty has set before me two great objects: the suppression of the slave trade and the reformation of manners."[77] In fact Clapham had a third, even greater ambition. This was nothing less than to spread Christianity throughout the Empire, if not the whole world.[78]

They were pragmatic visionaries—practical men, financiers, politicians, men of business—who tended to think of their relationship to God in contractual terms. Gladstone (who was brought up in a similar milieu) remarked that the evangelicals thought of Atonement as "a sort of joint-stock transaction."[79] As practical politicians, they admitted shades of gray. They were Tories, but they reluctantly accepted that their ally Pitt was obliged to temporize, even over slavery. They worked together with members of other Protestant denominations, most notably in the British and Foreign Bible Society. They were anti-Papist, but Wilberforce took the lead in arguing for Catholic representation in Parliament in 1812, hoping to promote peace in Ireland. This shocked Hannah More, but the Saints voted with Wilberforce.[80]

And yet they were still visionaries. Clapham launched famous crusades. A campaign to end slavery had been established under the leadership of Granville Sharp, an older MP, also based in Clapham. Soon after his conversion Wilberforce became the champion of the Abolitionists. In 1788 he and Pitt introduced the first anti-slavery measure in Parliament, a bill to regulate the number of slaves who could be carried in a ship of given tonnage. Opposition mounted as it became clear that the goal was emancipation. Wilberforce now drew together a brain trust from within the Clapham circle, with Zachary Macaulay as researcher in chief. ("Look it up in Macaulay," Clapham would say.)

The reaction to the French Revolution turned opinion in England against abolition for a time. Pitt temporized, but Clapham persevered. The Whig grandee Lord Brougham took up the cause. Wilberforce's diary of June 13, 1804, notes: "Brougham, Stephen, Babington, Henry Thornton, Macaulay, dining with us in Palace Yard most days of the Slave Trade debates."[81] The official Abolition Committee, which was revived in 1804, included the members of this inner circle and in addition the Claphamites Lord Teignmouth and Charles Grant's son, Robert. In 1807 Wilberforce faced a close election in York, and Clapham went north to lend a hand.[82]

That year, the Abolition Bill was passed. Celebrating with Wilberforce at Palace Yard were Stephen, Macaulay, Thornton, Robert Grant, and William Smith.[83] Wilberforce turned to Thornton: "Well, Henry, what shall we abolish next?" "The lottery, I think," Henry replied, for the reformation of public morals was high on the Clapham agenda.[84] The same small circle established a colony for freed slaves in Sierra Leone. The president of the Sierra Leone Company was Granville Sharp; Henry Thornton was chairman; and the directors included Wilberforce, Grant, Teignmouth, and Babington. They soon recruited as governor the young Zachary Macaulay.

Perhaps their greatest duty was to spread Christianity (and so to hasten the Second Coming). Charles Grant had a plan for evangelism in India. He won over Wilberforce, who lobbied Pitt to appoint Grant's friend and fellow evangelical, John Shore (later Lord Teignmouth), as Governor-General in India. However, the East India Company was reluctant to allow much scope to Christian missionaries. Clapham began to look for opportunities elsewhere.

"A Cabinet council on the business," Wilberforce's diary records early in 1797, meaning the inner council of Clapham that assembled in the library at Battersea Rise. "Henry Thornton, Grant, and myself, are the junto."[85] The great evangelical theologian Simeon urged them on, as did Venn, who was in attendance when the Clapham Cabinet discussed the propagation of the Gospel. In 1799, the Church Missionary Society was founded. The chairman was John Venn; Henry Thornton was treasurer; Wilberforce, Charles Grant, and James Stephen vice-presidents; and Babington a member of the committee. John Venn's son Henry served as chief secretary for thirty years.

But meanwhile paganism was gaining ground in England, and Clapham launched a series of religious tracts. They were aimed at the poor but were widely read by the rich. Hannah More was the star author, Thornton the business manager. In 1802 they established a magazine, the *Christian Observer*, with a governing committee of six including Wilberforce, Macaulay, Venn, Grant, and Thornton. Macaulay became editor. Hannah More was, again, a regular contributor. Clapham also supported the British and Foreign Bible Society, which was established at a meeting in 1804 chaired by Granville Sharp. Teignmouth became chairman of the committee, which included Wilberforce, Babington, Grant, Macaulay, Sharp, and Stephen. Henry Thornton, as usual, was treasurer.

THEY WERE collaborators, neighbors, fellow believers: they treated each other as members of an extended family. Sons, daughters, and grandchildren wrote biographies of the founding fathers.[86] But perhaps their most enduring bequest to the next generation was their network of intermarriages.

"Upper middle class Evangelical families couldn't supply the demand for pious young daughters," Standish Meacham comments in his biography of Henry Thornton. "Competition was intense . . . Intermarriage among friendly families proceeded on a grand scale."[87] Clapham was the most eminent, perhaps the most cohesive such set of friendly evangelical families, and their intermarriages both reflected and reinforced their bonds with one another. These bonds were direct—as they married each other's sisters—but also indirect, for they often married into the same families.

One particular provider of wives and husbands to Clapham was the Sykes family, evangelical business people who lived in Hull, the hometown of the Wilberforces and Thorntons.[88] The Sykeses were longtime associates of the Wilberforces. Nicholas Sykes had served as William Wilberforce's guardian, and it was his sister Marianne who married Henry Thornton, Wilberforce's lieutenant in Clapham. A daughter of Nicholas Sykes, Martha, married Henry Venn, son of John Venn, the rector of Clapham.[89] (In 1827 Wilberforce appointed him to the living of Drypool, a suburb of Hull.) Martha Sykes's sister, Fanny, married Matthew Babington, the son of Thomas Babington and Jean Macaulay, who was the sister of Zachary Macaulay.

The ties were renewed in the third generation. Matthew and Fanny's daughter, Rose Mary Babington, married Charles John Elliott, grandson of the Claphamite Charles Elliott and his wife, who was a sister of Henry Venn, who had married Martha Sykes. Henry Sykes Thornton, the eldest son of Marianne Sykes and Henry Thornton, married two sisters in succession, Harriet and Emily Dealtry. They were daughters of Venn's successor as rector of Clapham. His daughter, Emily Thornton, married Cam Sykes, the son of Martha and Frances Sykes's brother, Joseph Sykes. Another son of Joseph Sykes married Margaret Rose Dealtry, the sister of Henry Thornton's two wives. Even those who did not marry into Clapham remained tied to one another, and in different ways they re-created something of the old, exclusive, inward-looking society of their childhood. The spirit of coterie endured.

CHAPTER SIX

Difficulties with Siblings

$\mathcal{T}$he Claphamites were kindly if not indulgent parents—indeed, Thomas Babington published a remarkably liberal manual of child-rearing.[1] Boys and girls played blindman's bluff at the Wilberforces. They might enjoy a puppet show written for their entertainment—and instruction—by Hannah More and narrated by Henry Thornton. When they were older they could attend the fancy dress party thrown by Lord Teignmouth on Twelfth Night, to which young Wilberforce once went as the Pope, young Macaulay as Bonaparte, and young Thornton as Don Quixote.[2]

The boys started school locally, together with African children brought over to England from Sierra Leone to be trained for missionary work. (Lord Teignmouth's son recalled young William Wilberforce being lashed by an African prefect just as his father was rescuing "the negro from the similar usage of the white.")[3] Later they were not sent to public schools—according to Henry Thornton, "on account of that abatement of confidence and intimacy to which it almost necessarily leads."[4] Instead, they were privately educated by evangelical clergymen. The young men were then expected to attend university, usually being directed to one of the Cambridge colleges with a strong evangelical presence.

As adults, the men generally moved away from the pieties of Clapham. Social changes played their part. The sons and grandsons of Clapham were members of the consolidating bourgeois establishment, and they became alienated from the evangelical movement as it moved down-market after the death of Wilberforce. And they were exposed to new ideas. William Wilberforce's sons were attracted to the Oxford Movement, an intellectual revival of high church doctrine. Others put their faith in John Stuart Mill, or Charles Darwin.

Yet Clapham marked them for life. Even the skeptics held on to something of the old morality. Zachary's son, Thomas Babington Macaulay, summed up his private creed in a note written for his eyes only: "But if *to live strictly and think freely; to practise what is moral and to believe what is rational,* be consistent with the sincere profession of Christianity, then I shall acquit myself like one of its truest professors."[5] He spoke for other sons of Clapham. They remained faithful to their fathers' doctrine of social responsibility, and carried on Clapham's greatest crusade, the fight against slavery.

In private life, they respected the austerities of the Clapham tradition. "Did you ever know your father do a thing because it was pleasant?" James Stephen's wife asked her elder son, Fitzjames, when he was a small boy. "Yes, once—when he married you."[6] But Stephen turned his back on other, more frivolous pleasures. "He once smoked a cigar, and found it so delicious that he never smoked again," his younger son Leslie recalled. "He indulged in snuff until one day it occurred to him that snuff was superfluous; when the box was solemnly emptied out of the window and never refilled."[7]

Yet as Leslie Stephen remarked, his father "had discovered that Clapham was not the world, and that the conditions of salvation could hardly include residence on the sacred common."[8] The sons of Clapham moved in the most advanced intellectual circles. Sir James—as he later became—knew Carlyle and Mill. He described himself as a Latitudinarian.[9] "My opinion as to his opinions," Leslie's brother Fitzjames commented, "is that they are a sort of humility which comes so very near to irony that I do not know how to separate them."[10] The daughters of Clapham were more likely to remain loyal to the creed, but they were not inflexible. Lady Stephen might be the daughter of the Clapham rector John Venn, but Leslie Stephen remarked that "though her religious sentiments were very strong and deep, she was so far from fanatical that she accepted with perfect calmness the deviations of her children from the old orthodox faith."[11]

Nevertheless, Sir James looked back sadly to the world he had lost. As Leslie Stephen put it, "He wore the uniform of the old army, though he had ceased to bear unquestioning allegiance."[12] Writing to his wife in 1845, Sir James mourned: "Oh where are the people who are at once really religious, and really cultivated in heart and in understanding—the people with whom we could associate as our fathers used to associate with each other. No 'Clapham Sect' nowadays!"[13]

Yet the children of Clapham often kept up their old connections. No doubt in the interest of the highest principles, they went in for nepotism as their fathers had done. Charles Grant's son, also Charles Grant, later Lord Glenelg, was appointed Colonial Secretary, and he saw to it that James Stephen's son, also James Stephen, was appointed Permanent Under-Secretary. He became "King Stephen," or "Mr. Over-Secretary Stephen," or "Mr. Mother-Country Stephen," and it was said that he "literally ruled the Colonial empire."[14] And he served as a Clapham man.[15] He wrote in a letter to his cousin, Alfred Stephen, in 1829: "The last 10 years of my life have been very busy ones, devoted not exclusively but mainly to promoting, as far as was compatible with the duties of my office, the extinction of slavery. This task devolved upon me by inheritance."[16] Indeed, he had chosen to serve "partly with the view of gaining an influence upon the slavery question."[17] In 1833 he drafted the abolition of slavery bill in forty-eight hours over a single weekend, working for once on a Sunday.

Throughout his life, Sir James could rely on Clapham patronage. When his eldest son died, he became ill and retired from the Colonial Office. Clapham came to his rescue. Thomas Babington Macaulay, who had turned down the Regius Professorship of History at Cambridge, now put forward James Stephen's name.[18] Stephen was duly appointed, but at Cambridge he was accused of heresy—he had expressed doubts about eternal damnation—and he resigned. He then took a position at the East Indian training school at Haileybury, which had been founded by the Claphamite Charles Grant, the father of Sir James's first great patron, Lord Glenelg.

And the Claphamites renewed old connections by their marriages. Stephen himself married the daughter of the old rector, John Venn. For the rest of his life, his intimate circle was made up of his brothers and sisters and their families.[19] But if the extended family was central to their lives, it was not always a source of strength and comfort. Relationships could be too intimate, too intense. The marriage of a daughter could break a father's heart. Feelings between brothers and sisters were so charged that they could foment serious tensions between a man's sisters and his wife. Brothers and brothers-in-law were close, often partners in lifelong projects, but when breakups occurred they reverberated destructively through a series of connections.

IN THE case of the Wilberforce family, it was the relationship between brothers-in-law that caused the greatest problems. William Wilberforce had married at the age of thirty-eight, when Henry Thornton's marriage broke up the cozy bachelor household at Battersea Rise. His four sons, to whom he was devoted, were sent away to school relatively late, placed with clergymen who ran small educational establishments. Wilberforce hoped that they would make careers in the church, but his eldest son, William, was sent down from Cambridge for dissipation. The young prodigal then invested the family savings in a farming business, but it soon went under, leaving his father impoverished.

Disillusioned by William's misadventures in Cambridge, Wilberforce directed his younger sons, Robert, Samuel, and Henry, to Oriel College, Oxford, where Arnold, Newman, Pusey, and Keble were launching an Anglo-Catholic movement. The younger Wilberforces duly gained first class degrees, entered the church, and married into clerical families.

Robert Wilberforce married Agnes Wrangham, daughter of an archdeacon. When Agnes died, her aunt and her cousin—both, confusingly, named Jane Legard—came to live with Robert to look after his children. He married the cousin Jane, with Samuel Wilberforce officiating.

Samuel and Henry Wilberforce married two sisters, the daughters of John Sargent, rector of Lavington and Graffam in Sussex. There was a Clapham connection: Sargent was a disciple of their Cambridge saint, Charles Simeon. (Simeon officiated at Samuel's wedding.) And Samuel Wilberforce had known the Sargent family since childhood. He had been placed for a time at a school run by the Rev. Hodson, a cousin of the Stephens, who was a neighbor and close friend of Sargent.

John Sargent's two other daughters married George Dudly Ryder and Henry Edward Manning, who had been close friends of the Wilberforce brothers at Oxford. Ryder was the son of the first evangelical bishop in the Church of England, while Manning came from an evangelical banking family with Clapham connections. He was in fact distantly related to the Wilberforces: William Wilberforce's mother was Elizabeth Bird, and her sister, Mary, was Manning's maternal grandmother. And when Manning married into the Sargent family he was marrying a cousin, since the sister of his father's first wife had married the Rev. John Sargent, his wife's father. Samuel Wilberforce officiated again at the weddings of Manning and Ryder.

The four brothers-in-law became a close fraternity, but in a letter to Samuel Wilberforce, written in 1836, Manning prophesied that the relationship would not endure:

> God alone foresees what may be the lot of us four brothers, whether death, or the tiding undercurrents of life shall separate; or whether we shall be an exception, to the sad destiny which splits up early confidences, and intimacies . . . and narrows them to a rare correspondence, and a rarer intercourse. This seems now cold, and shocking, and to be impossible— and yet it is most true of brothers by blood, even the most affectionate—after the natural heads of the family are gone, and the faggot is broken up for want of a binder.[20]

They had been brought together by the Oxford Movement. In 1845 their mentor, Newman, converted to Catholicism. In the 1850s, Henry Wilberforce, Ryder, and Manning followed him into the Catholic Church. Manning was the last to convert, but he had been the first to foresee the direction in which the brotherhood was moving. "Twelve years ago," he wrote to Samuel, "I remember writing in a private book 'Of four brothers I am called to go first through this fire.'"[21] (He came through the fire rather well, becoming archbishop of Westminster and, like Newman, a cardinal.)

These conversions were particularly traumatic for Samuel Wilberforce, who remained in the Anglican fold and became a bishop. (His eldest daughter and her husband, however, went over to the Catholic Church.) But there were wider ramifications. The Wilberforces were cousins of the Sumner brothers, one of whom was Archbishop of Canterbury, the other Bishop of Winchester. The careers of the Wilberforce brothers had profited from Sumner patronage. They also had livings gifted to them by their father-in-law, John Sargent. The widowed Mrs. Sargent mothered them all. When Manning's wife died, Mrs. Sargent moved in with him for four years, only leaving in order to look after Samuel Wilberforce when his wife died.

Apostasy severed these connections. The converts were shunned. Mrs. Sargent cut them out of her will, leaving everything to Samuel. Ryder charged Samuel with exerting undue influence, but Samuel took the view that his sisters-in-law had lost their right to their inheritance through their conversion.[22] He turned away from the apostates and began to form a new connection with Charles Anderson, another clergyman's son. The Wilberforces and Andersons became godparents of each other's children. One of Samuel's sons married a daughter of Charles Anderson, while another married a second cousin of the family. The structure, the graft of kinship on friendship, endured, even after the catastrophic collapse of one constellation of relationships.

IN THE case of the Thornton children the problems lay elsewhere, in the relationship between the eldest son and his sisters, and, most difficult of all, the relationship between his sisters and his wife. Their father, Henry Thornton, Wilberforce's lieutenant, had died in January 1815 at the age of fifty, in Wilberforce's house at 4 Kensington Gore. His wife died in October of the same year. At the time of their parents' death the eldest of the nine Thornton children, Marianne, was eighteen; the oldest boy, Henry Sykes, fifteen.

Henry Thornton had determined that Sir Robert Inglis and his wife would be the guardians of the children. He might have opted for his brother, Samuel Thornton, but Henry thought he was socially ambitious. In any case, Sir Robert and his wife were childless, and ready to move into Battersea Rise. And they were in some crucial respects honorary Claphamites. Sir Robert was a member of Parliament, associated with the Wilberforce circle, and an opponent of the slave trade, which was the litmus test for Clapham. It is true that he was also a high churchman, committed to the supremacy of the Church of England, and that he had opposed the repeal of the Test and Corporation Acts and resisted the extension of civil rights to Jews. Yet he ran a liberal household and gave the children a taste for foreign travel. After an initial coolness, they grew fond of him. The eldest of the sisters, Marianne, eventually inherited Sir Robert's country estate at Milton Bryan. However, she stayed loyal to the values of her parents' generation and pressed William Wilberforce and Hannah More to act as honorary godparents to her younger siblings. "She once said, rather wryly, that she was the last representative of the Clapham Sect; all her brothers and sisters had followed Sir Robert elsewhere."[23]

In October 1818, Sir Robert Inglis and Zachary Macaulay escorted Henry Sykes Thornton, the eldest of the Thornton brothers, and his boyhood friend Thomas Babington Macaulay to Trinity College, Cambridge. They started off in a shared set of rooms on Jesus Lane. Henry was the more successful student, passing out as 4th Wrangler and top of the Trinity contingent. Shortly after going down from Cambridge he became an active partner in the Birchin Lane Bank, where his father had been a senior partner. It turned out that the bank had been poorly run for years, and Henry was almost immediately swept up in a financial panic. Despite his youth and inexperience, he took the helm during the storm. Bankruptcy was narrowly averted with the help of a political and banking ally, John Smith. (The Smiths had been partners of the Wilberforces in Hull and were connected by marriage to Samuel Thornton's family.) Henry emerged from the crisis with an excellent reputation. He established a new bank, with one of his Melville cousins as a partner.[24]

Henry was strongly attached to his six sisters, reluctant to see them married, and in no hurry to marry himself. The two eldest,

Marianne and Lucy, never did marry. The next oldest sister, Isabella, kept house for Henry when his first wife died. Only after he remarried did she find a husband, an impecunious archdeacon, when she was already forty-five years old.

The first to marry was the youngest of the sisters, Laura. Henry disapproved of her choice, a poor clergyman. Her grandson, E. M. Forster, has described how Laura's older sisters came to her rescue. They "formed themselves into a committee and wrote constantly to their future brother-in-law, informing him of Laura's state of mind and of his own prospects, warning him, encouraging him, giving him cause for caution or hope, transmitting messages provided they thought the messages suitable."[25] Henry eventually capitulated and negotiated a businesslike marriage settlement.

And then Henry immediately made his own move: he proposed to Harriet Dealtry, whose father, Dr. Dealtry, had succeeded John Venn as vicar of Clapham in 1813. It was apparently not a love match, at least on Henry's side. According to E. M. Forster, "He may have taken her to wife because he felt that the charmed circle of his youth had been broken by the defection of Laura."[26] The two weddings, Laura's and Henry's, were celebrated as a double event at the church on Clapham Common in August 1833.

The following year, Henry's sister Sophia married John Thornton Melville, who later became Earl of Leven. On the surface, this was a good match. The Melvilles and Thorntons were business associates, and John Melville had given Henry crucial support during the crisis at the bank. He was well-off. Henry respected him, and indeed he had insisted that Melville should be a partner in his new bank.

There was also a family link: the Thorntons and the Melvilles were cousins. John Melville's mother was Jane Thornton, the aunt of Henry and Sophia. (He was named John Thornton Melville, after his mother's father.) And there was yet a further connection, perhaps a complication. John Melville was a widower. His first wife had also been a first cousin: she was the daughter of Samuel Thornton, the brother of the first Henry Thornton. To put it another way, John Melville married twice, each time to a niece of his mother. Not only were both his wives his first cousins; they were also first cousins to each other.

Once again, Henry opposed the marriage. E. M. Forster speculates that he may have been troubled by the kinship relationships between the couple, although this is likely to be a twentieth-century prejudice. More persuasively, Forster cites the family tradition that Henry "was so fond of his sisters that he was always upset when they quitted his roof. He certainly made it difficult for Sophia to return to it. So preposterous was his behaviour that he alienated her."[27]

Henrietta was the next to marry, and once more, Henry objected. Henrietta's husband died five years later, leaving her with two small children: a boy, Inglis, named after his godfather Sir Robert Inglis, and a baby girl, named Marianne after Henrietta's mother and sister. Who was to be guardian of the two children? "The dying man thought that Henry would just do, that he had improved, that there

The Thorntons and the Melvilles.

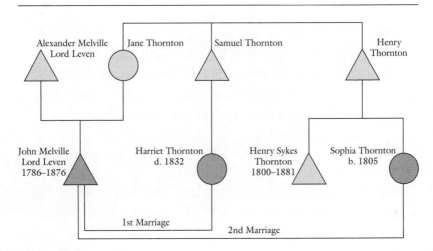

was sufficient agreement in religious outlook, but Henrietta, her baby-girl in her lap, cried 'No! Think of this poor little thing in a love affair, how he will use her!'"[28] After her husband's death she moved to a small rented house in Clapham, because she wanted the children to be close to Battersea Rise. When she died, in 1853, her sister Marianne took Henrietta's two children into her home.

After Henry's marriage his unmarried elder sisters continued to share his home at Battersea Rise. Then Henry's wife Harriet died in 1840, leaving three young children. This precipitated a crisis and led to an irreparable rift in the Thornton family.

Harriet's younger, unmarried sisters were regular visitors at Battersea Rise, helping to care for the children. The Thornton sisters began to suspect that their brother was courting the older of the sisters, Emily Dealtry ("Di"). When he decided to marry her, they were horrified. According to the Dealtry sisters, the Thornton women opposed the marriage because they did not want to part with Battersea Rise. That was certainly a factor, but the nature of the marriage worried them as well.

Since the passage of Lord Lyndhurst's Act in 1835, marriage with a deceased wife's sister had been illegal in England. Henry Thornton donated generously to the Marriage Law Reform Association, which promoted the second reading of the Marriage Bill of 1850. "To pass that Bill has become with him a 'furore'—it is almost what the abolition was to us," Marianne commented, "but unhappily he has a personal interest in the matter."[29]

Marianne accepted the theological argument against reform, but she admitted to a more personal antipathy. She wrote to an intimate friend:

> There are other feelings that I fear nothing can eradicate—for they seem like an instinct planted in ones very nature—that in this generation cannot be worn out. Should the law be altered,

probably the next will wonder at our scruples. I have never thought as alas all my family do that it is very wrong—only that it is an *impossible* sort of idea—in short it seems not a sin—but a shame—if indeed those two can be unconnected— a loss of taste and consideration and a want of refinement on the lady's side—nothing more. . . . Should the Bill not pass [Henry] talks of becoming an Alien and a foreigner.

Of course, she put the blame on Emily. Henry Venn, the son of the old vicar, reported (according to Marianne) that Henry was "the veriest slave of Emily that ever lived—& *yet*—he says he isn't in love with her—not one bit. He says he feels he has damaged her & owes it to her to make retribution."[30]

Writing to Henry, Marianne insisted that

I do not see the sinfulness of an alteration of the Law in the strong light that many people do—still I feel so differently about it from what you do that it would only be painful to both of us to enter upon it. My own brothers- and sisters-in- Law have always appeared to me so exactly like real brothers and sisters that any other connection seems an impossibility. I cannot realise a different state of feeling.[31]

Henry replied that the doctrine was uncertain, and that the law might soon be changed:

You cannot understand the marriage question or you would not write as you do. I will give you the substance of what the Archbishop told me was his advice to a friend of his— It is allowed by scripture and the prayer book is silent, but is made void by the act of 1835. If however you like to go abroad to obtain a bona fide residence there, it is without doubt a legal marriage.

If I were to go [abroad] merely to be married and return

its legality would be doubtful, and I am quite determined to have no doubt. . . .

I have quite made up my mind that I shall be much blamed for breaking up my establishment and going abroad. The person who has housed his sisters till he is 50 and has never crossed the channel is the very person who must expect to be blamed on these heads. . . .

I very much wish you would talk to me instead of to the children. Moreover the Lords may pass the Bill this session so that all this excitement may be quite uncalled for.—at all events it is clearly a question of time.[32]

The bill failed, however. Among the leaders of the opposition was Henry's former guardian, Sir Robert Inglis, who characterized the Deceased Wife's Sister Bill as "an alteration of the Law of the Land, an alteration of the Law of the Church, and an alteration if man could make it, of the Law of God."[33]

Henry's partners at the bank implored Tom Macaulay to intervene with his friend, but "I told them that he knew my opinion and that he carefully avoided the subject in my company. I could not with propriety introduce it, nor should I do any good by such officiousness."[34] In March 1852, Henry and Emily left England to marry, probably in Denmark, and settled abroad. "What a strange fatality has attended the eldest sons of the Clapham Sect!" Henry's sister Isabella Thornton wrote to Hannah Macaulay. "Henry and Tom Babington [a bankrupt] expatriated and [Wilberforce's son] W. W. excluded from respectable society."[35]

For a time it seemed as though Battersea Rise might be sold. This was perhaps the most distressing aspect of the whole business to the Thornton sisters. In the end the house was left empty, in the care of the faithful Thornton butler. Henry's partners at the bank insisted that he could not stay away for more than six months at a time, but when he made trips back to England, Emily was not received by Marianne and her sisters. (Even the butler refused to answer the door in person when Emily visited.) "The Thorntons continued to deny her the style of wife and insolently referred to her as E.D.," E. M. Forster records.[36]

Eventually Henry and Emily returned to live in Battersea Rise with their growing children. Henry died there in 1881. Presumably in order to prevent any legal challenge—since Emily was his deceased wife's sister—he willed Battersea Rise to his daughters by his first marriage. Emily rented it from them, and she lived there for the rest of her life. The Thornton sisters were never reconciled with her. Marianne reported that Emily soon abandoned her mourning cap, and that her younger sister Harty did not wear mourning at all, "for says she 'Henry was always saying sisters-in-law are no relations so I don't see why I am to mourn for him.'"[37]

THE RELATIONSHIP of Henry Thornton's friend Thomas Babington Macaulay with his two younger sisters was in its way equally fraught, problematic, and ultimately unhappy.

Tom Macaulay was born at Rothley Temple, the home of Thomas Babington, who had married his father's sister. Mr. and Mrs. Babington were the sponsors at his baptism, and he was named after his godfather.[38] When he was ennobled, he took the title Baron Macaulay of Rothley.

Tom and his brothers were prepared for the church or the law. John became a Rural Dean. Henry William benefited from Clapham patronage and became Commissioner of Arbitration in the Slave Court of Sierra Leone. The youngest of the Macaulay children, Charles, became a barrister and then Chief of the Audit Office in Somerset House.

Tom was extraordinarily precocious and far and away the cleverest of the brothers. Although he struggled with the mathematics element of his Cambridge course and gained only a pass degree, he soon won a fellowship at Trinity. He began to write for the intellectual reviews. But he had to earn a proper living. His father, Zachary, had passed his small firm on to his nephew, Thomas Babington, who had run it into the ground. By 1827 the Macaulay family was in serious financial difficulties. Tom was called to the bar, but he proved an unenthusiastic and unsuccessful lawyer. Political connections landed him a job as Commissioner of Bankruptcy, which together with his Trinity fellowship and earnings as a writer gave him an income of about £660 a year (roughly $70,000 in 2009).[39] In 1830 Lord Lansdowne invited him to stand for Parliament in a borough he controlled, which had only twenty-four electors. (Election from a rotten borough did not stop Macaulay from throwing his support behind the Reform Bill.)

Macaulay was soon to be a beneficiary of Clapham. Charles Grant, Lord Glenelg, a son of Clapham, now President of the Board of Control, kept an eye on the government of India. He was more religious than Macaulay. (They were the only two ministers in the government not to attend the Derby in 1833, but while Grant thought that it was a sin to go to the races, Macaulay merely thought it would be a bore.)[40] But Grant was loyal to Claphamites, even fallen brethren. When he was in charge of the Colonial Office, he had given a leg up to James Stephen. He appointed his untalented younger brother, William Thomas Grant, as his private secretary, and another brother, Robert Grant, was made a commissioner of the Board of Control. Now he made Macaulay Secretary to the Board, and so a government spokesman in Parliament on Indian matters. In 1834 Grant set up a supreme council for India, and he appointed Macaulay to the new position for a law member.

Macaulay returned to England in 1838, his financial situation now secure. He was reelected to Parliament and served briefly on the cabinet as Secretary at War and subsequently as Paymaster General.

After 1848 he devoted himself mainly to his multi-volume *History of England*, which was a huge success. He accepted a peerage from Palmerston in 1857, and when he died, in 1859, he was buried in Westminster Abbey, where Wilberforce had been interred a quarter of a century earlier.

Gladstone described Macaulay as "this favourite of fortune, this idol of society" and imagined that he lived in harmony with himself and the world,[41] but in fact Macaulay's private life was troubled. While at Cambridge he had been half in love with his cousin Mary Babington, the daughter of his father's sister, but nothing came of it—"her conversation soon healed the wound made by her eyes," Macaulay wrote in his journal when he heard of her death, in 1858.[42] He never showed a serious interest in any other marriageable women. Instead, he became emotionally obsessed with his two younger sisters.

The first, Hannah More Macaulay, ten years younger than Tom, was clever and highly strung. The second, Margaret, twelve years younger, was the warm-hearted baby of the family. His special relationship with them dated back to their childhood, and it blossomed when Tom came down from Cambridge to live with his family in Great Ormond Street.

In the summer of 1831, Macaulay wrote to Margaret: "The affection which I bear to you is the source of the greatest enjoyment that I have in the world. It is my strongest feeling."[43] His biographer, John Clive, suggests that Tom regarded the two young sisters almost as daughters,[44] but he expressed himself rather as a lover. "How sweet and perfect a love is that of brothers and sisters when happy circumstances have brought it to its full maturity," he wrote to both sisters, in June 1832. And he added a strange piece of doggerel:

> *My cousin is a bore,—*
> *My aunt she is a scold.—*

My daughter is too young,
My grammam is too old.
My mistress is a jilt—
My wife—uh! Bad's the best,
So give me my little sisters,
And plague take all the rest.[45]

Yet he was conscious of the risks. In a letter to Hannah written in
the fall of 1831 he had quoted from Byron's "Epistle to Augusta,"
published that year:

> *. . . two things in my destiny,*
> *A world to roam through and a home with thee.*

"The next page of the letter is torn," notes John Clive. "But sufficient fragments of the following line are preserved for it to be reconstructed. It reads: 'Lord [Byron to] his sister is the mids[t] of his
tro[ubles].'"[46]

Macaulay wanted to set up a home with one or both of his sisters.
He could not bear the thought that Margaret and Hannah might
marry. The two women were almost equally anxious. When in 1832
Margaret was making up her mind to become engaged to a Quaker
widower, Edward Cropper, Director of the Liverpool and Manchester Railway and active in the anti-slavery movement, she wrote
in her journal: "If my dearest, dearest Tom still loves me, and I am
not separated from him, I feel now as if I could bear anything."[47]
After her marriage, Margaret wrote to Hannah: "My love for [Tom]
is one which cannot know diminution, a feeling standing by itself
within me and in which is concentrated all the little romance of
which I am capable." She urged Hannah to devote herself to Tom.
"You will not know till you are parted from him as I am, how much
you love him." Margaret had kept a journal of her brother's doings
and sayings, and a few days after her marriage she read extracts to

her husband, "but I began some passages I could not get through, and I felt almost as I had broken faith, as if I was reading my love letters to my first love."[48]

After Margaret's marriage, Tom wrote to Hannah that "husbands and wives are not so happy and cannot be so happy as brothers and sisters." She passed the letter on to Margaret, who responded: "I cannot quite agree with him, and yet I think there is much in that relation which is the best part of married life."[49]

Tom himself was brokenhearted. "Shortly before leaving England, in a letter that he could not trust himself to finish without locking the door—lest he be found crying like a child—Tom wrote [to Margaret] that the separation that made him weep was not that which would result from his going to India, but that which had taken place a year earlier, when she married . . . 'My loss is all pure loss. Nothing springs up to fill the void. All that I can do is to cling to that which is still left to me.'" "She is dead to me," he wrote to Hannah. "The bitterness of that death is past . . . Instead of wishing to be near her, I shrink from it."[50]

Macaulay now focused all his love on Hannah. He was determined to take her with him to Calcutta, telling her that he was accepting a position in the Council of India only for her sake, "so that I may surround her with comforts, and be assured of leaving her safe from poverty."[51] But within six months of their arrival in India Hannah became engaged to a brilliant young civil servant, Charles Trevelyan, who was working with Macaulay.

Macaulay acquiesced in Hannah's engagement, but he wrote to Margaret:

> My parting from you almost broke my heart . . . My Margaret and my Nancy [his nickname for Hannah] were so dear to me and so fond of me that I found in their society all the quiet social happiness of domestic life. I never formed any se-

rious attachment—any attachment which could possibly end in marriage. I was under a strange delusion . . . I could not see that others might wish to marry girls whose society was so powerfully attaching to keep me from marrying. I did not reflect—and yet I well know—that there are ties between man and woman dearer and closer than those of blood, that I was suffering an indulgence to become necessary to me which I might lose at any moment, that I was giving up my whole soul to objects the very excellence of which was likely to deprive me of them. I have reaped as I have sowed. At thirty-four I am alone in the world. I have lost everything and I have only myself to blame. The work of more than twenty years has vanished in a single month. She was always most dear to me. Since you left me she was everything to me. I loved her, I adored her. For her sake more than for my own, I valued wealth, station, political and literary fame. For her sake far more than for my own I became an exile from my country. . . . She was everything to me: and I am to be henceforth nothing to her."[52]

He confided that he had agreed to live with the Trevelyans, but only because they made it a condition of their marrying. However, before his letter arrived in England Margaret had died, of scarlet fever. The Trevelyans now felt more than ever responsible for Tom.[53] Hannah remained besotted with her brother. As late as 1839, she was worrying that she loved Tom more than God. "I cannot endure the thought of ever loving him less than I do at this moment, though I feel how criminal it is—But I must leave off."[54]

Macaulay and the Trevelyans returned together to London. Tom continued to live with them until the Trevelyan family moved to the suburbs (in fact to Clapham). In 1839, concerned that Trevelyan would be sent back to India, Macaulay engineered his appointment as assistant secretary to the Treasury.[55] Eventually, in 1858, Sir Charles

Trevelyan, as he had become, was appointed governor of Madras. He took his wife and children back to India. The following year, Macaulay had a heart attack and died. He was fifty-nine years old. At Hannah's prompting, her son, George Otto Trevelyan, eventually produced the *Life and Letters of Lord Macaulay.*

PART III

the intellectuals

CHAPTER SEVEN

The Bourgeois Intellectuals

*I*n March 1831, when Parliament was debating the first Reform Act, and factions maneuvered for tactical advantage, Thomas Babington Macaulay rose to set the franchise question in a large historical perspective.

> All history is full of revolutions, produced by causes similar to those which are now operating in England. A portion of the community which had been of no account expands and becomes strong. It demands a place in the system, suited, not to its former weakness, but to its present power. If this is granted, all is well. If this is refused, then comes the struggle between the young energy of one class and the ancient privileges of another.

Such conflicts had pitted the plebeians against the nobles in ancient Rome, the colonists in North America against the mother country, the Third Estate against the aristocracy in France, the slaves against "an aristocracy of skin" in Jamaica.

> Such, finally, is the struggle which the middle classes in England are maintaining against an aristocracy of mere locality,

against an aristocracy the principle of which is to invest a hundred drunken potwallopers[1] in one place, or the owner of a ruined hovel in another, with powers which are withheld from cities renowned to the furthest ends of the earth, for the marvels of their wealth and of their industry.[2]

To be sure, the disabilities of the urban middle class could hardly be compared to slavery. Nor should the rather limited extension of the franchise in 1832 be compared to the abolition of slavery in the British territories that was mandated in 1833. The Reform Act did away with rotten boroughs controlled by country landowners, gave the vote to more property owners, and extended parliamentary representation in the towns and cities, but it did not bring the middle classes to power. The landed interest did not go away.

Contemporaries nevertheless felt that great changes were inevitable in the way that the country was run, although there was much disagreement about what changes were desirable. Intellectuals were divided between the party of industry and the party of culture. The Utilitarians taught that government was like a machine, or rather that it should be. The engine of government should be rendered more and more efficient in order to produce maximum happiness for the greatest number. Obsolete models were to be tossed aside.

The prospect of a rational, mechanical, and urban civilization was not, however, to everyone's taste.

> But civilisation is itself but a mixed good [Samuel Taylor Coleridge proclaimed], if not far more a corrupting influence, the hectic of disease, not the boom of health, and a nation so distinguished more fitly to be called a varnished than a polished people, where this civilisation is not grounded in cultivation, in the harmonious development of those qualities and faculty that characterise our humanity. We must be men in order to be citizens.[3]

Macaulay concurred. "As civilisation advances," he mourned, "poetry almost necessarily declines."[4] And he mounted a devastating charge against Utilitarian materialism. "All that is merely ornamental—all that gives the roundness, the smoothness, and the bloom, has been excluded. Nothing is left but nerve, and muscle, and bone."[5] John Stuart Mill did his best to synthesize the materialism of Bentham and the idealism of Coleridge, but not everyone was persuaded.[6]

Yet the intellectuals agreed on one fundamental premise: the traditional ruling class was unfitted to lead an urban, industrial Britain. Feudal privilege had no place in an efficient Benthamite state. Nor could the rural aristocracy provide spiritual guidance to the urban masses. Darwin and Galton believed that the nobility was in any case done for, condemned by their inefficient breeding habits and their anti-competitive rule of primogeniture. Natural selection would finish them off. A new elite was required, a leading cadre of educated and cultivated men.

Coleridge had called for a true clerisy—"the sages and professors of . . . all the so called liberal arts and sciences."[7] Macaulay was in favor of greater democracy, but only if it was guided by men of culture. Thomas Carlyle demanded "a new real Aristocracy of fact, instead of the extinct imaginary one of title."[8] Matthew Arnold damned the Gradgrind men of business as Philistines, and imagined a cultivated elite that could be charged with the nation's soul, its culture.[9] Francis Galton put his faith in a hereditary aristocracy of talent.[10]

But George Meredith sounded a warning:

How soothing it is to intellect—that noble rebel, as the Pilgrim has it—to stand, and bow, and know itself superior! This exquisite compensation maintains the balance: whereas that period anticipated by the Pilgrim, when science shall have produced an *intellectual aristocracy,* is indeed horrible to contemplate. For what despotism is so black as one the mind cannot challenge? 'Twill be an iron Age.[11]

Looking back a century later, Noel Annan argued that an intellectual aristocracy did in fact establish itself in England.[12] "A section of the Victorian middle class rose to positions of influence and respect as a range of posts passed out of the gift of the nobility into their hands," he wrote. "They naturally ascended to positions where academic and cultural policy was made."[13] The reform of the civil service in the middle of the nineteenth century was "their Glorious Revolution." "No formal obstacle then remained to prevent the man of brains from becoming a gentleman."[14]

And Annan judged that Meredith's prophecy had been too gloomy. He remarked approvingly that the new men were reformers but not revolutionaries. Their writers undertook the great work of moral improvement, "criticising the assumptions of the ruling class above them and forming the opinions of the upper middle class to which they belonged."[15] They renewed the public schools and the universities, and they made public policy, if only behind the scenes. He might have added that they carried forward Clapham's liberal projects in India and Africa.

This intellectual aristocracy was not a hereditary caste of men of genius, as Galton believed. Annan insisted that its leading lights were made, not born, formed by families that prized brains and honored public service. And where Galton was obsessed by descent, Annan was more impressed by lateral connections. The eminent men he singled out were linked by recurring ties of marriage, and he proposed to illustrate how "certain families gain position and influence through persistent endogamy."[16]

Updating Galton's genealogies, Annan chased up the links between the intellectual dynasties. His approach was decidedly impressionistic, however, and not only as compared to Galton's statistical treatment. The running metaphor is a fox hunt—"We had better first draw a covert in the Macaulay country"—"Now we are in open fields and the pace is tremendous"—"Though this fox would run much further we had better hack back to the Babingtons where there is a gap in the hedge for us to jump into the Stephen country."[17]

The metaphor—remote from the lived experience of most of his readers—may suggest that Annan was also a snob, which he was, and indeed his essay reads at times very like an old-fashioned society column.

> The following Wedgwoods are cousins of the Darwins. Dr Ralph Vaughan-Williams, O.M., whose maternal grandparents were a Wedgwood and a Darwin; the novelist Arthur Wedgwood; Sir Ralph Wedgwood, railway director, and his daughter, the historian and literary editor of *Time and Tide,* Miss Veronica Wedgwood; Mrs Irene Gosse, a Wedgwood through her mother and second wife (though the marriage was later dissolved) of Mr Philip Gosse, son of Sir Edmund Gosse, critic and author of the brilliant description of a nonconformist childhood, *Father and Son.* Finally there were the children of the first Lord Wedgwood, who married the daughter of the judge Lord Bowen: his son the artist and second baron; his fourth daughter, the anthropologist the late Hon. Camilla Wedgwood; and his eldest daughter Helen, who married Mr Michael Pease, the geneticist and son of E. H. R. Pease, the secretary and chronicler of the Fabian Society and grandfather of Mrs Andrew Huxley.[18]

Nonetheless, Annan was on to something. An intelligentsia had emerged in England: not an aristocracy but a thoroughly bourgeois class. A surprising number of intellectuals were descended from families of the Clapham Sect and their Quaker and Unitarian allies—or perhaps unsurprisingly, since they inherited their public conscience and puritan habits, and benefited from successive generations of patronage. They often had day jobs as university professors, or senior civil servants, or lawyers. Some were members of Parliament. Others were vicars and even bishops. (Annan neglected the theologians, although the Victorians were great readers of sermons, and Coleridge had placed the clergy "at the head of all" the "sages.")[19] Annan left out the intellectuals' less famous brothers, sons, and nephews (let alone their sisters and daughters, unless they married intellectuals). However, they were also typically professional men, or company directors, or even members of Parliament, quite capable of publishing essays in the quarterly reviews or the occasional novel.

Nor were their private arrangements unusual. Intellectual coteries shared common values, intermarried, and often settled near to one another, but then so did the Clapham Sect, and the Lake Poets, and the Pre-Raphaelite Brethren, and also the dynasties of bankers and industrialists. But while they were gentlemen, and seldom bohemians or revolutionaries, they were public intellectuals, who served in the front line in the battle of ideas.

THE SONS of Clapham, who came of age in the 1830s, were obsessed with the reformation of political and economic organization. The next generation faced a challenge to religion. In the 1850s the close associates of Samuel Wilberforce were converting to Catholicism. By the end of the decade, educated men were encountering unprecedented challenges to Christianity itself. Shaken by the publication of Darwin's *The Origin of Species* in 1859, they were probably still more discomfited in the following year when *Essays and Reviews* appeared, the first significant English work of modern biblical criticism.[20] Samuel Wilberforce, by then Bishop of Oxford, provoked a famous public confrontation with Huxley over the descent of man.

(He asked whether Huxley was descended from an ape on his mother's side of the family, or on his father's.)[21] He also moved to have *Essays and Reviews* condemned in the Convocation of Canterbury.

Younger men were readier to adopt the new doctrines. When Sir James Stephen's son Leslie followed his older brother Fitzjames to Cambridge, in 1850, he discovered that the tone there was now decidedly Broad Church. "At Cambridge . . . by my time the epithet 'evangelical' generally connoted contempt," he recalled. "The 'Oxford Movement' might be altogether mistaken, but we agreed with it that the old 'low church' position had become untenable."[22] In 1854 Leslie took holy orders, but only because this commitment was required for appointment to a college fellowship. "I took this step rather—perhaps I should say very—thoughtlessly . . . My real motive was that I was very anxious to relieve my father of the burthen of supporting me."[23]

Nearly thirty years younger than Samuel Wilberforce, and two generations removed from Clapham, Leslie Stephen read the new books and discovered that he no longer believed in the flood or in miraculous interventions. Indeed, he came to believe that the doctrines of Clapham led ineluctably to skepticism. "Protestantism in one aspect is simply rationalism still running about with the shell on its head," he remarked. "This gives no doubt one secret of the decay of the evangelical party. The Protestant demand for a rational basis of faith widened among men of any intellectual force into an inquiry about the authority of the Bible or of Christianity."[24]

He confessed his doubts to the Master of his college and had to resign his tutorship, but even though he had lost both his faith and his job he had a sense of liberation. "In truth, I did not feel that the solid ground was giving way beneath my feet, but rather that I was being relieved of a cumbrous burden. I was not discovering that my creed was false, but that I had never really believed it."[25] Only in retrospect did he recognize how much had changed—"only when I

. . . remind myself that we are all now evolutionists, and that orthodox divines accept the most startling doctrines of *Essays and Reviews,*
I feel as though I must have lived through more than one generation."[26]

Even a grandson of John Venn, the vicar of Clapham, another in
the long line of clerical John Venns, became a follower of John Stuart Mill and abandoned holy orders. (A distinguished logician, he
went on to write a number of books, notably *The Logic of Chance*
[1866].) Yet like Tom Macaulay, the first great intellectual from a
Clapham family, these men acknowledged the force of the old moral
imperatives. And the evangelical legacy left other indelible traces.
"The effect of the religious training is apparently perceptible in a
great tendency to self-analysis,"[27] Leslie Stephen wrote of his older
brother, adding that although Fitzjames became a rationalist and a
follower of Mill and Bentham, "the superstructure of belief was a
modified evangelicism."[28] He might have described himself in the
same terms.[29] The Stephen brothers also carried on Clapham's campaign against slavery. Fitzjames led the prosecution of Governor
Eyre for the bloody suppression of a rebellion in Jamaica, while Leslie was a passionate advocate of the North in the American civil war.

THE STEPHEN brothers became important public intellectuals.
James Fitzjames Stephen served as legal member of the Indian vice-
roy's council in succession to Macaulay and his friend, Henry Maine
—in fact Maine recommended him for the post. Like Macaulay and
Maine, Fitzjames also made a name for himself as a polemical journalist. In the publication's early years, a contemporary remarked,
Stephen "*was* the Pall Mall Gazette."[30] And the *Pall Mall Gazette*
was a distinguished forum. "We address ourselves to the higher circles of society: we care not to disown it," says one of Thackeray's
conspiratorial characters; "the Pall Mall Gazette is written by gentle-

men for gentlemen; its conductors speak to the classes in which they live and were born. The field-preacher has his journal, the radical free-thinker has his journal: why should the Gentlemen of England be unrepresented in the Press?"[31]

After his false start as a Cambridge don, Leslie Stephen moved back to London in 1864, "intending to support myself by my pen."[32] He wrote biographies and books of literary criticism, moral philosophy, and intellectual history, and he also became an indefatigable contributor to the *Pall Mall Gazette* and to Thackeray's *Cornhill Magazine*, which he was to edit from 1871 to 1882. In 1881 he was appointed founding editor of the *Dictionary of National Biography*, which he directed for ten years.

When Leslie began his literary career in London, Fitzjames and his Cambridge friend, the economist and politician William Fawcett, were already well known for their journalism. Leslie was later to write the biographies of both men. Now, at the start of his career, they offered him a ready entrée into the intellectual society of London.[33] As ever, networks yielded patronage, and neighbors, and wives. But, as ever, dependence on family support had its darker side, its barely controlled emotional tensions.

Like the Claphamites, the Stephen brothers and their friends and cousins tended to look for houses near one another, in their case mainly in the professional milieu of Kensington, a district lovingly evoked by Leslie Stephen's sister-in-law Anny Thackeray in her best-known novel, *Old Kensington*. Fitzjames bought a huge and ugly house in De Vere Gardens, just off Kensington High Street, and Leslie moved in nearby. "We all live within a few minutes' walk of each other and with sundry cousins we form a little colony in the neighbourhood of the South Kensington Museum," he wrote to Oliver Wendell Holmes in 1867.[34]

Their networks were dense, made up of multiple, overlapping

links, often connected to their Clapham roots. When Leslie Stephen explained to his children how he and his brother had found their wives, he began by sketching the circles through which they moved.

Fitzjames married a daughter of J. W. Cunningham, vicar of Harrow. The Rev. Cunningham had started his career as John Venn's curate at Clapham parish church. (He wrote a popular novel, *The Velvet Cushion,* which glorified the evangelical movement. Venn appears in it as Berkely.) Cunningham became editor of the *Christian Observer* on the suggestion of Sir James Stephen. This was a mark of real esteem: the *Christian Observer* was virtually the official organ of the Clapham Sect, and Sir James had first thought of taking on the editorship himself in partnership with his son Fitzjames. All in all, Cunningham "belonged, therefore, by right, to the evangelical party," Leslie Stephen wrote, "and had been more or less known to my father for many years. There were thus various links between the Cunninghams and ourselves."[35]

The Cunningham family soon absorbed Fitzjames. Leslie remarked diplomatically that "the marriage had the incidental advantage of providing him with a new brother and sister; for Henry (now Sir Henry) Stewart Cunningham, and Emily Cunningham (now Lady Egerton), were from this time as dear to him as if they had been connected by the closest tie of blood relationship."[36] Henry Cunningham was another lawyer and author, whose first novel, *Wheat and Tares,* described a clerical household based very obviously on that of his uncle and aunt. He became a government advocate in the Punjab, collaborated with Fitzjames in the codification of Indian law, and ended up a high court judge in Calcutta.

The relationship between Fitzjames and his wife's sister was more problematic: they were evidently in love with each other. Emily Cunningham lived with her brother Henry until his marriage in 1877, but she herself married only in 1883, when she was fifty years old. In copying Fitzjames's letters after his death, Lady Stephen censored the emotional tone of his correspondence with Emily.[37]

None of Fitzjames's daughters married, but the eldest, Katherine, became a notable academic. His three sons all became lawyers. His first son, Herbert, an authority on criminal law and practice, married his cousin, Hermione Cunningham, when he was seventy years old, commenting "we Stephens mature late."[38] The second son, James Kenneth, was passionately in love with Leslie Stephen's stepdaughter, Stella Duckworth. The third son, Harry, a judge of the high court of Calcutta, married a niece of Florence Nightingale.

"AT CAMBRIDGE I had learnt to consider myself as rather an old bachelor," Leslie Stephen recalled. "I looked no further."[39] But when he moved to London he was free of the celibacy rule that still bound Cambridge dons, and he began to meet young women in the social circle of his mother and sister, and in Fitzjames's literary milieu.

Fitzjames was an associate of the novelist William Makepeace Thackeray, and both his mother and his sister knew Thackeray's daughters, Anny and Minny. When Anny and Minny were small children Mrs. Thackeray had gone mad and was placed in care; the girls were brought up by their father. After Thackeray's death, the sisters set up a household together. Anny was already an established author, and Minny became her devoted helper. "The relation between them might be compared to the relation between a popular author and his wife," wrote Leslie Stephen, who was to marry the younger sister. "My Minny, of course, played the part of wife in the little household. That is, she was to all appearance entirely dependent upon her sister. She both loved Anny and believed in her with the most unstinted warmth."[40]

Through another twist of family ties, the Thackeray sisters had become foster parents. When they were in their early teens Thackeray had brought Amy Crowe, the daughter of a friend, into the house to act as their companion. Virtually an adopted sister, Amy married Thackeray's cousin, Edward Thackeray, a soldier in India. (Thackeray was so upset after giving away the bride that he spent the afternoon in tears in Millais's studio.)[41] Amy went off to India with her husband but corresponded regularly with the Thackeray sisters. Anny was named godmother of her first child. Then the young mother suddenly sickened and died. Her two small children were sent back to London, and Anny and Minny took them in. The "husband" and "wife" were now father and mother.

Eventually Edward Thackeray remarried, returned to London, and reclaimed his daughters, very much against the wishes of their foster parents. But the sisters remained close to the girls. Their relationships were later reinforced by two marriages: Anny's goddaughter married a cousin of the Thackerays, Gerald Ritchie, and Anny herself married Gerald's brother Richmond, so becoming her goddaughter's sister-in-law.[42]

Leslie Stephen and Minny married in 1867. He moved into the Thackeray house, alongside Anny and their two little foster daughters. Leslie dutifully made the rounds of their connections, but as Anny's biographer, Henrietta Garnett, notes, he "found the business thoroughly muddling, simply because so many of the sisters' friends were also their relations."[43] However, the joint household was a failure. Leslie and Anny quarreled continuously. She was feckless; he worried obsessively about money. At last even Minny agreed that Anny should set up home on her own. "The scheme showed no decline of [Minny's] love for Anny, but a growing closeness to me," Leslie Stephen told his children. "In the earlier days she would have dreaded the most partial separation from her sister. She now thought of it, chiefly on the ground that it might make Anny more prudent in money matters."[44] But the new household was short-lived. Following two miscarriages and the premature birth of a daughter, Minny died suddenly, of eclampsia, in the course of a new pregnancy, in 1875. She was buried at Kensal Green cemetery, beside Leslie's father and mother.[45]

Leslie was shattered by Minny's death, but two women in his most intimate network were ready to care for him and his infant daughter. He turned first to Anny, his deceased wife's sister. Leslie and Anny moved to a small house in Hyde Park Gardens, which belonged to the Thackeray sisters. At once the chronic rows over money started up again. They were also divided about the best way of dealing with Minny's daughter, Laura, who was already showing unmistakable signs of the mental illness that was to blight her life (and which Leslie feared was hereditary, given the madness of her Thackeray grandmother). But when the crisis came, it was for a completely different reason. Anny had been carrying on a flirtation with her cousin, Richmond Ritchie, who was seventeen years her junior. One afternoon, as Leslie put it, "the catastrophe occurred." "To speak plainly, I came into the drawing-room and found Richmond kissing Anny. I told her at once that she ought to make up her mind one way or other."[46]

The Ritchie family were less easily shocked, but they also regarded this development as a calamity. Thackeray's father's sister, Charlotte, had married John Ritchie. Richmond was their grandson, and he was therefore Anny's second cousin. That was not regarded by anyone concerned as an impediment to their marriage. Nor did the Ritchies object that Richmond was so much younger than Anny. Rather, they blamed Leslie for pushing the couple into a premature marriage, so forcing Richmond to give up his studies at Cambridge. They were mollified when Sir Henry Cole, a lifelong friend of the Thackerays, found Richmond a place in the India Office, where he went on to have a distinguished career.[47]

Leslie's own objections to the marriage were more emotional, more violent, and more obviously selfish. "The fact was that if they hated the marriage, I positively loathed it," he confessed to his children.

> I hated it perhaps, as Julia [Duckworth] suggested to me, partly because all men are jealous and I might feel that I was being put at a lower level in Anny's affections; I certainly thought that it would make a widening gulf between us; I hated it because men at least always hate a marriage between a young man and a much older woman; and I hated it because the most obvious result would be the breaking up of my own household. I knew very little of and carried very little for Richmond. Well, it all seems absurd now. The marriage, as Julia foretold, has been a very happy one.[48]

The second woman to whom Leslie turned was his only surviving sister, Caroline Emelia Stephen. Known as Milly, she had lived a sheltered life with her parents, caring for her father in his frail old age and nursing her mother, who died shortly before Leslie's wife Minny. While her brothers became rationalists, she had (Leslie said) "taken up with the Quakers, finding something sympathetic in their quietism and semi-mystical tendencies."[49] Milly had published a book, *The Service of the Poor*, drawing on a correspondence with Florence Nightingale (whose niece had married a son of Fitzjames Stephen), and she was already set on a career of charity.

But there was not much she could do for Leslie, admittedly a difficult man, who had just suffered a tragic loss. Leslie thought that Milly was too besotted with him, perhaps too much like him, to be helpful.

> Now Milly has loved me all her life; she has been more like a twin than a younger sister; and Julia [Duckworth] used to say

—of course affectionately—that she was altogether silly about me. Yet, as I found myself saying at the time, she was too like me to be helpful. If I put an argument in order to have it contradicted, she took it so seriously that I thought there must be something in it; if I was in doubt, she fell into utter perplexity; if I was sad, she began to weep . . . Consequently, though a most affectionate, she was a most depressing companion.[50]

After only a month, Milly moved out and set up house in Chelsea, where she founded the Metropolitan Association for Befriending Young Servants together with her first cousin Sara Stephen.

Alone once more with his disturbed daughter, Leslie now turned to a third woman in his network, a widow, Julia Duckworth. Leslie had known her late husband, Herbert Duckworth, at Cambridge, where they had friends in common (a cousin of Leslie and a cousin of Duckworth).[51] And Julia was one of Anny Thackeray's closest friends. When Julia's husband died, Anny was one of the few people whose presence the young widow could tolerate.[52] When Minny died, Anny had depended on Julia's support.

Julia was a beauty. Her mother was one of the seven famously lovely Pattle sisters, descended on their mother's side from an aristocratic French exile, the Chevalier de l'Étang. "Old Madame de l'Étang was extremely handsome," according to Julia's daughter, Virginia Woolf. "Her daughter, Mrs. Pattle, was lovely. Six of Mrs. Pattle's seven daughters were even more lovely than she was."[53] Mr. Pattle, however, was an embarrassment. Virginia Woolf described him as "a gentleman of marked, but doubtful, reputation, who after living a riotous life and earning the title 'the biggest liar in India,' finally drank himself to death and was consigned to a cask of rum to await shipment to England."[54] The story was no doubt embroidered,[55] but in any case the Pattle sisters "created some stir in Victorian society," according to one of their grandsons, Herbert Fisher, "by their good looks, warm hearts, and high-spirited and unconventional ways."[56]

Two of the sisters married into the aristocracy; others married into the Anglo-Indian establishment. The most talented of the sisters, Julia Pattle, married Charles Cameron, a member of the Supreme Council of India, and on their retirement to England she became a pioneering photographer. Sara Pattle married Henry Thoby Prinsep, a Director of the East India Company and author of several books. Maria Pattle married less grandly—her husband was a physician in Calcutta, a Dr. Jackson—and they retired to England to live a moderately prosperous life near Tunbridge Wells. Dr. Jackson's position in his own family puzzled Leslie Stephen. "Somehow he did not seem to count—as fathers generally count in their families . . . The old doctor was respected or esteemed rather than ardently loved . . . And this was the more obvious because of the strength of the other family affections."[57]

By these "other family affections" Stephen meant the close relationship between the Pattle sisters. Mrs. Jackson herself was particularly attached to Sara Prinsep. Her daughter, Julia Prinsep Jackson—named after her mother's two favorite sisters—was a regular presence at the grand establishment of the Prinseps, Little Holland House in Kensington. It was one of the artistic and literary centers of London. Thackeray was a regular visitor, as were Tennyson, Browning, and Meredith. The artist G. F. Watts actually lived in their house; Burne-Jones was taken in when he was ailing; and other members of the Pre-Raphaelite circle, including Holman Hunt, were frequent guests.[58]

"Little Holland House was her education," according to Julia's daughter, Virginia Woolf.[59] But Julia made an impression in her own right. The artists were dazzled by her. Watts drew Julia as a child, and she modeled for Burne-Jones's painting of the Annunciation.

Two members of the Pre-Raphaelite Brethren, Holman Hunt and the sculptor Thomas Woolner, "felt a more than artistic admiration for Julia and made offers," Leslie recalled.

> I may add that Woolner and Hunt married two sisters and that Hunt's marriage of a third sister, upon the death of his first wife, led to a quarrel between them. I used to be told, though obviously such reports are not to be taken as worth anything, that these two were attracted to the said sisters by their likeness to Julia. Probably this was a conjecture of some ingenious person; but it is true, though to me not very intelligible, that the present Mrs Holman Hunt and Julia were not infrequently taken for each other.[60]

Abandoned by Anny, disappointed in Milly, Leslie now laid siege to Anny's friend Julia Duckworth. After a strange courtship conducted largely by correspondence, she agreed to marry him. The wedding took place in the church where Richmond and Anny had celebrated their marriage only a few months earlier. Anny noted, however, that Leslie was still mourning the loss of Minny. "He says Julia has healed his wound, but she cannot staunch the blood."[61]

ANNAN'S "INTELLECTUAL aristocracy" was in fact a specialized wing of the bourgeoisie. Its members were drawn largely from established clans of professionals, civil servants, and clergymen. Like their more conventional relatives, they drew on family connections and they created their own tight, localized networks, cross-cut with recursive marriage ties, intimate but sometimes oppressive.

Some of these networks endured over several generations, turning into clans of intellectuals. The Stephens (and their Venn and Dicey cousins), all directly descended from the Clapham Sect, formed one of the more eminent of these. Another, also directly descended from Clapham, was the Macaulay-Trevelyan clan. Aristocratic, featuring civil servants and politicians, it was notable above all for its historians —Macaulay himself; his nephew and biographer, George Otto Trevelyan; and George Otto's son, George Macaulay Trevelyan.[62] The Darwin-Wedgwoods were another of the intellectual clans, with a hereditary bent for the sciences.

These clans continued to produce leading writers, scientists, and dons until the middle of the twentieth century. Their localized, intermarried networks were typical of their bourgeois contemporaries. However, the next generation of intellectuals developed a rather different form of association in the less constrained milieu of Edwardian London.

CHAPTER EIGHT

The Bloomsbury Version

*I*n an essay written in 1929, E. M. Forster described Bloomsbury as "the only genuine *movement* in English civilization" of his day.[1] He did not attempt to defend this large claim in any detail. Perhaps he did not think it necessary, and indeed his assertion would not have seemed entirely extravagant at the time. Forster himself was regarded as a major novelist, Virginia Woolf as a pioneering modernist, Maynard Keynes as a great economist and also a weighty—and witty—commentator on current affairs. Roger Fry had a reputation as a very advanced art critic. His Omega Workshops were becoming fashionable. Assisted by Clive Bell and Desmond MacCarthy, he had organized the sensational exhibition "Manet and the Post-Impressionists" in 1910, which brought the revolutionary new art from Paris to London. The Woolfs' Hogarth Press seemed to be publishing every important new highbrow writer. Bloomsbury's house magazine, *The Nation*, largely funded by Keynes and edited for some time by Leonard Woolf, was a bible to the liberal intellectuals.

But if Bloomsbury was important, it was not universally popular. Forster was particularly concerned to defend it from charges of snobbery, although he conceded that its members were all very much of a certain class: "Essentially *gentlefolks*. Might occasionally open other people's letters, but wouldn't steal, bully, slander, blackmail, or resent generosity as some of their critics would, and have required a culture in harmony with their social position."[2]

They were generally comfortably off, enjoying at least Virginia Woolf's famous minimum standard for a writer—five hundred pounds a year and a room of one's own (that is, an income of around $32,000 today).[3] Clive Bell had a wealthy family behind him. Keynes became rather rich through his investments. E. M. Forster and the Stephen siblings had modest but helpful private incomes, boosted by legacies from maiden aunts. Others struggled, notably Duncan Grant and also Lytton Strachey until the success of his *Eminent Victorians*, but they were both bailed out regularly by Keynes and another moneyed bachelor in their circle, Harry Norton. "The class war," declared Keynes, "will find me on the side of the educated *bourgeoisie*."[4] He spoke for them all.

IN 1910, Lytton Strachey noted in his diary that he passed an evening at Lady Ottoline Morrell's home but found "no Bloomby" there.[5] The term "Bloomsberries" was coined in 1910 or 1911 by Molly MacCarthy. E. M. Forster himself preferred "Bloomsburies."[6] The more familiar term "Bloomsbury Group" recurs in later Bloomsbury letters, diaries, and memoirs, typically accompanied by reservations about the real existence of a "group," or the possibility of establishing who were its members. This ambivalence is perhaps suggestive. Raymond Williams discerned in it "the clue to the essential definition" of Bloomsbury: "It was united by an ideology, but paradoxically by an ideology which claimed that individuals should resist ideologies."[7]

However, the sociologically acute Leonard Woolf denied that

there was any ideological bond at all. Nor was Bloomsbury an artistic movement, as E. M. Forster claimed. It was simply a set of friends.

> There have often been groups of people, writers and artists, who were not only friends, but were consciously united by a common doctrine and object, or purposes artistic or social. The utilitarians, the Lake poets, the French impressionists, the English Pre-Raphaelites were groups of this kind. Our group was quite different. Its basis was friendship, which in some cases developed into love and marriage.[8]

Yet Woolf also once described his circle as "a company of personal friends whose residential roots were in Bloomsbury and their spiritual roots in Cambridge."[9] This was to admit an ideological kinship of some kind, and indeed to pinpoint its origin. "The colour of our minds and thought had been given to us by the climate of Cambridge and Moore's philosophy."[10]

Unsympathetic contemporaries described Bloomsbury as a coterie or clique. "Group" is, at least, a neutral term. So too is Forster's "movement," which also suggests the avant-garde temper of Bloomsbury and hints, perhaps, at its public role. A more precise term, however, is "network." Bloomsbury was a network made up, as Leonard Woolf remarks, of friends and lovers. Friends and lovers are not necessarily mutually exclusive categories. In Bloomsbury they were often hard to tell apart; friends and lovers might also be neighbors, lodgers, painters and subjects, patrons and clients. But there was nothing casual about this confusion. Friendship and love were idealized. Friends and lovers were sacred figures in a cult of personal relationships. In short, the network was heavily charged. "I see in the collection each of us connected up with each of the others by particular peculiar links," one of the more obscure members of the set, Saxon Sydney-Turner, wrote to Virginia Woolf in 1919; "some are more and some less important but they all have some meaning."[11]

Rather than radiating out from a single center, like a spider's web, the Bloomsbury network had two nodes, each rooted in a set of siblings. The first was constituted by Thoby Stephen and his sisters Vanessa (Bell) and Virginia (Woolf). After Thoby died in 1906 the Stephen sisters became central figures, although which sister was the queen of Bloomsbury was a matter of some dispute. E. M. Forster described Bloomsbury as "matriarchal" and asserted that "at the centre of the maze sat the unwobbling pivot, Vanessa Bell."[12] T. S. Eliot, however, thought that "without Virginia Woolf at the centre of it, [Bloomsbury] would have remained formless or marginal."[13] Their younger brother, Adrian, was a birthright member of this wing of Bloomsbury, and when the sisters married, their husbands became members of the Stephen moiety. Both Vanessa's husband, Clive Bell, and Virginia's husband, Leonard Woolf, had been close to Thoby Stephen in Cambridge. (Thoby and Clive Bell enjoyed

The Stephen siblings and spouses.

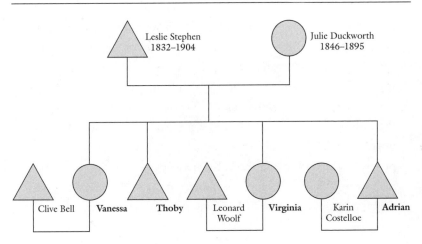

smoking cigars together and talking about hunting—not in general Bloomsbury tastes.)

The second node formed around Lytton Strachey. Closely associated with Lytton were his younger brother, James, and their cousin —and lover—Duncan Grant. Their young sister, Marjorie Strachey, and sometimes their older sisters were also included in their brothers' circle. ("Marjorie Strachey's party trick was to sing shockingly filthy songs with a completely straight face and lady-like demeanour.")[14]

THE STORY of the Bloomsbury network must accordingly begin with the Strachey and Stephen families at the end of the nineteenth century, both long established in Kensington (and on visiting terms with each other).

> "Who was I then?" [asked Virginia Woolf, reflecting on her childhood in Kensington]. "Adeline Virginia Stephen, the second daughter of Leslie and Julia Prinsep Stephen, born on 25th January 1882, descended from a great many people, some famous, others obscure; born into a large connection, born not of rich parents, but of well-to-do parents, born into a very communicative, literate, letter writing, visiting, articulate, late nineteenth century world."[15]

Lytton Strachey might have described his background in similar terms, although the Strachey lineage was rather grander than the Stephen line. When Leonard Woolf, a Jewish scholarship boy, visited the Stracheys he felt that "whereas I was living in 1902, they were living in 1774–1902 . . . The atmosphere of the dining-room at Lancaster Gate was that of British history and of the comparatively small ruling middle class which for the last 100 years had been the principal makers of British history."[16]

Members of the Strachey family were accustomed to see themselves almost as a biological species. "The Stracheys are most strongly the children of their fathers, not of their mothers," Mrs. St. Loe Strachey wrote in 1930. "'It does not matter whom they marry,'" said one of St. Loe's aunts to me when I was quite young, "'the type continues and has been the same for three hundred years.'"[17] Responding to Francis Galton's questionnaire to leading members of the Royal Society, Richard Strachey charaterized the Stracheys in the following way:

> All the males are intelligent above average, and decidedly peculiar though it is difficult to say in what way, the present tendencies are distinctly discernable in the preceding generation and may possibly have existed further back. Besides the intellectual qualities of tendency towards acquisition of precise knowledge in detail, capacity for business, active political interest, with an absence of piety, want of sporting interests, general inaptitude for squire life and indisposition to personal exaltation there is a certain eccentricity of manner . . . combined with most decided opinions.[18]

The nineteenth-century Strachey men were administrators in India, while the Stephens were writers and lawyers. But both families were equally eminent. Leslie Stephen's *Dictionary of National Biography* (the first volume of which appeared in 1885) had entries for his brother, his father, his father's father, and two of his father's brothers. Leslie wrote these himself, and his entry on his brother, James Fitzjames, included a note on Fitzjames's son, James Kenneth Stephen, Leslie's favorite nephew. He also wrote the entry on James Fitzjames's father-in-law, J. W. Cunningham. Leslie's mother's father, John Venn, had an entry (as did John Venn's father, Henry Venn). A long entry was devoted to the novelist W. M. Thackeray, the father of Leslie's first wife. This was also written by Leslie himself. Leslie's second wife, Julia, contributed the entry on her aunt, the photographer Julia Cameron (after whom she was named). There were also entries on Julia's uncle, Henry Thoby Prinsep (after whom her son Thoby Stephen was named), and on Prinsep's son Valentine. A supplement published after Leslie Stephen's death included an entry on Leslie himself, with a note on his sister Caroline, and an entry on Leslie's wife's sister, Anny Thackeray.

The Stracheys featured hardly less prominently in the *DNB*. Lytton Strachey's great-grandfather, Edward, had an entry which included a note on his son, Lytton's grandfather, also Edward. There was an entry as well on Lytton's father, Sir Richard, and on two of his father's brothers, Sir Edward and Sir John, "the most powerful pair of brothers in the Raj."[19] All these Stracheys had been distinguished administrators in India. Two of Sir Edward's sons had their own entries. Lytton's mother's father and one of her brothers also made enough of a name for themselves in India to warrant entries in the *DNB*, and there was a brief entry on Lady Strachey's father's father, a pioneering physician, William Grant. (Duncan Grant, the Bloomsbury artist, was his great-grandson.)

Virginia Woolf and Lytton Strachey both described their family milieux as Victorian.[20] "Hyde Park Gate in 1900 was a complete model of Victorian society," Virginia wrote. "If I had the power to lift out of the past a single day as we lived it about 1900, it would give a section of upper middle class Victorian life, like one of those sections with glass covers in which ants and bees are shown going about their task."[21]

This way of life was already anachronistic in the last years of the nineteenth century. "Two different ages confronted each other in the drawing room at Hyde Park Gate," according to Virginia. "The Victorian age and the Edwardian age. We were not [Leslie Stephen's] children; we were his grandchildren . . . But while we looked into the future, we were completely under the power of the past . . . we lived under the sway of a society that was about fifty years too old for us."

Victorian, no doubt—certainly in the eyes of their children—the Stracheys and the Stephens were more particularly representative of London's liberal, educated Victorian bourgeoisie, a distinctive breed. "The solid bourgeois qualities were interpenetrated by intellectualism and eccentricity," Lytton Strachey remarked of his own family.[22] Although both of Lytton's parents came from what they proudly described as "Anglo-Indian" families, his father, Richard Strachey, was a meteorologist and geographer of some distinction, a Fellow of the Royal Society, and a friend of Joseph Hooker, T. H. Huxley, George Darwin, and Francis Galton. Richard Strachey was an agnostic and an intellectual. So too was Leslie Stephen, and both men accepted knighthoods with some reluctance.

Leslie Stephen and Richard Strachey were also both rather deaf, which allowed them to ignore a great deal of what was going on around them, and as they got older neither exercised great authority in their homes. In 1901 the young Lytton Strachey visited his friend Thoby Stephen, who was on holiday with his family in the country. He reported back to Leonard Woolf: "It is a nice though wild family—two sisters very pretty—a younger brother Adrian, and Leslie with his ear-trumpet and tam-o-shanter. What is rather strange is the old man—older than he really is—among so young a family. He is well kept in check by them, and they are well bustled by him. They know each other very well I think."[23]

Certainly the Strachey and Stephen children were accustomed to being heard as well as seen. The Stephen girls felt that their mother had submitted too easily to Leslie's moods and demands, but many of the women in these families were notably independent and assertive. Jane Strachey was an active feminist who smoked the ultra-modern "American" cigarettes and was apt to regard domestic du-

ties as a nuisance. She confessed to Virginia Woolf that her ideal life
"would be to live entirely in boarding houses."[24]

She had reason to complain. A distinctively Victorian feature of
both households was their scale. The Stracheys had ten surviving
children, produced over a period of thirty years. Richard Strachey's
first wife died within a year of his marriage, and he married for the
second time at the age of forty-one, at the height of his career in
India. His wife was then only eighteen years old. The older children
were born in India and sent home to join the households of Jane
Strachey's married sisters. By the time the youngest children were
born, Richard Strachey had returned to England. After recouping,
with difficulty, from a financial disaster, he settled in London. When
Lytton was born in 1880, his father was already well into his sixties,
although he was not to retire for another thirty years. Jane Strachey
was over forty, and increasingly active in feminist causes. However,
two more children were to follow Lytton—a daughter, Marjorie,
and, in 1887, Jane Strachey's favorite child, James.

The Stephen household was smaller, but its structure was more
complicated. There were eight children—the oldest was fifteen when
the youngest was born—and they belonged to three distinct family
clusters. There was one child from Leslie Stephen's first marriage.
This was the unfortunate Laura Stephen, who was severely mentally impaired. (She was institutionalized permanently in 1891.) Julia
brought with her the three children from her marriage with Herbert
Duckworth: George, Stella, and the delicate Gerald, born after his
father's death. And Leslie and Julia had four children together—
Vanessa, Thoby, Virginia, and Adrian.

The younger children formed distinct cells in both of these households. Lytton, James, and Margaret Strachey were very close to each
other. The four Stephen children were not only significantly younger than their Duckworth half-siblings, but temperamentally very
different. As children, Vanessa and Virginia formed "a very close

conspiracy," Virginia wrote.[25] The sisters were also very competitive, but their loyalties and avocations diverged. Vanessa preferred
her mother, Virginia her father.[26] Perhaps influenced by her mother's position as the darling of the Pre-Raphaelites, Vanessa was to be
an artist. Virginia was to be a writer like Leslie, and quite early she
became her father's amanuensis. The focus of their rivalry was their
brother Thoby—a year younger than Vanessa, two years older than
Virginia. "Even as a little boy he was dominant among us," Virginia
recalled. "He could impose himself." He was sent away to a prepara-
tory school, Evelyns, and Virginia wrote that when he came home
on holiday he "told me stories about the boys at Evelyns. These
stories went on all through Evelyns, through Clifton [his public
school], and through Cambridge."[27]

Vanessa and Virginia Stephen were not given a formal education
and were not sent to university, although Vanessa did attend art
school. The reason may have been Leslie's chronic worries about
money, for he encouraged Virginia to study Greek and gave her the
run of his library. Leslie's brother, James Fitzjames Stephen, who
was no friend of the women's movement, did allow his eldest daughter, Katharine, to go to university. She became a pioneer of higher
education for women, eventually succeeding one of the Strachey sisters, Pernel, as Principal of Newnham College, Cambridge.

The feminist Jane Strachey sent all her daughters to a progressive
London school which was run by a French educator, Marie Souvestre, with whom Jane was besotted. When Marie Souvestre's relationship with her lesbian partner broke up, she established a new
school at which one of the Strachey daughters, Dorothy (also in love
with Marie) was to teach.[28] The two youngest sisters, Pernel and
Marjorie, studied at Oxford and Cambridge, respectively, and both
had distinguished academic careers.

The eldest Strachey sister, Elinor, married young; her husband
was James Rendel, the son of a close colleague of her father. The

second sister, Dorothy, was in love with her married cousin Sidney
Foster, but eventually married a penniless French artist when she
was in her late thirties. The three younger Strachey sisters never married.

LARGE HOMES were required to accommodate these complex families, and they were sprawling, shapeless, and almost defiantly not
smart. "To house the lot of us, now a storey would be thrown out
on top, now a dining room flung out at bottom," Virginia Woolf
wrote. "My mother, I believe, sketched what she wanted on a sheet
of notepaper to save the architect's fees . . . Here then seventeen or
eighteen people lived in small bedrooms with one bathroom and
three water-closets between them."[29] Lytton Strachey described the
scale of the nearby Strachey family house at Lancaster Gate as "size
gone wrong, size pathological; it was a house afflicted with elephan-
tiasis."[30] The Stracheys and their ten children and famously odd servants occupied seven floors, but with only one bathroom and lava-
tory between them.

Friends and relatives would assemble in the drawing room, which
Lytton Strachey described as "the most characteristic feature of the
house—its centre, its summary, the seat of its soul, so to speak."[31]
Recalling how he tried to kiss one of his grown-up nephews there
one afternoon, Strachey remarked that it was "a family room." It was
"on Sunday afternoons, when my mother was invariably at home,
that the family atmosphere, reinforced from without, reached its in-
tensest and its oddest pitch. Then the drawing room gradually grew
thick with aunts and uncles, cousins and connections . . . One saw
that it had indeed been built for them—it held them all so nicely, so
naturally, with their interminable varieties of age and character and
class."[32] Virginia Woolf described similar Sunday afternoons at Hyde
Park Gate, with relatives and old friends crowding around the sacred
center, the tea table.[33]

The sprawling households took considerable management. Jane Strachey ran her home at Lancaster Gate eccentrically but independently, with little interference from her much older husband. Julia Stephen was forced to contend with Leslie's extreme anxiety when the household accounts were presented. When she died, in 1895, the profoundly depressed Leslie gradually ceded his responsibilities to the eldest of the Duckworth siblings, George. "George Duckworth had become after my mother's death, for all practical purposes, the head of the family," Virginia Woolf recalled. "My father was deaf, eccentric, absorbed in his work, and entirely shut off from the world. The management of affairs fell upon George. It was usually said that he was father and mother, sister and brother in one—and all the old ladies of Kensington and Belgravia added with one accord that Heaven had blessed those poor Stephen girls beyond belief."[34]

In all these families it was the eldest daughter who had to take the mother's place. Katharine Stephen, Fitzjames's eldest daughter, looked after her siblings and nephews when they needed help, and she became the legal guardian of Leslie's incapable daughter, Laura, all in addition to her own distinguished career at Cambridge. The oldest unmarried Strachey daughter, Phillipa ("Pippa"), looked after her parents in their old age and later made a home for all the unattached Stracheys in Bloomsbury, while always working hard in the feminist movement.

Stella Duckworth naturally succeeded Julia as the female head of Leslie Stephen's household. She looked very much like her mother, and when Leslie once suggested that Julia treated Stella more harshly than her brothers, Julia replied that it was because she felt Stella was "part of myself."[35] Stella's responsibilities included the care of her egocentric, emotionally demanding, and chronically depressed stepfather. "Stella is my great support now," the incorrigibly solipsistic Leslie wrote to a friend soon after Julia's death:

She is very like her mother in some ways—very sweet and noble and affectionate to me. I am sometimes worried by thinking that she ought to be a wife and mother and that she may find sufficient reasons for leaving me. I ought to wish for it and sometimes I do but from a purely selfish point of view the event would be disastrous almost for me. However I suppose that I should submit and indeed there would be compensations.[36]

Stella did have a number of suitors, but when taking stock of his family immediately after Julia's death Leslie noted rather smugly that Julia had set very high standards for a prospective husband for Stella, and that nobody had shaped up.[37] Leslie's favorite nephew, "Jem" Stephen, the son of his brother Fitzjames, a brilliant young man, might have been a very acceptable suitor from Leslie and Julia's point of view. He was, however, subject to fits of madness. His pursuit of Stella was violent; eventually he had to be locked up in a mental hospital, where he died young. But Virginia suggested that after her mother's death Stella "became far less exacting, as indeed she lost interest in her fate."[38] In 1897, twenty-eight years old, she agreed to marry a persistent suitor, Jack Hills, an Eton friend of her brother George. Shortly after returning from their honeymoon Stella and Hills moved into a house in Hyde Park Gate, just a few doors away from the Stephen household.

Leslie was nevertheless deeply upset by Stella's marriage. He wrote to her on the eve of her honeymoon:

The world seems to have turned topsy-turvy with me since this morning and I feel as I felt once when I picked myself up after a fall—I cannot tell whether I am hurt or healed of a wound or simply dazzled . . . Well, dearest, I am quite clear about one or two things. I know that we love each other and

shall continue to love each other. I know that you will do all
you can for me and that your husband will help you.[39]

But after just three months of marriage, Stella suddenly died. Shattered, Leslie now looked to Vanessa to take over the role that Stella
herself had inherited from Julia.

Stella and Vanessa, the eldest daughters of Julia's two marriages,
were linked with each other within the family. Stella was ten years
older than Vanessa, but they shared a birthday and Vanessa's name
had been suggested by Stella's.[40] Stella "found in Vanessa both in
nature and in person something like a reflection of her mother,"
according to Virginia.[41] Leslie also associated each of them with Julia. He completed the family memoir written for his children (which
they mockingly called the *Mausoleum Book*) on May 30, 1895, a few
months after Julia's death and, he noted, on "the birthday of Stella
and Vanessa." The manuscript ended with the symbolic conferral of
Julia's memory on the eldest daughters of her two marriages. "I
have given to Stella a chain which I gave to her mother upon our
marriage; and to Vanessa a photograph by [Julia's aunt] Mrs. Cameron which, as I think, shows her mother's beauty better than any
other. We will cling to each other."[42] Or as Virginia put it, Leslie
Stephen was "quite prepared to take Vanessa for his next victim."[43]

Vanessa was just eighteen years old and did not yet have serious
suitors. But Stella's widower, Jack Hills, was unable to tear himself
away from the Stephen household and in 1900 he and Vanessa became romantically involved, Vanessa following in the wake of Stella
once more. Stella's brother George Duckworth was horrified—he
complained that a marriage between Hills and his deceased wife's
sister would be against the law. Leslie ruled that Vanessa should do
whatever she wanted to do.[44] However, she did not marry Hills. She
was to marry only after Leslie's death precipitated the breakup of the
lugubrious household at 22 Hyde Park Gate.

A potent mixture of emotion and latent sexuality marked relationships within the Stephen household, even before Julia's death. Leslie abandoned himself to depressive self-pity, although he only really let himself go when he was alone or with his wife and daughters—"the breast beating, the groaning, the self-dramatisation," Virginia Woolf believed, were laid on only for them. "He needed always some woman to act before; to sympathise with him, to console him."[45] But it was Duckworth sentimentality that particularly provoked her mockery: "It was quite a common thing to come into the drawing room and find George on his knees with his arms extended, addressing my mother, who might be adding up the weekly books, in tones of fervent adoration."[46]

George also expressed an extravagant regard for his stepsisters. He did his best to introduce Vanessa and Virginia into society, escorting them to dinners and dances. He gave them jewels and dresses, and closely supervised their appearance and demeanor. According to Virginia, he also forced himself upon them sexually.

This charge was made in a talk that she gave to the Bloomsbury Memoir Club in 1920, and she concluded with what reads like a parody of Gothic fiction: "Yes, the old ladies of Kensington and Belgravia never knew that George Duckworth was not only father and mother, brother and sister to those poor Stephen girls; he was their lover also."[47] Her excellent biographer Hermione Lee throws some doubt on this charge,[48] and Maynard Keynes commented to Virginia Woolf after the reading of her Memoir Club paper that it was the best thing she had ever done—"You should pretend to write about real people and make it all up."[49] Virginia later gave a less damning account of George's displays of affection: "There would be a tap at the door; the light would be turned out and George would fling himself on my bed, cuddling and kissing and otherwise embracing me in order, as he told Dr. Savage [Virginia Woolf's psychiatrist] later, to comfort me for the fatal illness of my father—who was dying three or four storeys down of cancer."[50] In any event Leonard Woolf, a sober judge, did not disapprove of George. When Virginia had a serious breakdown in 1913, Leonard moved her into George Duckworth's country house for two months to allow her to recuperate.

Virginia also claimed that George's younger brother, Gerald Duckworth, had fondled her groin when she was six years old and he was eighteen.[51] Hermione Lee finds this more plausible, although she questions the significance given to this episode by some commentators.[52] When they were all grown up, Gerald became a publisher and took on Virginia Woolf's first two novels. Leonard Woolf described him as "a kindly, uncensorious man who had considerable affection for Virginia."[53]

And then there were Virginia's feelings about her sister Vanessa. "But with you I am deeply, passionately, unrequitedly in love—and thank goodness your beauty is ruined, for my incestuous feelings may then be cooled—yet it has survived a century of indifference."[54] This obsession with Vanessa was to resurface, transmuted, in a long flirtation with Vanessa's husband, Clive Bell.

THE ADORED brother of Vanessa and Virginia, the charming Thoby Stephen, nicknamed the Goth, went up to Trinity College, Cambridge, in 1899. Lytton Strachey arrived at Trinity at the same time. He took up Thoby and introduced him to "The Reading Club," whose five members, including Leonard Woolf and Saxon Sydney-Turner, had begun to meet in the college rooms of Clive Bell. (A well-off country gentleman, Bell's aesthetic interests were signaled by a Degas reproduction on his wall.) The same small circle of first-year undergraduates at Trinity were also members of other little clubs, the Midnight Society and the X Society. These five men—Lytton Strachey, Thoby Stephen, Clive Bell, Leonard Woolf, and

Saxon Sydney-Turner—were later to be founding members of the Thursday Club, the original incarnation of Bloomsbury.

Societies, secret or merely exclusive, were central to their Cambridge experience, but the epitome, the most prestigious and influential of these Cambridge societies, was the Cambridge Conversazione Society, familiarly known as the Apostles, or sometimes simply The Society.[55] Among the 255 members elected between its inauguration in 1820 and 1914 were a remarkable number of the famous men who passed through the university. Strachey and Leonard Woolf (the first Jewish Apostle) were elected in 1902. Maynard Keynes, three years their junior, was elected in the following year, supported by Strachey and Woolf.

Largely through the force of his personality, capable of Svengali-like manipulation of his friends' emotions, Lytton Strachey became, in the words of Leonard Woolf, "the dominating influence upon three or four generations of Cambridge undergraduates."[56] In a very different style, Maynard Keynes was also a master of personal politics. The two men formed a close partnership. "In one respect, Strachey was the most important friend Maynard ever had," according to Keynes's biographer, Robert Skidelsky. "He was the only one who exerted on him an appreciable moral authority."[57] Together they engineered a takeover of the Society, which was then controlled by George Macaulay Trevelyan, Macaulay's great-nephew. Already a young don at Trinity, four years older than Lytton, Trevelyan had befriended Strachey when he came up, but although relations remained cordial they had very different ambitions for the Apostles. Trevelyan was interested in liberal politics, while Strachey and, at the time, Keynes were beginning to foster a cult of personal relations. "There was a long drawn out battle between George Trevelyan and Lytton Strachey," recalled Bertrand Russell, another older Apostle. "Lytton Strachey was on the whole victorious."[58]

Strachey and Keynes dominated the Society for a decade and managed the elections of new "embryos" (the Apostle code for candidates), bringing in several of their close friends. When Strachey became Secretary, in 1902, he immediately introduced Leonard Woolf and Saxon Sydney-Turner. Later Lytton's brother James Strachey was elected. Keynes brought in a young mathematician, Henry Norton, and, against Lytton's bitter opposition, a fellow economist from King's, Gerald Shove. Even Keynes sensed that recruitment to the Society was becoming somewhat incestuous—"we want fresh blood," he complained to Strachey in January 1906, "at present we are too much inclined to marry our first cousins."[59] However, all these men were to become lifelong Bloomsberries.

Strachey and Keynes introduced two significant changes into the Society. Both men were homosexual, indeed were convinced that homosexual relations (the Higher Sodomy, they called it) were morally and aesthetically superior to the common bonds between heterosexual men and women. A slightly older Apostle, Bertrand Russell, claimed that after the Strachey/Keynes takeover of the Society "homosexual relations among the members were for a time common, but in my day they were unknown."[60] Russell perhaps did not know it, but in the cohort before Strachey's there had been a number of active homosexuals in the Society. Goldsworthy Lowes Dickinson, elected in 1885, had published an account of homosexuality in ancient Greece (*The Greek View of Life,* which appeared in 1896). Painfully shy, in private a boot-fetishist, Dickinson was inclined to hopeless romantic attachments to young men, but he also had an affair with Roger Fry, a fellow Apostle. It is clear, however, that open discussions of homosexuality became central to the life of the Apostles in the heyday of Strachey and Keynes. This was daring. In 1885 the Criminal Law Amendment Act had criminalized any male homosexual activity, even in private. Oscar Wilde was tried and imprisoned for homosexuality in 1895, and he died in disgrace, in exile in Paris, in 1900.

Russell also noted that Strachey and Keynes brought about a change in the "mental climate" of the Society:

> The tone of the generation some ten years junior to my own was set mainly by Lytton Strachey and Keynes. It is surprising how great a change in mental climate those ten years had brought. We were still Victorian; they were Edwardian. We believed in ordered progress by means of politics and free discussion . . . The generation of Keynes and Lytton did not seek to preserve any kinship with the Philistine. They aimed rather at a life of retirement among fine shades and nice feelings, and conceived of the good as consisting in the passionate mutual admirations of a clique of the élite. This doctrine, quite unfairly, they fathered upon G. E. Moore . . . but those who considered themselves his disciples . . . degraded his ethics into advocacy of a stuffy girls-school sentimentalizing.[61]

G. E. Moore, a fellow of Trinity, seven years older than Strachey, had been brought into the Apostles by his mentor, the philosopher McTaggart, and Bertrand Russell. Russell remarked that "for some years he fulfilled my ideal of genius. He was in those days beautiful and slim, with a look almost of inspiration, and with an intellect as deeply passionate as Spinoza's."[62] Moore's *Principia Ethica* appeared in October 1903, soon after Keynes and Strachey had been elected to the Apostles. It bowled them over. In a letter to Moore, Strachey declared: "I date from October 1903 the beginning of the Age of Reason."[63]

Recalling their enthusiasm thirty years later, Maynard Keynes was prepared to admit some reservations about Moore's "religion," but he insisted that "its effect on *us*, and the talk which preceded and followed it, dominated, and perhaps still dominate, everything else. We were at an age when our beliefs influenced our behaviour . . . and the habits of feeling formed then still persist in a recognisable degree. It is those habits of feeling, influencing the majority of us, which make this Club [the Bloomsbury Memoir Club] a collectivity and separate us from the rest."[64]

He nevertheless conceded the gist of Russell's criticism: "What we got from Moore was by no means entirely what he offered us . . . We accepted Moore's religion, so to speak, and discarded his morals . . . Nothing mattered except states of mind, our own and other people's of course, but chiefly our own . . . Broadly speaking we all knew for certain what were good states of mind and that they consisted in communion with objects of love, beauty and truth."[65]

This was lighthearted, even ironic, but it is not too far from Moore's own canonical statement of his doctrine: "By far the most valuable things which we know or can imagine, are certain states of consciousness which may be roughly described as the pleasures of human intercourse and the enjoyment of beautiful objects." And Moore added that "it is only for the sake of these things—in order that as much of them as possible may at some time exist—that anyone can be justified in performing any public or private duty."[66]

"The two things Clive [Bell] cared about were art and friends," Frances Partridge recalled,[67] and these were indeed the two sacred objects of the creed. The young Apostles (and later the core members of Bloomsbury) were imbued with a conviction that they represented a small band of the saved. Anyone outside the Society was described, in their private code, as merely phenomenal. And they agreed that private duty trumped public responsibilities. E. M. Forster was famously to remark that "if I had to choose between betraying my country and betraying my friend, I hope I should have the guts to betray my country."[68] Keynes had already acted on Forster's principle in a dramatic fashion. Early in World War I he had financed a fellow Apostle, Ferenc Békássy, who wanted to join up with the Hungarian army to fight against Russia. This was despite the fact that Britain was at war with the Austro-Hungarian Empire.[69] (Békássy was killed in action in 1915.)

AFTER CAMBRIDGE, London. This was the traditional next step in the life of an educated English gentleman. The move of Thoby Stephen and his Cambridge friends to London coincided with the breakup of the Stephen family household at Hyde Park Gate.

Leslie Stephen succumbed finally to bowel cancer in February 1904. The Duckworth men now went their own way. George Duckworth, who had entered into a gentlemanly and unpaid apprenticeship as private secretary to Charles Booth,[70] married an aristocrat, Lady Margaret Herbert. Gerald Duckworth found a bachelor flat for himself and started a publishing house. Vanessa shepherded her two brothers to a new home, at 46 Gordon Square, Bloomsbury. Following her father's death Virginia had the first of her major psychotic episodes. She was hospitalized for several months, but was well enough by December to move in with her sister and brothers.

Virginia discovered that Vanessa had created in Gordon Square the antithesis of their childhood home at Hyde Park Gate, with its Victorian décor and rituals.

> Needless to say the Watts-Venetian tradition of red plush and black paint had been reversed; we had entered the Sargent-Furse era; white and green chintzes were everywhere; and instead of Morrow wall-papers with their intricate patterns we decorated our walls with washes of plain distemper. We were full of experiments and reforms. We were going to do without table napkins . . . we were going to paint; to write; to have cof-

fee after dinner instead of tea at nine o'clock. Everything was
going to be new; everything was going to be different. Everything was on trial.[71]

The very choice of neighborhood was an act of rebellion against
their own background. Leonard Woolf's middle-class Jewish parents
had both grown up in Bloomsbury—"my maternal and paternal
grandparents, my father, my mother, and I myself all lived in or practically in Tavistock Square."[72] But when Leonard's father became a
successful barrister he had moved his family to Kensington, with its
civil servants, scientists, and scholars (though the Woolfs lived in
Lexham Gardens off the Earls Court Road, not the smart part of the
district). Viewed from Kensington, Bloomsbury was down-market,
raffish, bohemian, not quite respectable.

Thoby and his friends were trying to find their feet in London.
Thoby himself began to read for the bar. Lytton Strachey tried for a
fellowship at Trinity, failed, and was at a loose end, reviewing for
weekly papers. Sydney-Turner and Keynes entered the Civil Service,
but without enthusiasm. Keynes was hoping for a vacancy in Cambridge.

Vanessa and Virginia kept open house for Thoby's friends on
Thursday evenings at Gordon Square, offering cocoa and biscuits.
The young men drifted in and sat in gloomy silence, or talked on
and on about Moore's philosophy, or read plays aloud, in the Cam-
bridge style. Vanessa, who had entered the Painting School of the
Royal Academy in 1901, studying with John Singer Sargent, also be-
gan a "Friday Club" for artists and art critics, at which Thoby's
Cambridge friend Clive Bell became a regular visitor.

Vanessa's son Quentin Bell identified the "essential element in the
situation" as "the sense of liberation at 46, Gordon Square. The Stephen children were orphans. They had escaped from an extremely
depressing Victorian home. They were young. In that uncontrolled,

uncustomed environment Thoby Stephen's friends might continue the conversation which had begun at Cambridge."[73] In a letter
to her nephew Julian Bell, Virginia remembered

> the burst of splendour, those two years at Gordon Square . . . a
> kind of Elizabethan renaissance, much though I disliked the
> airs that young Cambridge gave itself. I found an old diary
> which was one violent shriek of rage at Saxon [Sydney-Turner]
> and Lytton sitting there saying nothing, and with no emo-
> tional experience, I said.[74]

"But it could not have gone on," Virginia realized later. "Even if
Vanessa had not married, even if Thoby had lived, change was inevitable."[75]

In the autumn of 1906, in the course of a family holiday in Greece
and Turkey, Thoby Stephen contracted typhoid fever, dying that
November. Just before setting off for Greece, Vanessa had refused
an offer of marriage from Thoby's close friend Clive Bell. Clive
helped Vanessa to nurse Thoby during his last illness. Two days after
Thoby's death, she agreed to marry him.

Thoby's death and Vanessa's marriage, which was followed almost
immediately by her first pregnancy, were extremely difficult for the
vulnerable Virginia to deal with. She began an intense (though unconsummated) flirtation with her brother-in-law, Clive Bell. This
became serious shortly after the birth of Clive and Vanessa's son Julian. And Virginia moved out of Gordon Square with her younger
brother, Adrian, who was down from Cambridge and reading for
the bar. Together they established a new base on the bohemian
northern side of the Tottenham Court Road, in Fitzroy Square.
Most of the houses there had been divided into offices, workshops,
and flats. According to Duncan Grant, Virginia and Adrian were the
only people who had an entire house to themselves in the square.[76]

They made a rather discordant and improvident couple, but still they acted as a focus for their network. Adrian entertained his friends at poker parties which attracted some of Thoby's old circle, among them Gerald Shove, Saxon Sydney-Turner, and Maynard Keynes, and even a few young women, including Noel Olivier and the sisters Karen and Ray Costelloe.[77] Virginia established her own at-homes. The Thursday evenings, starting at ten, often prolonged long past midnight, fueled by whisky, buns, and cocoa, now continued on alternate weeks at 46 Gordon Square and 29 Fitzroy Square. The sisters were competitive hostesses. "Nessa [Vanessa] and Clive live, as I think, much like great ladies in a French salon," Virginia wrote to a friend; "they have all the wits and the poets: and Nessa sits among them like a Goddess."[78] But the same people came to both salons, and the atmosphere was much the same. "And people talked to each other," Duncan Grant recalled. "Conversation; that was all."[79]

The nature of the conversation changed, however, after the death of Thoby, who had been a mildly constraining influence on the sisters, and Vanessa's marriage. There was a new freedom. Vanessa Bell attributed this particularly to the influence of Lytton Strachey.[80] Virginia had an anecdote to prove it.

It was a spring evening. Vanessa and I were sitting in the drawing room. The drawing room had greatly changed its character since 1904. The Sargent-Furse age was over. The age of Augustus John was dawning. . . . The door opened and the long and sinister figure of Mr Lytton Strachey stood on the threshold. He pointed his finger at a stain on Vanessa's white dress.

"Semen?" he said.

Can one really say it? I thought and we burst out laughing. With that one word all barriers of reticence and reserve went down. A flood of the sacred fluid seemed to overwhelm us. Sex permeated our conversation. The word bugger was never far from our lips. We discussed copulation with the same excitement and openness that we had discussed the nature of good.[81]

IN OCTOBER 1911 Virginia and Adrian moved to 38 Brunswick Square, renting out rooms to Keynes and his lover Duncan Grant and to Gerald Shove. (With Duncan's help, Adrian decorated his sitting room with life-size nude figures of tennis players.)[82] When Leonard Woolf, on leave from the colonial service in Ceylon, moved in with them at the end of the year he remarked on the great alteration in the manners of his friends since their Cambridge days— a change that was apparent even, and most remarkably, in front of ladies.

> The social significance of using Christian instead of surnames and of kissing instead of shaking hands is curious . . . They produce a sense—often unconscious—of intimacy and freedom, and so break down barriers to thought and feeling. It was this . . . that I found so new and so exhilarating in 1911. To have discussed some subjects in the presence of Miss Strachey or Miss Stephen would seven years before have been unimaginable; here for the first time I found a much more intimate (and wider) circle in which complete freedom of thought was now extended to Vanessa and Virginia, Pippa and Marjorie [Strachey].[83]

Above all, they now began to talk about love and sex. This came as a great relief to the young women after the long evenings of abstract discussions of Moore's philosophy, despite the fact that (perhaps even because) most of the young men were homosexuals. "It never struck me that the abstractness, the simplicity which had been so great a relief after Hyde Park Gate were largely due to the fact

that the majority of the young men who came there were not attracted by young women," Virginia remarked. "I did not realise
that love, far from being a thing they never mentioned, was in fact a
thing which they seldom ceased to discuss."[84]

But some *were* attracted to young women. In this free and unchaperoned atmosphere, Virginia was courted by several of the
young Cambridge men.[85] Her suitors were orchestrated by her
brother-in-law Clive Bell, with whom she nevertheless continued to
carry on a serious flirtation for many years. Lytton Strachey himself
impulsively asked Virginia to marry him when his adored Duncan
Grant left him for his friend Maynard Keynes. Virginia accepted but
Lytton withdrew his offer the following day, to their mutual relief.
("I should like Lytton as a brother in law better than anyone I
know," Vanessa commented, "but the only way I can perceive of
bringing that to pass would be if he were to fall in love with
Adrian—& even then Adrian would probably reject him.")[86] However, Lytton had been writing to Leonard Woolf in Ceylon urging
him to propose to Virginia, whom Leonard had only met, briefly,
once or twice. And when he returned from Ceylon, a month after
becoming a lodger at Brunswick Square, Leonard did propose to
Virginia. They were married in August 1912. Leonard suggested to
Lytton that he and Clive Bell had fallen in love with Thoby's sisters
because they were, in a way, in love with Thoby.[87] Virginia herself
remarked that Leonard reminded her of Thoby.[88]

THE PRECISE membership of "Old Bloomsbury" has been exhaus-
tively debated by participants in the salons of the two sisters, as well
as by biographers and historians. They did form little clubs, on the
Cambridge model—the Play-reading society, the Friday Club, the
Novel Club, and so on—but Bloomsbury was a network rather than
a formal group or society, and so there cannot be a definitive answer
to the question of membership; and, of course, there were shifts

over time. However, one generally accepted model is the sketch by Quentin Bell, reproduced below, of Bloomsbury as it was in 1913.[89]

If the younger Stephens and Stracheys formed the core of Bloomsbury, more complex links, interlocking and recursive, brought others into the circle, beginning with slightly older members of the Apostles—E. M. Forster, Roger Fry, and Desmond MacCarthy. "Looking back I see that I converged upon 'Bloomsbury' by three ways," Desmond MacCarthy recalled, "through making friends with Clive Bell, through getting to know some Cambridge 'Apostles' junior to me, and through my introduction into the home-life of Miss Vanessa and Miss Virginia Stephen."[90] His wife, Molly MacCarthy, born Warre-Cornish, was the daughter of an Apostle. Fellow Apostles were called brothers, and so her marriage to Desmond MacCarthy seemed "somewhat incestuous," Lytton Strachey joked in a letter to Leonard Woolf.[91] Moreover, two of Molly's actual brothers had been close friends of MacCarthy at Cambridge. She was also a

The Bloomsbury circle.

E. M. Forster

David Garnett

Molly MacCarthy

Sydney Waterlow   Desmond MacCarthy

Roger Fry

Vanessa Bell

Duncan Grant   Virginia Woolf

Clive Bell   Saxon Sydney-Turner

Leonard Woolf

Lytton Strachey   Adrian Stephen

John Maynard Keynes

Gerald Shove

James Strachey   H. T. J. Norton

Marjorie Strachey

Francis Birrell

sort of cousin to the Stephens.[92] Molly's marriage to Desmond Mac-Carthy was a long and evidently happy one, although she had an affair with Clive Bell, the husband of her cousin Vanessa.[93] And so the network kept curling in on itself.

Husbands, wives, and lovers were absorbed into the network. Leonard Woolf's list of the people associated with a later phase of Bloomsbury included Adrian Stephen's wife, Karin Costelloe, whom he married in 1914, and James Strachey's wife, Alix Sargent-Florence, whom he married, after a long courtship, in 1920.[94] (Adrian Stephen, James Strachey, and their wives all underwent psychoanalysis, James and his wife by Freud himself, and all four became psychoanalysts. Assisted by his wife, James became the leading translator of Freud into English.) Such reiterated links tend to reinforce the impression that Old Bloomsbury was made up at its core by the Stephen and Strachey siblings, and indeed Leonard Woolf added that the children of Vanessa and Clive Bell (Julian, Quentin, and Angelica) were incorporated as they grew up. Woolf omitted some of the more marginal Cambridge associates—Shove, Norton, and Waterlow—again reinforcing the view of inner Bloomsbury as a Stephen/Strachey network with its dual base, the two sets of siblings.

Over time there were further changes in the structure of the network. Leonard Woolf later suggested that Bloomsbury really came into existence only after he returned to London from Ceylon, in the period 1912–1914. However, he called this period "ur-Bloomsbury," partly because only eight of its members actually lived in Bloomsbury at the time. "It was not until Lytton Strachey, Roger Fry, and Morgan Forster came into the locality so that we were continually meeting one another, that our society became complete," he wrote, "and that did not happen until some years after the [First World] war."[95] In 1919, when the Strachey family moved to Gordon Square, Lytton wrote to Virginia Woolf: "Very soon I forsee that the whole square will become a sort of College. And the rencontres in the garden I shudder to think of."[96]

Certainly Bloomsbury, and in particular Gordon Square, became a tightly packed precinct for the elect in the interwar years. David Garnett made a list in his autobiography:

> Adrian Stephen married and came to live in No 51 Gordon Square; the Strachey family left Hampstead and took No 50 next door; James Strachey married and took No 41 Gordon Square. Maynard Keynes married and took over the lease of No 46. Clive took a flat at the top of Adrian's house and Vanessa took a lease of No 37. Roger Fry went to live in Bernard Street, and Morgan Forster had a *pied-à-terre* in my mother-in-law's house, No 27 Brunswick Square.[97]

And even this left out the fact that Lytton Strachey, Ralph Partridge, and Dora Carrington made regular forays to James Strachey's house at No. 41, and that Vanessa Bell and Duncan Grant were often guests of the Keyneses at No. 46, where Norton also had a flat.

There was also a country extension, Bloomsbury by the Sea, near Lewes in Sussex. Vanessa and Virginia rented Asheham House, four miles southeast of Lewes, from 1912 to 1914. Virginia and Leonard Woolf then leased Monk's House in Rodmell, three miles south of Lewes. Later Vanessa moved to Charleston, a farmhouse six miles east of Lewes, where she lived during the war with her family and Duncan Grant. Keynes was at the Treasury, and "Charleston became Maynard's chief wartime family. He would arrive on a Friday or Saturday evening, recount his war news, and then stay in bed till lunch the following morning, by which time he would have worked through his files."[98] When Keynes married, he bought a farmhouse half a mile from Charleston.

Even if Bloomsbury was most completely localized in the 1920s,

Virginia Woolf and Quentin Bell prefer to talk about "Old Bloomsbury" as a phenomenon of the prewar period. After the war, as some
of its central figures became well known and influential, new people
were attracted to the group and the network expanded. Nevertheless, the core remained stable for three decades. Mary MacCarthy
formed the Memoir Club in 1920. "It is a secret club," she wrote
to Clive Bell's mistress, Mary Hutchinson, inviting her to join.[99]
But Mary Hutchinson dropped out, and Leonard Woolf's list of its
members corresponds very closely to Quentin Bell's census of "Old
Bloomsbury": in addition to himself and his wife, he lists Clive
and Vanessa Bell, Lytton Strachey, Maynard Keynes, Duncan Grant,
Roger Fry, E. M. Forster, Saxon Sydney-Turner, Adrian Stephen,
and Desmond and Molly MacCarthy.[100] (Bertrand Russell was
elected but never attended any meetings.)

This exclusiveness was jealously guarded. When the Memoir Club
was set up E. M. Forster wrote to Molly MacCarthy, "Please do be
severe about us only being the original bunch, and let it be widely
known that if Nell this and Gwynne that are brought, all the readers
[of memoirs] will discover that at the last moment they have mislaid
their papers."[101] Desmond MacCarthy agreed, telling Clive Bell that
"after all *we*—at any rate for ourselves—are the best company in the
world."[102] When Keynes married Lydia Lopokova in 1922, Vanessa
Bell wrote to him: "Clive says he thinks it is impossible for any of
us . . . to introduce a new wife or husband into the existing circle
. . . We feel that *no one* can come into the sort of intimate society we
have without altering it."[103] Ideally the restriction of membership
to Old Bloomsbury would make for complete frankness, although
Leonard Woolf pointed out that "absolute frankness, even among
the most intimate, tends to be relative frankness."[104]

With the sole exception of Duncan Grant, all the men in Quentin Bell's Old Bloomsbury had been undergraduates at Cambridge.

Moreover, they all came from two colleges: nine from Trinity College, where Lytton Strachey and Thoby Stephen were undergraduates, and five from King's, Maynard Keynes's college. Ten of them were Apostles.[105] In addition, two of the women, Marjorie Strachey and James Strachey's wife, Alix, had studied at Newnham College, Cambridge. Many though not all of the men were both Apostles and homosexuals, and it was important to them to be able to talk openly about the Apostles and about homosexual love, both of which were taboo topics outside the circle of the initiated.

And they shared what Keynes termed a "religion." (Gertrude Stein described the circle to Edith Sitwell as "The Young Men's Christian Association—with Christ left out, of course.")[106] Not that they were all disciples of G. E. Moore. Roger Fry was critical of Moore's ideas. The Stephen sisters were not much interested in philosophy. Duncan Grant had only the vaguest idea of what it was all about. But they shared a faith in reason and a suspicion of instinct; they venerated personal relations; and they championed modernity in the arts. "Lytton Strachey is *their* Moore," Molly MacCarthy commented astutely.[107]

They were often accused of smugness, and Keynes had to admit that D. H. Lawrence's revulsion against Bloomsbury chatter had some force. Keynes's Memoir Club address, "My Early Beliefs," was framed as a response to Lawrence. When Clive Bell published his brief *Civilization: An Essay* in 1928, Virginia Woolf remarked that civilization turned out to be a lunch party at 50 Gordon Square. But she could also write, in a letter to her nephew Julian Bell in 1936: "I sometimes feel that old Bloomsbury though fast dying, is still our bulwark against the tawny flood."[108]

They also shared a common project, and so thought it only right to give each other a helping hand. Starting off, they had relied on family connections. At the beginning of his career Lytton Strachey was employed as a reviewer for the *Spectator* by his cousin St. Loe Strachey, who was the editor. His brother James was also taken on to the staff of the magazine. At the start of her career, Virginia Woolf had her first two novels published by her half-brother Gerald Duckworth.

It is true that the writers in the group freely disparaged one another's books, at least among themselves, but the Bloomsbury authors were published by the Woolfs' Hogarth Press or were commissioned by Leonard Woolf to write reviews for *The Nation*, which Keynes had founded and where Woolf was employed as literary editor. Keynes also had an interest in the *New Statesman*, where he was to place Desmond MacCarthy and Bunny Garnett successively as literary editor, and they loyally commissioned contributions from Bloomsbury friends. The Bloomsberries wrote memoirs that obsessively recalled Bloomsbury, and also wrote critical (but not very critical) essays on other members. Virginia Woolf wrote a biography of her sister's lover, Roger Fry. Many of their novels featured characters based on their Bloomsbury friends.

The artists formed a united front, which Wyndham Lewis not unjustly called a cabal. Roger Fry was the impresario, forming the Omega Workshops around Duncan Grant and Vanessa Bell and writing a book on Grant's paintings. He and Clive Bell promoted each other's work and the paintings of Grant and Vanessa Bell. When Fry organized his two Post-Impressionist exhibitions, in 1910 and 1912, he dutifully found jobs as secretary for Desmond MacCarthy, on the first occasion, and for Leonard Woolf on the second. Keynes was, as always, ready to help out, handing out personal subsidies and using his organizational skills and connections. With help from Samuel Courtauld, Keynes started the London Artists' Association in 1926 to provide artists with funds and help in their careers. Duncan Grant, Roger Fry, and Vanessa Bell were all early beneficiaries. When Grant was given a major commission, to decorate the Russell Chantry in Lincoln Cathedral, Vanessa Bell was a member of the jury.

THE IDEOLOGICAL and professional bonds between the members of "Old Bloomsbury" were reinforced by a remarkable range of sexual liaisons—a remarkable variety too, since a number of the men and women, indeed a majority, were bisexual. They tended to pass partners around between themselves. Infidelity, even promiscuity, were not regarded as moral failings. Nevertheless, their affairs were typically love affairs. Sex might even be marginal. Two of the most enduring and loving Bloomsbury "marriages," between Leonard and Virginia Woolf and between Lytton Strachey and the androgynous Dora Carrington, were sexless, in both cases after disappointing initial experiments.

There is no obvious path through this maze, but perhaps a good starting point is Lytton Strachey, whose love affairs were central to the evolution of Bloomsbury. Both Lytton Strachey and his younger brother, James, had brief affairs with Maynard Keynes between 1905 and 1908. However, Keynes and Lytton were more usually rivals in love. An early object of Strachey's passion at Cambridge was a young Etonian, Bernard Swithinbank, Keynes's closest school friend and former lover. When Keynes and Lytton were orchestrating recruitment to the Apostles they competed for the affections of attractive young candidates, with Keynes always the winner. This would regularly throw his friendship with Lytton into a state of crisis. A particular quarrel occurred over a young man named Hobhouse, and they were reconciled only when Lytton's cousin Duncan Grant admitted that he had become Hobhouse's lover.

But it was Duncan Grant himself who was the most important object of rivalry between Keynes and Strachey. Duncan Grant's father was a rackety Scottish aristocrat, a military man with a taste for music and women. His mother was the sister of Jane Strachey, Lytton's mother (and therefore Duncan and Lytton were cousins). Duncan Grant's parents were often posted abroad, and he was sent to boarding school, at Rugby, with James Strachey. (Another contemporary at Rugby was Rupert Brooke. James Strachey had passionate attachments to Grant and, more enduringly, to Brooke, whose own circle, the "Pagans," was a louche and short-lived equivalent to early Bloomsbury, with which it overlapped.)[109]

Duncan later lived for some time with the Stracheys while attending St. Paul's school as a day boy. He struggled academically and was rescued by Jane Strachey, who persuaded his parents to allow him to study painting in London and then in Paris. Between 1905 and 1907 the two cousins, Lytton Strachey and Duncan Grant, had a passionate affair. Although the relationship was by then petering out, certainly on Duncan's part, Lytton was devastated to discover that in the summer of 1908 Duncan had begun an affair with Keynes and that they had gone on "honeymoon" to Rackawick, an island in the Orkneys. (Quite unsuspecting, Lytton had been writing to Keynes confiding that Duncan was irresponsible, and to Duncan describing Keynes as passionless.) It was Lytton's discovery of their affair that precipitated his own rash proposal of marriage to Virginia Stephen.

At the end of 1909 Duncan Grant leased a ground floor flat in Virginia and Adrian Stephen's house in Fitzroy Square, and he and Adrian began an affair. "You're married to Adrian now, which you weren't before," Keynes wrote to him, "I'm feeling very wretched and don't know what I ought to do."[110] In the end he accepted Duncan's infidelities and rented a back bedroom in the Fitzroy Square house for his own visits to London. Keynes now began to be drawn into the Bloomsbury group. The fact that Duncan had moved on emotionally made Keynes's entry into Bloomsbury more acceptable to Lytton.

Lytton now entered into what was to prove an enduring relationship with the bisexual painter Dora Carrington, who managed to extricate Lytton from his family home in 1916. Although they only briefly slept together, Lytton and Carrington became virtually a married couple with a country home, first at Mill House, Tidmarsh, and then, after 1924, at Ham Spray.

In 1919 this cozy arrangement was complicated by the arrival on the scene of Ralph Partridge. Lytton pursued Partridge, but with no success; Partridge was infatuated with Carrington. She was attracted to him, in part evidently because of his connection with her much-loved brother Noel, who had been killed at the front. Noel and Partridge had been friends at Oxford, and Partridge had also served as an officer in France. Determined to keep both Carrington and Partridge with him, Lytton encouraged Carrington to marry Partridge. Partridge bought a major share in Ham Spray, and after the marriage the three continued to live there together. Lady Ottoline Morrell commented bitchily but acutely that this was clever of Lytton—"for he will retain his maid & attendant & he will also have a manservant too—'Married Couple' in fact."[111] (Advertisements for servants would often ask for a married couple.) Virginia Woolf thought that Partridge would be a "despotic" husband but encouraged Carrington to marry him precisely in order to keep Lytton's household intact.

The first rift in this rural idyll was caused by a visit from Partridge's army friend, the writer Gerald Brenan, who fell in love with Carrington and seduced her. Lytton helped to patch matters up between Partridge and Brenan, but Partridge now began a passionate affair with Frances Marshall. Frances was already linked to Bloomsbury: her father had been a friend of Leslie Stephen, taking part in his marathon "Sunday tramps," and her mother was a suffragist, an ally of Lady Strachey. At school her best friend was Oliver Strachey's daughter, Julia. Frances then went on to Newnham College, where

Pernel Strachey was the principal. Coming down from Cambridge, she took a job in David "Bunny" Garnett's bookshop, patronized by the elect, which he ran in partnership with his lover, the Bloomsberry Francis Birrell. Frances Marshall's sister Ray was also taken on as an assistant in the bookshop, and she later married Bunny Garnett (who had also been Duncan Grant's lover).

Partridge's relationship with Frances Marshall posed a greater threat to the Ham Spray arrangements than the Brenan-Carrington affair had done. Lytton did his best to stop Partridge from taking a flat with Frances in James Strachey's house in Bloomsbury. He even summoned Frances to a meeting at the Oriental Club, where he solemnly told her that if Partridge left Ham Spray he would have to leave himself, abandoning Carrington, who would not be able to survive the breakup of their ménage. In the end Carrington wrote to Frances to say that the Ham Spray trio had signed "a Treaty," and that Partridge was at liberty to leave—although he was expected to make regular visits, preferably, Lytton later intimated, alone.[112]

Lytton now took the ground floor in his brother's house as a base for his London visits, where Frances found herself sharing a bathroom with him. Lytton also persuaded Leonard Woolf to give Partridge a job in the Hogarth Press, and arranged for Partridge and Frances to edit the Greville Memoirs under his supervision.

Lytton later fell briefly in love with Philip Ritchie and then had a final, passionate, sadomasochistic affair with Ritchie's friend Roger Senhouse. He died in 1932. Almost immediately after Lytton's death, Carrington committed suicide. Ralph Partridge married Frances Marshall, and she later had an affair with Lytton's younger brother, James.

James Strachey had been actively homosexual as a young man, but after leaving Cambridge he became interested in women and began to look for a wife. One possible candidate was Noel Olivier. She was a childhood friend of David Garnett and a lover of the poet Rupert Brooke, with whom James had been in school and with whom he was infatuated for many years. He also courted Alix Sargant-Florence, whom he eventually married in 1920. During this courtship Alix was carrying on simultaneous affairs with Bunny Garnett and another member of "Old Bloomsbury," Harry Norton. Carrington fell for her too. "Oh Alix, I wish you were a Sappho," she wrote to her. "We might have had such a happy life without these Stracheys."[113] It was, however, only after some years of marriage to James Strachey that Alix entered into a lesbian relationship, which made Carrington very jealous. Meanwhile, James's early love, Noel Olivier, had married. In the late 1930s she suddenly fell in love with James, and they had a child together. James later had other affairs, including one with Ralph Partridge's wife, Frances Marshall.

While Lytton was almost exclusively homosexual, and James first homosexual and then heterosexual, their elder brother, Oliver, was a classic Edwardian ladies' man.[114] An Apostle of Moore's generation, Oliver began to make a career in India, in the Strachey tradition, but he shocked his family by marrying Ruby Meyer, the daughter of a Swiss tradesman in India. Ruby complained that Oliver forced her into elaborate wife-swapping arrangements, and in 1908 she left him for another man. Oliver returned to England and in 1911 married Ray Costelloe, a niece of Bertrand Russell. Ray seems to have fallen in love with the Strachey family before meeting Oliver, and when Oliver continued to have affairs after their marriage she concentrated her affections on his sister, Pippa Strachey, who was, however, enamored of Vanessa Bell's lover Roger Fry. (Ray Costelloe's sister, Karin, married Adrian Stephen.)

Vanessa Bell's affairs also reconfigured the Bloomsbury network. She and Virginia had married two of the unequivocally heterosexual men in their brother's circle. Virginia and Leonard Woolf stopped having sex soon after they married, and Virginia had her first passionate affair, with a woman, Vita Sackville-West, when she was forty-three years old. Vanessa, in contrast, was both heterosexual and intensely sensual, but her husband, Clive Bell, was hardly ever without a mistress. Shortly after the birth of their first child, Bell began his long and passionate, though unconsummated, flirtation with his sister-in-law, Virginia. Vanessa was undeceived though by no means complaisant, but it was some time before she began to have affairs of her own.

Beginning to find her feet as an artist, she came under the influence of Roger Fry, an Apostle and aspiring artist who would come to be better known as a critic and impresario. In the spring of 1911 Vanessa and Clive took a holiday in Turkey, accompanied by Roger Fry and Harry Norton. Fry's wife had gone mad and had been institutionalized just a few months earlier. Although he was just beginning an affair with Lady Ottoline Morrell, Fry and Vanessa fell in love with each other. They had a serious and sexually fulfilling relationship that lasted for two years. They also continued their artistic collaboration in the Omega Workshops, a center of design masterminded by Fry, in which Duncan Grant also participated. It was set up at 33 Fitzroy Square, close to the old house of Virginia and Adrian Stephen.

When Vanessa fell in love with Fry she half-hoped that Clive and Virginia would now finally become lovers, but, according to her son Quentin, "such is the perversity of things, that affair seemed to be cooling off. In fact there was a moment—or so I suspect—when Vanessa feared that her much loved but agonisingly exasperating sister might set herself to charm Roger."[115] However, Virginia was now able to make an independent move at last, and she married Leonard Woolf. (It was Lytton Strachey's sister Pippa who fell, hopelessly, in love with Fry.)

Vanessa's affair with Roger Fry lasted until 1913. She then took up with Duncan Grant. In the middle of 1914, Duncan was depressed by the marriage of Adrian Stephen and perhaps for that reason more inclined to make love to Adrian's sister, Vanessa. Almost immediately, however, he started another affair, with David "Bunny" Garnett. Clive Bell, meanwhile, had begun an affair with a married woman, Mary Hutchinson, a cousin of the Stracheys. Her husband put up with it, and in April 1915 the whole set—Clive, Vanessa, Duncan, and Bunny—went to stay with the Hutchinsons at their country house. (Mary Hutchinson was later to carry on simultaneous affairs with Aldous Huxley and his wife Maria, which lasted for many years.)[116]

At this stage the outside world impinged upon the insistently unworldly and private recesses of Bloomsbury. Conscription was introduced early in 1916. Lytton Strachey made a famously comical appearance before the recruitment board, bringing along an inflatable cushion because he was suffering from piles. Although a general's son, he was clearly unfit for military service. On the advice of Keynes, the youthful and robust Duncan Grant (also the son of a general) and his lover Bunny Garnett established themselves as farm workers, in order to gain exemption from the call-up. They worked on an abandoned farm belonging to Duncan's family, where they were joined by Vanessa with her two young sons, together with a cook and a nurse, and then moved to Vanessa's country base, Charleston, near Lewes in Sussex.

As in Lytton Strachey's ménage à trois at Ham Spray, relationships became extremely complicated. Duncan Grant was sleeping with both Bunny Garnett and Vanessa Bell. Bunny made an attempt, perhaps successful, to seduce Vanessa.[117] And whenever he went up to London he slept with Alix Sargent-Florence (who was simultaneously in pursuit of James Strachey, whom she married after the war).

Further complicating matters, Vanessa became pregnant by Duncan. Their child, Angelica, was born on Christmas Day, 1918, shortly after the Armistice. Vanessa regarded Duncan as little more than a boy, and certainly not as capable of taking on the role of father; and in any case, after Angelica's birth Duncan told her that he was no longer able to have sexual relations with her. Vanessa's husband, Clive Bell, agreed to pretend to the world that he was Angelica's father. Despite the Bloomsbury cult of truthfulness in personal relations, Angelica herself was not told the facts about her birth until she was an adolescent. Despite these strains and complications, Vanessa managed to keep her hold over her three men. "Even when she ceased to be 'in love,' she needed evidence of her power over the loved one," her daughter Angelica wrote. "Clive and Roger both hovered nearby, compelled by her need, as later did Duncan. Luckily all were, in their different ways, equal to saving their skins."[118]

Bunny Garnett was oddly moved by the birth of his lover's daughter. He wrote to Lytton, "I think of marrying it; when she is twenty I shall be 46—will it be scandalous?"[119] "No one took him seriously," Angelica was to write in her own memoir, "and neither Duncan nor Vanessa was in the habit of analysing other people's behaviour. But Bunny meant it literally, and did not forget it, and, knowing his nature, I find it impossible to believe that it was unconnected with jealousy, and perhaps with a desire to assimilate one who had been a part of both Duncan and Vanessa. . . . It seems clear enough now that when he carried me off to live as his wife and be a stepmother to his sons, his purpose was, at least in part, to inflict pain on Vanessa."[120] (Bunny Garnett was not the only intimate who had ambivalent feelings about Vanessa and her children. Virginia joked—in a letter to Vanessa—that when Angelica grew up she would "rape" her.)[121]

THEY SAW themselves as Edwardians, in revolt against the social code and artistic standards of the Victorians. To be sure, they could be unexpectedly conventional in their social judgments. And there were limits to their modernism. Proust was admired, but James

Joyce and D. H. Lawrence were undervalued, perhaps for snob-
bish reasons. They championed the Post-Impressionists, but Picasso
tended to be a puzzle. ("Also—the other day at G[ordon] Square—
lunch with Derain and Picasso," Lytton Strachey wrote to Carrington in 1919. "Not so enjoyable.")[122] They adored Diaghilev but
had little contact with modernist movements in music. They were
Francophile in principle, but there were limits here too. Lytton Strachey, for instance, did translations from French with ease but refused
to speak the language even to his sister's husband, Simon Bussy,
whose English was much less good than Strachey's French.

Their avant-garde moment lasted into the 1920s. By the 1930s they
had become unfashionable. Walking through Bloomsbury shortly
after World War II, a character in Anthony Powell's *Dance to the
Music of Time*, the musician Moreland, remarks:

> . . . what a lost opportunity within living memory. Every house
> stuffed with Moderns from cellar to garret. High-pitched
> voices adumbrating absolute values, rational states of mind,
> intellectual integrity, civilized personal relationships, signifi-
> cant form . . . the Fitzroy Street Barbera is uncorked. *Le Sacre
> du Printemps* turned on, a hand slides up a leg . . . All are at
> one now, values and lovers.[123]

Yet they always saw themselves as moderns, and enjoyed Lytton
Strachey's lampoon of the old icons in *Eminent Victorians*. When it
was suggested to a more loyal descendant of Clapham, G. M. Trevelyan, that he should publish in full the diaries of Lord Macaulay, a
son of Clapham, Trevelyan was horrified. "Over my dead body," he
said. "I'm not going to have those Bloomsbury people laughing at
my great-uncle."[124] Yet the Stephen family was very conscious of its
Clapham roots. When Virginia Woolf entered her final psychological
crisis in 1940–41, she chose as her doctor her second cousin Octavia
Wilberforce, a great-granddaughter of William Wilberforce, the sage

of Clapham. ("I rather think I've got a new lover, a doctor, a Wilberforce, a cousin," she wrote to Vita Sackville-West.)[125] E. M. Forster wrote a loving biography of his great-aunt, Marianne Thornton, who claimed to be the last survivor of the Clapham Sect.

And some commentators have identified continuities between the values of Clapham and Bloomsbury, despite the obvious differences. "Each generation renounce their father's beliefs," Noel Annan commented, "but the spirit of the coterie is so strong that there remains an outlook, an attitude, not unlike that of the Sect itself."[126]

> Bloomsbury, like Clapham was a coterie. It was exclusive and clannish. It regarded outsiders as unconverted and was contemptuous of good form opinions. Remarks which did not show that grace had descended upon their utterer were met with killing silence. Like the Claphamites they criticised each other unsparingly but with affection. Like Clapham, Bloomsbury had discovered a new creed: the same exhilaration filled the air, the same conviction that a new truth had been disclosed, a new Kingdom conquered.[127]

Both Clapham and Bloomsbury can be fairly described as sects, even cults. The borders of the network were strictly policed. Personal relationships within the group had something of the sacred about them. Beyond were the unsaved. Both groups had a charismatic leader.

Despite Leonard Woolf's protestations, it is evident that there was a Bloomsbury ideology, almost indeed a religion (as Keynes admitted). It had distinct echoes of the Clapham doctrines. Keynes pointed out that Moore's thought attracted him and his friends because they "closely followed the English puritan tradition of being chiefly concerned with the salvation of our own souls. The divine resided within a closed circle. There was not a very intimate connection between 'being good' and 'doing good'; and we had a feeling that there was some risk that in practice the latter might interfere with the former."[128] Keynes himself came from Noncomformist stock; Roger Fry was a scion of a great Quaker dynasty; E. M. Forster and the Stephens were descendants of Clapham.

Although the projects of Bloomsbury and Clapham were very different, they were equally "spiritual," though never less than practical. Members of these networks helped each other out as a matter of course. The Bloomsberries promoted one another's work and careers just as the original Claphamites did, as well as the intervening generations of their grandparents and parents.

And there was a sense of family in both Clapham and Bloomsbury, although it took very different forms. Brothers and sisters sustained a lifelong intimacy. Wilberforce encouraged marriages within his circle. Lytton Strachey urged Leonard Woolf to marry Virginia, and he manipulated the liaisons of his friends and lovers. Yet marriages within the Clapham sect were stable, while the polymorphous sexuality of Bloomsbury and its baroque entanglements created a kaleidoscope of shifting patterns. There was jealousy and some real anguish as discarded lovers moved on to affairs with other insiders. At the same time, the homosexuals in the group enjoyed the intimacy of something like an extended family. Yet Bloomsbury had few of the enduring relationships between brothers- and sisters-in-law on which previous generations had relied (although Clive Bell's long flirtation with his sister-in-law Virginia Woolf recalls the erotic tension that sometimes marked those relationships).

Bloomsbury was nevertheless firmly grounded. Its original base was the fictive brotherhood of Apostles. Later it was anchored by the two sets of siblings—the Stephens and the Stracheys. They did not intermarry, although Lytton was engaged to Virginia for a fraught twenty-four hours, and the priapic Duncan Grant had affairs with James and Lytton Strachey and with Vanessa and Adrian Stephen. Adrian Stephen's wife's sister married Oliver Strachey, an older brother of Lytton and James. In any case, the Strachey-Stephen alliance remained solid. It was the core of Bloomsbury. Geographic concentration, regular gatherings, and house parties nourished the more extended network, and sustained the shared values that separated it from the wider society, sufficiently to keep things going for a generation. Bloomsbury could not survive beyond that, if only because it produced so few children.

Some of those children did marry into Bloomsbury, or renewed old relationships. Vanessa Bell's son, Quentin Bell, married the daughter of a peripheral Bloomsbury figure, Brynhild Olivier, a sister of Noel Olivier, who was once James Strachey's lover. Vanessa's daughter Angelica, fathered by Duncan Grant, married Grant's lover, Bunny Garnett. Their daughter Henrietta married her first cousin, Burgo Partridge. Burgo's mother was Frances Marshall, the sister of Garnett's first wife; his father was Ralph Partridge, Carrington's lover, with whom Lytton Strachey had been infatuated. Henrietta Garnett wrote a novel, *Family Skeletons*, in which the heroine marries a cousin. Later she discovers that she is the incestuous child of her "uncle," who had brought her up, and his sister.[129]

The End of the Line

$\mathcal{T}$he English bourgeoisie were not unique. Their counterparts in other European countries also favored marriages within the kinship network.[1] Sigmund Freud specialized in the incestuous fantasies of the Viennese bourgeoisie, but he was not bothered by the marriage of close relatives outside the nuclear family. Indeed, two years after the marriage of his favorite sister, Anna, to Eli Bernays, he married Eli's sister Martha. Later there was gossip about Freud's special fondness for his wife's sister, Minna Bernays. Mitzi, a younger sister of Freud, married her cousin, Moritz Freud.

And, as in England, novelists wove stories around the love of cousins. Johann Wolfgang von Goethe's novella *The Man of Fifty* was first published as part of *Wilhelm Meisters Wanderjahre* in 1829.[2] In the novella a retired major takes over a country estate from an improvident elder brother, in partnership with his sister, a widowed baroness. They plan to pass the property on to their children (the major's son, Flavio, and the baroness's daughter, Hilarie). The cousins are expected to marry each other in order to preserve their patrimony.

However, a complication arises. The baroness tells the major that Hilarie—her daughter, his niece—has fallen in love with him.

"I would not have thought that such a natural soul could be capable of something so unnatural," replied the major.

He is not troubled by the fact that they are uncle and niece—nor, indeed, does it worry him that the young woman had been accustomed to call him "father." What concerns him rather is that he is so much older than Hilarie. This is what makes her love seem "unnatural" to him. "It's not so unnatural," said his sister. "I remember that as a young woman I loved a man who was even older than you."

The major has been worrying about getting older—turning fifty. Despite his misgivings, he is flattered and tempted by Hilarie's adoration. But what is he to tell his son Flavio? Luckily for him, Flavio confesses that he has fallen in love with a rich widow, who is much older than himself.

"You place me in a great predicament," the father began after a pause. "The entire agreement between the remaining members of our family depends on the condition that you marry Hilarie. If she marries a stranger, then the elegant and artful consolidation of such a considerable fortune is annulled and you in particular are not terribly well provided for. There is perhaps still another way, although it might sound somewhat strange and you admittedly gain little: I must marry Hilarie despite my old age, but this could hardly give you great pleasure." "The greatest pleasure in the world!" the lieutenant cried out.

Relieved and delighted, the major sets off to inspect the estate. Meanwhile, Flavio is rejected by the widow. In a desperate state, he takes refuge in his aunt's home. His cousin Hilarie nurses him. At first he calls her "sister," which wounds her. But soon the young couple fall in love.

The major accepts their relationship with fortitude. Through the discrete intervention of his sister he is united with Flavio's rich widow, who is, at least, the right age for a man growing older.

ANDRÉ GIDE'S *La Porte Étroite,* a semi-autobiographical account of his near-marriage with his cousin, appeared in France in 1909, toward the end of the era of cousin marriage.[3] (The English translation was undertaken by Lytton Strachey's sister, Dorothy Bussy, who had once been in love with a married cousin. She later married a French artist and moved to France, where in good Bloomsbury style she fell hopelessly in love with the homosexual Gide.)

Gide was brought up as a Protestant, and in this, his first novel, he developed an intricate plot involving four Protestant cousins. Alissa and Juliette are the daughters of Pastor Vautier, whose flighty wife has deserted him. Jerome, the only child of the Pastor's widowed sister, falls in love with Alissa. Alissa loves the serious and talented Jerome, but she discovers that her younger sister, Juliette, is also in love with him. Alissa is in any case concerned that she is two years older than Jerome, and that one day she will be too old for him. She tells him that they cannot become engaged until Juliette is married.

Pastor Vautier also has a brother, whose son, Abel, is in love with Juliette. Jerome encourages Abel, and this forces Juliette to recognize that Jerome is indifferent to her, perhaps even unaware of her love. Devastated, Juliette marries a vintner who loves her but whom she does not love. The unhappy Abel publishes a cynical but successful novel.

Alissa is now free to accept Jerome. However, she renounces marriage and becomes a religious ascetic. Mysteriously, she suddenly ages and dies. After her death Jerome visits Juliette, whose baby, Alissa, has just been born. They realize with sadness that they might have been happy together.

It is remarkable, and telling, that for both Goethe and Gide discrepancies of age represented a natural bar to marriage while close kinship did not.

COUSIN MARRIAGE was common in some communities in the United States, and not only in elite circles. In the first half of the nineteenth century, for instance, nearly 10 percent of marriages among planters in North Carolina were with first cousins.[4] In the same period, one in five Protestant Northern Irish immigrants to the midwest married a first cousin.[5] Cousin marriage continued to be common in some pockets of rural America even in the second half of the nineteenth century. Between 1850 and 1879, 14 percent of the women in a Blue Ridge community in Madison County, Virginia, married first cousins, and a further 33 percent married second cousins.[6] But the closest parallel to the English pattern of upper-middle-class kin marriage was to be found among the east coast urban bourgeoisie. The Boston Brahmins set a particularly high standard, in this as in so much else.

Partners in New England merchant firms were commonly related to one another. Fathers took their sons into business; brothers carried on in partnership. From the second half of the eighteenth century, cousins and brothers-in-law were even more likely to set up as partners, drawing on the capital of two families.[7] And families were often bound together by repeated marriages, as in comparable circles in England.[8]

In 1702 two immigrants from the Channel Island of Jersey to Salem, Massachusetts, John Cabot and Anne Orne, were married. This was the first of several marriages between Cabots and Ornes over the generations. The eldest son of John and Anne married into another merchant family, the Higginsons. Two of his sisters married brothers of his wife. A younger brother married his sister's stepdaughter, Elizabeth Higginson. In the next generation there were two first-cousin marriages between the families. Another alliance, sealed by marriages, was forged with the Lee family, who were drawn into partnership in the Cabot concern. In the fourth and fifth generations there were further first-cousin marriages, but the couples might now be related to one another along several different lines as the Cabots, Higginsons, and Lees became more and more intertwined.[9]

In his study of five prominent New England families, Peter Dobkin Hall counted both cousin marriages and the marriages between brothers- and sisters-in-law as "close kin" marriages, and found that they were roughly equally popular.[10] The incidence of marriage between close relatives fluctuated in this circle of prosperous merchants, but the mean was 40 percent of marriages for much of the eighteenth century. There was a remarkable spike of kin marriages during the Revolutionary period, when the future looked particularly uncertain for the Bostonian upper classes. Two-thirds of Brahmin men who reached marriageable age around that time married their cousins or their sisters-in-law,[11] and these marriages cemented the new elite after the Revolution. Of the first twelve directors of the new Massachusetts Bank, nine were related by blood or by marriage, including, of course, a Cabot and a Higginson. Following the introduction of more flexible rules of incorporation and the institution of family trusts, the rate of close kin marriage declined, but it was a still significant 20 percent of Boston Brahmin marriages for most of the nineteenth century.[12]

As in England, related families coalesced into clans that persisted for several generations, sometimes establishing a residential base. Writing in the second half of the nineteenth century, Henry Lee recalled:

> In Boston in my boyhood the houses were for the most part detached garden houses; there was no quarter for the rich; they and the poor, successful and unsuccessful members of the same family, perhaps,—at least of the same stock,—dwelt in

the same quarter . . . families and friends built courts (no thor-
oughfares) to dwell in together, and there was a personal recognition and co-operation in all affairs . . . which was wholesome. We all lived in this little world; all our work and all our
play were there.[13]

So too were many of their marriages.

THE CLIMATE of opinion changed, however, in mid-nineteenth-
century America. Scientific studies, notably the Bemiss report to the
American Medical Association in 1858, claimed that marriages between cousins were responsible for a number of birth defects.[14] Despite their slapdash methodology, these studies got wide publicity.[15]
Citing unreliable but terrifying statistics, politicians and journalists
began to demand a ban on cousin marriage.[16] Judges and clergymen
weighed in with solemn warnings.

Kansas was the first state to ban the marriage of first cousins, in
1861. Ten of the states that joined the union in the second half of
the nineteenth century passed similar legislation (although not Cali-
fornia or Texas). Several of the older states also introduced a ban
on first-cousin marriage, beginning with New Hampshire in 1869.
Others, notably Massachusetts, New York, and Pennsylvania, still allowed cousins to marry, but everywhere in America cousin marriage
became less common. (More recently, first-cousin marriage has been
banned in Kentucky [1946], Maine [1985], and Texas [2005].)

The regulation of marriage was being tightened up in other ways
as well. A number of states raised the minimum age of marriage. In
some cases, the freedom of mentally handicapped people to marry
was restricted. And after the Civil War, measures were taken to prevent interracial sex and marriage.[17]

The term "miscegenation" was coined in 1864. It referred to all
mixing of the races, but above all to intermarriage.[18] Democrats

campaigned against black-white marriages. In the 1870s, there were moves to restrict marriages between whites and Indians. The campaigns against cousin marriage and miscegenation both warned against mixing the wrong types of "blood."[19] White people, so the argument went, should not mingle their blood with that of other races, because it was too alien, or in some vaguely specified way inferior. Reverend McIlvaine, a distinguished Presbyterian minister who later became principal of the Princeton Theological Seminary, explained that there were also dangers if the blood was too similar. The "degradation and inferiority" of the American Indian peoples had come about because they married cousins and "the blood, instead of dispersing itself more and more widely, is constantly returning upon itself."[20] In short, there was a feeling, apparently supported by science, that marriages should not unite either close kin, or people of different races. In the one case the "blood" was too similar, in the other too alien. In either event, the mixture would cause problems.

In Britain, scientific opinion about close-kin marriage was divided. George Darwin had reported in 1875 that first-cousin marriages did not represent a significant risk to the offspring. His cousin, Francis Galton, the founding father of eugenics, was persuaded. Galton's protégé, Karl Pearson, reached the same conclusion.

It was only after the First World War that the counter-argument gained ground. By the 1920s, eugenicists routinely condemned cousin marriage. Leonard Darwin, another son of Charles Darwin, followed his cousin Francis Galton as president of the Eugenics Education Society and joined the chorus of disapproval, despite the fact that he was himself the son of cousins and had married a first cousin once removed.[21] In the 1930s eugenic racial theories were denounced by the liberal geneticists J. B. S. Haldane and Lionel Penrose, both scions of famous intellectual clans with ties to Bloomsbury. Nevertheless, they agreed that cousin marriages should be discouraged because of their link to recessive disorders, notably congenital deaf-mutism and certain mental defects.[22]

These scientific concerns passed into the general culture. In Thomas Hardy's novel *Jude the Obscure* (1896) Jude, the self-made intellectual, courts his cousin Sue Bridehead, but he is troubled by the vague worry that "it is not well for cousins to fall in love."[23] By 1921, when the cousins Holly Forsyte and Val Dartie marry in the third novel of Galsworthy's *Forsyte Saga,* they bow to the eugenic imperative: "Being first cousins they had decided, or rather Holly had, to have no children."[24] Cousin marriage soon became almost unthinkable. In 1924 Christopher Tietjens, the hero of a novel sequence by Ford Madox Ford, defends his wife against a charge of adultery: "She's Rugeley's mistress, isn't she?" his brother asks. Christopher says: "No, she isn't. I should certainly say she wasn't. Why should she be? She's his cousin."[25]

If anything, these prejudices are stronger than ever today. There is a common feeling that a liaison between cousins is incestuous, and if it is not forbidden it should be, if only because it carries unacceptable risks of genetic damage to offspring. However, this attitude is not justified by the science. Any mating is risky to some degree, one danger being that offspring may be born with a defect if parents have a deleterious recessive gene in common. The chances of birth defects and of infant mortality are roughly doubled for the children of first cousins, but in normal circumstances that means that only an additional 2 percent of children may be affected.[26] According to the geneticists A. H. Bittles and U. E. Makov, "The risks to the offspring of inbred unions generally are within the limits of acceptability. For first cousin progeny, it also must be admitted that they appear to be in remarkably close agreement with the levels calculated by [George] Darwin in 1875."[27] In the United States, the National Society of Genetic Counselors recently convened a panel of experts to review the risks of first-cousin marriage. They reported that the small background risk of congenital defects is raised by some 1.7 to 2 percent in the case of children of first cousins. There is also an additional 4.4 percent chance of pre-reproductive mortality.[28] (The risks are significantly higher, however, if cousin marriages are repeated over several generations.)[29]

IN THE English upper and upper-middle classes the prevalence of first-cousin marriage remained steady at between 4 and 5 percent for much of the nineteenth century—that is, one marriage in every twenty to twenty-five. However, after the First World War cousin marriage became very unusual in England. By the 1930s, only one marriage in 6,000 was with a first cousin.[30] And a study of a middle-class London population conducted in the 1960s found that just one marriage in 25,000 was between first cousins.[31]

The decline in cousin marriage was not due entirely to considerations of health risks. It may even be that medical opinion was only of marginal significance. (After all, in that same period the age of childbearing rose, which introduced more serious risks.) At any rate, other factors were at least as compelling. First, the business environment was gradually liberalized. Restrictions on the issue of shares were lifted in the 1840s.[32] Legislation in the 1850s and 1860s made limited liability a useful option even for medium-sized firms. Provincial stock exchanges flourished. It took some time for the new structures to become widely diffused, but by 1913 domestic companies were a major component of the securities quoted in the London Stock Exchange. Once a partnership did not bear the full risk of failure, and capital could be raised and shares traded on the stock market, there was less incentive for businessmen to marry their cousins or sisters-in-law.

Then the economic foundations of the country were rocked by the First World War. In 1914 Britain had been the largest trading nation in the world and also the world's leading lender. But the war created an economic crisis, or perhaps hastened changes that were already in the making. "The most serious problems for England have been brought to a head by the war, but are in their origins more fundamental," Keynes wrote. "The forces of the nineteenth century have run their course and are exhausted. The economic motives and ideals of that generation no longer satisfy us."[33] Many old family firms were swept away in the postwar depression.

Less obvious, but perhaps even more significant, were the demographic changes. One in three British men aged between nineteen and twenty-two at the outbreak of World War I did not live to see the peace.[34] Men of the upper and upper-middle classes were most likely to volunteer. They could expect to be given commissions, and young officers, drawn disproportionately from the public schools and Oxbridge, were in the greatest danger. As G. R. Searle notes, "The higher up the social scale, the greater the casualty rate."[35] The death rate was not much lower among senior officers in elite regiments: one in five Old Etonian officers was killed during the war, and another one-quarter wounded. Following the introduction of conscription the officer corps became less selective, more broadly middle class, and young solicitors and accountants began to suffer comparable casualty rates.

As a result, young women in the upper and upper-middle classes lost brothers and cousins, and after the war they greatly outnumbered marriageable men. Their chances of marriage were accordingly reduced. Moreover, a significant number of women had engaged in war work, and were less inclined to seek, or to accept, conventional marriages—for instance with their cousins.

Another demographic factor, more long-established, also reduced the chances of cousins marrying: families were having fewer children. The average couple marrying in England and Wales between 1860 and 1870 had six children, but this dropped to about four children in the 1900–1910 cohort and three for the cohort marrying between 1910 and 1920.[36] The upper-middle classes had still smaller families. By the last decades of the nineteenth century doctors had on average 2.8 children, clergymen three.[37] Bourgeois families generally had fewer children as the century progressed, as the table below indicates. (The age of marriage of women rose in all but one of the cohorts.)[38]

Birth dates (men)	Number of married men and women in sample	Age at marriage (men)	Age at marriage (women)	Average number of children
before 1790	289	30.8	25.4	4.4
1791–1820	132	34.8	27.3	5
1821–1850	106	31.4	28.8	3.6
1851–1880	68	27.0	23.8	2.6
after 1880	28	32.8	28	2.8

The smaller the family, the fewer the brothers and sisters. In the next generation, the number of uncles and aunts drops, and they in turn produce fewer cousins (and fewer brothers- and sisters-in-law). In the middle of the nineteenth century a person might have around forty first cousins. By the end of the century, the average number of cousins would be only about a dozen.[39] Only half, of course, were of the right sex, and a number were disqualified by age difference. In the first decades of the twentieth century most young women would have had only a couple of marriageable first cousins, and the chances of these men surviving the war were not good.

THE DECLINE of cousin marriage is at once an index and a cause of a more fundamental social change: the end of the great Victorian clans in England. There were other causes in addition to demographic changes and the new structures of business enterprises. Universal adult franchise was introduced after the First World War, broadening participation in politics. Then, in the 1930s, came the great depression, which again devastated family businesses and impoverished rentiers. The end of the age of the bourgeois clans was if anything overdetermined.

Virginia Woolf, a daughter of one of the leading intellectual dynasties, documented this transformation just as it was becoming apparent. During the years of breakdowns and invalidism that followed the publication of her first novel, she painfully composed her second, *Night and Day,* which appeared in 1919. This was her most traditional novel—"a deliberate exercise in classicism," E. M. Forster called it, not altogether approvingly.[40] Backward-looking, it ignored the war. And yet it documents the end of the dynastic age. As Hermione Lee comments, it is a "long, melancholy comedy of the break with Victorianism."[41]

The central character in the novel, Katharine Hilbery, belongs to one of the Victorian bourgeois dynasties. Her grandfather was a great poet, and Katharine and her mother are writing his biography in a desultory but consuming fashion. "The quality of her birth oozed into Katharine's consciousness from a dozen different sources as soon as she was able to perceive anything. Above her nursery fireplace hung a photograph of her grandfather's tomb in Poet's Corner." The house is full of relics. "There were always visitors—uncles and aunts and cousins 'from India,' to be reverenced for their relationship alone."[42]

Katharine is based on Virginia Woolf's sister, Vanessa Bell. Mrs. Hilbery is drawn even more directly drawn from her aunt, Anny Thackeray. The clan itself is reminiscent of the Stephens and Stracheys:

Denham had accused Katharine Hilbery of belonging to one of the most distinguished families in England, and if anyone will take the trouble to consult Mr Galton's *Hereditary Genius,* he will find that this assertion is not far from the truth. The Alardyces, the Hilberys, the Millingtons, and the Otways seem to prove that intellect is a possession which can be tossed from one member of a certain group to another almost indefinitely, and with apparent certainty that the brilliant gift will be safely caught and held by nine out of ten of the privileged race. They had been conspicuous judges and admirals, lawyers and servants of the State for some years before the richness of the soil culminated in the rarest flower that any family can boast, a great writer . . . Whatever profession you looked at, there was a Warburton or an Alardyce, a Millington or a Hilbery somewhere in authority and prominence.[43]

And "on the whole, in these first years of the twentieth century, the Alardyces and their relations were keeping their heads well above water . . . One finds them at the tops of professions . . . they sit in luxurious public offices . . . they write solid books . . . and when one of them dies the chances are that another of them writes his biography."[44]

But the weight of the past is difficult to bear, the pressure of expectations stifling. Katharine escapes. She gives up her appropriate suitor—passes him on, in fact, to her cousin—and marries a middle-class self-made intellectual, Ralph Denham, the young man who had "accused" her of "belonging to one of the most distinguished families in England." (Katharine's marriage recalls Helen Schlegel's—more adventurous—romance with Leonard Bast in E. M. Forster's *Howards End,* which had appeared in 1910.) Katharine is still rather conventional, however, compared to Mary, who is also in love with Ralph but renounces marriage and devotes herself to feminist work. Mary represents the new woman.

The old pattern lingered on here and there. In *Period Piece,* her memoir of life in Edwardian England, Charles Darwin's granddaughter Gwen Raverat evokes Darwin's five sons: "A solid block of uncles, each more adorable than the other. There was a great family likeness among them . . . they all had the same kind of presence; the same flavour, and the same family voice."[45] Three of the brothers built houses in the grounds of an estate that Emma Darwin bought in Cambridge after she was widowed. The extended family came together at Christmas, for family parties, and on long summer visits to Emma at Down House. Two of the brothers, Leonard and Horace, married cousins (respectively, a first cousin once removed and a second cousin once removed). However, none of Charles and Emma's grandchildren married a relation.

In a more recent book, the novel *Camomile Lawn,* nostalgically set in the last summer before the Second World War, Mary Wesley evokes an enchanted holiday in which cousins fall in love, "sitting round a table lit by candles, with the moon rising over the sea."[46] Yet it was all over by then—not only cousin marriages, but the whole structure of intermarrying networks of kin, engaged in great family projects. A generation earlier, the age of the bourgeois dynasties had come to an end.

Notes

Prologue

1. Frederick Burkhardt and Sydney Smith, eds., *Correspondence of Charles Darwin* (Cambridge, 1986), vol. 2, 444.
2. Ibid., 445.
3. Janet Browne, *Charles Darwin: Voyaging* (London, 1996), 392.
4. Ibid., 391.
5. *Emma Darwin: A Century of Family Letters,* ed. Henrietta Litchfield (London, 1915), vol. 2, 1.
6. Barbara Wedgwood and Hensleigh Wedgwood, *The Wedgwood Circle 1730–1897: Four Generations of a Family and Their Friends* (London, 1980), 233.
7. *Emma Darwin: A Century of Family Letters,* vol. 2, 2–3.
8. Browne, *Charles Darwin: Voyaging,* 392.

Introduction

1. In a letter to his friend and partner, Thomas Bentley, in 1776. Eliza Meteyard, *The Life of Josiah Wedgwood* (London, 1865), vol. 1, 351.
2. E. A. Wrigley, "British population during the 'long' eighteenth century, 1680–1840," in Roderick Floud and Paul Johnson, eds., *The Cambridge Economic History of Modern Britain* (Cambridge, 2004), vol. 1, 64.
3. See ibid., 87–90; Boyd Hilton, *A Mad, Bad & Dangerous People? England 1783–1846* (Oxford, 2006), 6–7.
4. See Floud and Johnson, eds., *The Cambridge Economic History of Modern Britain,* vol. 1, *Industrialisation, 1700–1860;* E. A. Wrigley, *Continuity, Chance, and Change: The Character of the Industrial Revolution in England* (Cambridge, 1988); Hilton, *A Mad, Bad & Dangerous People?,* 2–24.
5. D. N. McCloskey, "The industrial revolution 1780–1860," in R. Floud and D. McCLoskey, eds., *The Economic History of Britain since 1700,* vol. 1, *1700–1860* (Cambridge, 1981).

6. Stephen Quinn, "Money, finance and capital markets," in Floud and Johnson, eds., *The Cambridge Economic History of Modern Britain,* vol. 1, 173–174.

7. Hilton, *A Mad, Bad & Dangerous People?,* 6–7.

8. Nicholas Crafts, "Long-run growth," in Floud and Johnson, eds., *The Cambridge Economic History of Modern Britain,* vol. 2, 4.

9. For reviews of the structure of the upper-middle classes, see Paul Langford, *A Polite and Commercial People, England 1727–1783* (Oxford, 1989), especially chap. 3; Hilton, *A Mad, Bad & Dangerous People?,* 124–161; K. Theodore Hoppen, *The Mid-Victorian Generation, 1846–1886* (Oxford, 1998), particularly chap. 2.

10. Langford, *A Polite and Commercial People,* 668.

11. Harold Perkin, *The Origins of Modern English Society,* 2nd ed. (London, 2002), 287.

12. Leslie Stephen, *The Life of James Fitzjames Stephen* (London, 1895), 7.

13. Leslie Stephen, *The English Utilitarians* (London, 1900), vol. 1, 111–112.

14. Asa Briggs, *Victorian Cities* (London, 1963); Derek Fraser, *Urban Politics in Victorian England: The Structure of Politics in Victorian Cities* (Leicester, 1976); Hilton, *A Mad, Bad & Dangerous People?,* 152–166.

15. W. D. Rubenstein, "The Victorian middle classes: Wealth, occupation, and geography," *Economic History Review,* 30, no. 4 (1977), 602–623.

16. Jenny Uglow, *The Lunar Men* (London, 2002).

17. Joel Mokyr, "Accounting for the industrial revolution," in Floud and Johnson, eds., *The Cambridge Economic History of Modern Britain,* vol. 1, 17–27.

18. Cited in Uglow, *The Lunar Men,* 77.

19. G. R. Searle, *A New England? Peace and War 1886–1918* (Oxford, 2004), 129.

20. Perkin, *The Origins of Modern English Society,* 425–426.

21. Noel Annan, "The intellectual aristocracy," in J. H. Plumb, ed., *Studies in Social History: A Tribute to G. M. Trevelyan* (London, 1955), 247.

22. Darwin to J. D. Hooker, October 23, 1859, letter 2509, Darwin Correspondence Project *(http://www.darwinproject.ac.uk).*

23. Ernst von Hesse-Wartegg, "Bei Charles Darwin" [At Charles Darwin's], trans. R. Keynes. *Frankfurter Zeitung und Handelsblatt,* July 30, 1880, 1–2. Darwin collection, Cambridge University Library.

24. Ibid.

25. Noel Annan, *Leslie Stephen: The Godless Victorian* (London, 1984), 198.

26. Leslie Stephen, *The Life of James Fitzjames Stephen,* 198–199.

27. See particularly Peter Laslett and Richard Wall, eds., *Household and Family in Past Time* (Cambridge, 1972); Richard Wall, Jean Robin, and Peter Laslett, eds., *Family Forms in Historic Europe* (Cambridge, 1983).

28. Lutz Berkner, "The use and misuse of census data for the historical analysis

of family structure," *Journal of Interdisciplinary History,* 5(4) (1975), 721–738.

29. Lawrence Stone, *The Family, Sex and Marriage in England 1500–1800* (New York, 1977); but cf. Alan McFarlane, *Marriage and Love in England: Modes of Reproduction, 1300–1840* (Oxford, 1986).

30. J. L. Flandrin, *Families in Former Times* (Cambridge, 1979), 110.

31. Michael Anderson, *Approaches to the History of the Western Family 1500–1914* (Cambridge, 1980). Cf. Lawrence Stone, "Family history in the 1980s," *Journal of Interdisciplinary History,* 12:1 (1981), 521–587.

32. Jane Turner Censer, "What ever happened to family history?" *Comparative Studies in Society and History,* 33:3 (1991), 529.

33. See, for instance, Valerie Sanders, *The Brother-Sister Culture in Nineteenth-Century Literature: From Austen to Woolf* (London, 2002); Susan Annes Brown, *Devoted Sisters: Representations of the Sister Relationship in Nineteenth-Century British and American Literature* (Aldershot, 2003); Ellen Pollack, *Incest and the English Novel, 1684–1814* (Baltimore, 2003); Ruth Perry, *Novel Relations: The Transformation of Kinship in English Literature and Culture 1748–1818* (Cambridge, 2004).

34. Pat Jalland, *Women, Marriage, and Politics, 1860–1914* (Oxford, 1986), chap. 4.

35. Ibid., 255. For age of marriage in the general population, see Wrigley, "British population during the 'long' eighteenth century," 73.

36. Jalland, *Women, Marriage, and Politics,* 59–72.

37. Richard Grassby, *Kinship and Capitalism: Marriage, Family, and Business in the English-Speaking World, 1580–1740* (Cambridge, 2001), 70–75, 85–88.

38. Jalland, *Women, Marriage, and Politics,* 59.

39. Leonore Davidoff and Catherine Hall, *Family Fortunes: Men and Women of the English Middle Class, 1780–1850,* rev. ed. (London, 2002), 206–209.

40. Cited in Stephen Cretney, *Family Law in the Twentieth Century* (Oxford, 2003), 92. See also Mary Lyndon Shanley, *Feminism, Marriage, and the Law in Victorian England* (Princeton, N.J., 1989), especially 57–128.

41. Cited in Cretney, *Family Law in the Twentieth Century,* 97.

42. See Naomi Tadmor, *Family and Friends in Eighteenth-century England: Household, Kinship, and Patronage* (Cambridge, 2001), Introduction.

43. Brown, *Devoted Sisters;* Sanders, *The Brother-Sister Culture in Nineteenth-Century Literature;* Claudia Nelson, *Family Ties in Victorian England* (Westport, Conn., 2007), chap. 4.

44. Nelson, *Family Ties in Victorian England,* 137.

45. Sanders, *The Brother-Sister Culture in Nineteenth-Century Literature,* 105.

46. Francis Galton, *Memories of My Life* (London, 1908), 158.

47. George Darwin to Charles Darwin, February 6, 1874. The Darwin Correspondence, University of Cambridge Library.

48. The table in the text shows the percentage of marriages between first and

second cousins for different age cohorts. The families documented in this table occur in genealogies that I collected as my research progressed. A rolling sample, not a random sample, it draws mainly on well-known families and their connections.

49. E. A. Smith, "Caroline" [Princess Caroline of Brunswick-Wolfenbüttel] (1768–1821), *Oxford Dictionary of National Biography.*

50. Judith Schneid Lewis, "Princess Charlotte Augusta," *Oxford Dictionary of National Biography.*

51. Alan Palmer, "Ernest Augustus" (1771–1851), *Oxford Dictionary of National Biography.*

52. Hilton, *A Mad, Bad & Dangerous People?,* 500.

53. H. C. G. Matthew and K. D. Reynolds, "Victoria," *Oxford Dictionary of National Biography.*

54. Randolph Trumbach, *The Rise of the Egalitarian Family: Aristocratic Kinship and Domestic Relations in Eighteenth-Century England* (New York, 1978), 18–21.

55. John Wilmot, Lord Rochester, *Letter from Artemisia in the Towne to Chloe in the Country* (1679).

56. T. H. Hollingsworth, *The Demography of the British Peerage,* Supplement to *Population Studies,* XVIII, 2 (1964), 9–10.

57. Samuel Dugard, *The Marriages of Cousin Germans Vindicated* (Oxford, 1673), cited in Trumbach, *The Rise of the Egalitarian Family,* 19.

58. Trumbach, *The Rise of the Egalitarian Family,* 19.

59. Jeremy Taylor, *Ductor Dubinantium* (London, 1660), cited in Trumbach, *The Rise of the Egalitarian Family,* 19–20.

60. Perry, *Novel Relations,* 123.

61. Trumbach, *The Rise of the Egalitarian Family,* 18–30.

62. George H. Darwin, "Marriages between First Cousins in England and their Effects," *Journal of the Statistical Society,* xxxviii (1875).

63. Hilton, *A Mad, Bad & Dangerous People?,* 133.

64. David Sabean, Simon Teuscher, and Jon Mathieu, eds., *Kinship in Europe: Approaches to Long-Term Development, 1300–1900* (Oxford, 2007), 188.

65. Pat Hudson, "Industrial organisation and structure," in Floud and Johnson, eds., *The Cambridge Economic History of Modern Britain,* vol. 1, 50–51.

66. £30,000 in 1854 is the equivalent of £2 million (or $2.9 million) at the end of 2007, calculated by using the retail price index. *www.measuringworth.com/ppoweruk/.*

67. W. Byng Kenrick, *Chronicles of a Nonconformist Family: The Kenricks of Wynne Hall, Exeter and Birmingham* (Birmingham, 1932).

68. See Eric Hobsbawm, *Industry and Empire: An Economic History of Britain since 1750* (London, 1968); Joseph E. Inikori, *Africans and the Industrial Revolution in England: A Study in International Trade and Economic Development* (Cambridge, 2002).

1. The Romance of Incest and the Love of Cousins

1. Janet Browne, *Charles Darwin: Voyaging* (London, 1996), 392.
2. Ibid.
3. Jane Austen, *Catharine and Other Writings,* ed. Margaret Anne Doody and Douglas Murray (Oxford, 1998), 3.
4. Ibid., 6.
5. Jane Austen, *Pride and Prejudice* (London, 1813), vol. 1, chap. 13.
6. Jane Austen, *Persuasion* (London, 1817), chap. 9.
7. Cited in Paul Langford, *A Polite and Commercial People, England 1727–1783* (Oxford, 1989), 96.
8. Anna Barbauld, *The British Novelists,* 2nd ed. (London, 1820), vol. I, 47–48.
9. Ruth Perry cites a number of eighteenth-century examples. Ruth Perry, *Novel Relations: The Transformation of Kinship in English Literature and Culture 1748–1818* (Cambridge, 2004), 122.
10. For instance, in Trollope's *Can You Forgive Her?* (1864–1865), George Vavasor marries his cousin Alice. In *Sir Harry Hotspur of Humblethwaite* (1870), Emily Hotspur wants to marry *her* cousin George. In *The Eustace Diamonds* (1873), Lizzie Eustace tries to entice her cousin Frank Greystock into marriage. In *The Way We Live Now* (1875), Roger Carbury is in love with his cousin Hetta. Her mother is in favor of the marriage, but Hetta falls for Roger's rather unreliable friend. Ever the gentleman, Roger gives her up, but wills his country estate to Hetta's son.
11. Margaret Oliphant, *Hester* (1883; Oxford, 2003), 6.
12. Elizabeth Gaskell, *The Moorland Cottage* (London, 1850), chap. 4.
13. William Makepiece Thackeray, *The Newcomes* (London, 1854), chap. 59.
14. Beatrix Potter, *The Tale of the Flopsy Bunnies* (London, 1909).
15. Francis Darwin, ed., *The Life and Letters of Charles Darwin,* 3 vols. (London, 1887), I, 101.
16. Deirdre Le Faye, *Jane Austen's Outlandish Cousin* (London, 2002), 123, 143, 150–151.
17. Nancy Fix Anderson, "Cousin marriage in Victorian England," *Journal of Family History,* 11:3 (1986), 290.
18. Algernon Charles Swinburne, *The Sisters: A Tragedy* (London, 1892), 15–16.
19. Rikky Rooksby, *A. C. Swinburne: A Poet's Life* (Aldershot, 1997), 266–267.
20. Deirdre Le Faye, ed., *Jane Austen's Letters* (Oxford, 1995), 283.
21. Cherry Durrant, "Coleridge, Henry Nelson," *Oxford Dictionary of National Biography.*
22. Henry Nelson Coleridge, *Six Months in the West Indies in 1825* (London, 1826), 112.
23. An autograph note, published in *Collected Letters of Samuel Taylor Coleridge,* ed. Earl Leslie Griggs, 6 vols. (Oxford, 1956–1971), vol. 6, 590 (n. 1).

24. Kathleen Jones, *A Passionate Sisterhood: The Sisters, Wives and Daughters of the Lake Poets* (London, 1998), 240–241.

25. *Specimens of the Table Talk of the Late Samuel Taylor Coleridge*, ed. H. N. C. [Henry Nelson Coleridge], 2 vols. (London, 1835), vol. 1, 55: entry for June 10, 1824.

26. Augustine, *The City of God against the Pagans*, trans. and ed. R. W. Dyson (Cambridge, 1998 [first edition 426 CE]), 667.

27. Anderson, "Cousin marriage," 289.

28. Cherry Durrant, "Coleridge."

29. Leonore Davidoff and Catherine Hall, *Family Fortunes: Men and Women of the English Middle Class 1780–1850*, rev. ed. (London, 2002), 467–468.

30. See Nancy Fix Anderson, "The 'Marriage with a Deceased Wife's Sister Bill' Controversy: Incest anxiety and defence of family purity in Victorian England," *Journal of British Studies*, 21:2 (1982); Anderson, "Cousin marriage"; Margaret Morganroth Gullette, "The puzzling case of the deceased wife's sister," *Representations*, 31 (1990); Glenda Hudson, *Sibling Love and Incest in Jane Austen's Fiction* (New York, 1992); Elizabeth Rose Gruner, "Born and made: Sisters, brothers, and the Deceased Wife's Sister Bill," *Signs*, 24(2) (1999); Valerie Sanders, *The Brother-Sister Culture in Nineteenth-Century Literature: From Austen to Woolf* (London, 2002); Susan Annes Brown, *Devoted Sisters: Representations of the Sister Relationship in Nineteenth-Century British and American Literature* (Aldershot, 2003); Ellen Pollack, *Incest and the English Novel, 1684–1814* (Baltimore, 2003); Perry, *Novel Relations;* and Mary Jean Corbett, "Husband, wife, and sister: Making and remaking the early Victorian family," *Victorian Literature and Culture*, 35 (2007).

31. Anderson, "Cousin marriage," 286.

32. The psychoanalyst John Bowlby wrote a biography of Darwin, and did not suggest that he had a disturbed or unbalanced attachment to his sisters. John Bowlby, *Charles Darwin: A New Life* (New York, 1991).

33. Pollak, *Incest and the English Novel*, 1.

34. See Perry, *Novel Relations,* especially 400–401.

35. Several of these examples are taken from Hudson, *Sibling Love and Incest in Jane Austen's Fiction.*

36. Perry, *Novel Relations*, 162.

37. Mary Shelley, *Frankenstein* (London, 1818), chap. 1.

38. Frances Wilson, *The Ballad of Dorothy Wordsworth* (London, 2008), 143.

39. F. W. Bateson, *Wordsworth: A Re-interpretation* (London, 1954).

40. Wilson, *The Ballad of Dorothy Wordsworth*, 3–4.

41. Ibid., 146.

42. Jane Austen, *Persuasion* (1817), chap. 11.

43. £3,000 in 1814 is the equivalent in purchasing power to £160,000 in 2007 (or $231,000 in 2009). Lawrence H. Officer, "Purchasing Power of British

Pounds from 1264 to 2007," MeasuringWorth, 2008. *www.measuringworth. com/ppoweruk/.*

44. Jane Austen, *Mansfield Park* (1814), vol. I, chap. 1.
45. Ibid., vol. III, chaps 15. and 17.
46. Ibid., chap. 17.
47. Ibid.
48. Ibid., vol. II, chap. 6.
49. Hudson, *Sibling Love and Incest in Jane Austen's Fiction,* 37.
50. Austen, *Mansfield Park,* vol. III, chap. 17.
51. Emma Wedgwood to Charles Darwin, January 3, 1839, Darwin Correspondence Project, University of Cambridge.
52. George Eliot, *Daniel Deronda* (London, 1876), Book I, chap. 3.
53. Ibid., chap. 4.
54. William Makepeace Thackeray, *The History of Henry Esmond: Written by Himself* (London, 1852), Book 1, chap. 1.
55. Ibid., Book 2, chap. 8.
56. Ibid., Book 3, chap. 3.
57. Ibid., Book 2, chap. 15.
58. Ann Monsarrat, *An Uneasy Victorian* (London, 1980), 281–284. Cf. D. J. Taylor, *Thackeray* (London, 1999), 284.
59. Cited in John Tilford, "The 'Unsavoury Plot' of 'Henry Esmond,'" *Nineteenth-Century Fiction,* 6:2 (1951), 122.
60. Cited in ibid.
61. Anthony Trollope, *Thackeray* (London, 1879), 126–127.
62. Ibid.
63. Austen, *Mansfield Park,* vol. III, chap. 17.
64. Cited in John Tosh, "Domesticity and manliness in the Victorian middle class: The family of Edward White Benson," in Michael Roper and John Tosh, eds., *Manful Assertions* (New York, 1991), 54.
65. Charlotte Brontë, *Villette* (1853), chap. 37.
66. Tosh, "Domesticity and manliness," 57–59.
67. Mark D. Chapman, "Benson, Edward White," *Oxford Dictionary of National Biography.*
68. Ibid.
69. See Sanders, *The Brother-Sister Culture in Nineteenth-Century Literature,* 13, 25.

2. The Law of Incest

1. Frederick Pollock and Frederic William Maitland, *The History of English Law before the Time of Edward I,* 2 vols. (Cambridge, 1895), vol. 2, 372, 542.
2. Roger Lee Brown, "The rise and fall of the Fleet marriages," in R. B. Outhwaite, ed., *Marriage and Society* (London, 1981), 117–136.
3. Ibid., 117, 123.

4. Ibid., 126.
5. Stephen Cretney, *Family Law in the Twentieth Century: A History* (Oxford, 2003), 4–5.
6. Eric Josef Carlson, *Marriage and the English Reformation* (Oxford, 1994), 20–21.
7. Pollock and Maitland, *The History of English Law before the Time of Edward I*, vol. 2, 368–369.
8. Ibid., 135–136. See also Cretney, *Family Law in the Twentieth Century*, pp. 5–6.
9. J. C. D. Clark, *English Society 1688–1832* (Cambridge, 1985), 89.
10. Cretney, *Family Law in the Twentieth Century*, chap. 1.
11. John Morley, *The Life of William Ewart Gladsone*, 3 vols. (London, 1903), vol. 1, 155.
12. Cretney, *Family Law in the Twentieth Century*, chap. 1.
13. Cynthia Fansler Behrman, "The annual blister: A sidelight on Victorian social and parliamentary history," *Victorian Studies*, xi (1967–68), 484.
14. G. H. Gordon, *The Criminal Law of Scotland*, 2nd ed. (Edinburgh, 1978), 896–900.
15. Martin Ingram, *Church Courts, Sex, and Marriage in England, 1570–1640* (Cambridge, 1987), 245–246.
16. Robert Hole, "Incest, consanguinity and a monstrous birth in rural England, January 1600," *Social History*, 25: 2 (2000), 189.
17. Chris Durston, "'Unhallowed Wedlocks': The regulation of marriage during the English revolution," *The Historical Journal*, 31: 1 (1988), 45–59.
18. Keith Thomas, "The Puritans and adultery: The act of 1650 reconsidered," in Donald Pennington and Keith Thomas, eds., *Puritans and Revolutionaries* (Oxford, 1978), 257–282.
19. William Blackstone, *Commentaries on the Laws of England*, 4 vols. (Oxford, 1769), vol. 4, 64.
20. Joyce Hemlow, *The History of Fanny Burney* (Oxford, 1958), 282–283.
21. Fiona MacCarthy, *Byron: Life and Legend* (London, 2002), 276.
22. Thomas Moore, *Life of Lord Byron*, 3 vols. (London, 1854), vol. 3, 180.
23. MacCarthy, *Byron*, 275.
24. Louis Crompton, *Byron and Greek Love* (Berkeley, 1985), 223–224.
25. Moore, *Life of Byron*, vol. 3, 180.
26. Polly Morris, "Incest or survival strategy? Plebeian marriage within the prohibited degrees in Somerset, 1730–1835," *Journal of the History of Sexuality*, 2 (1991), 242.
27. Heathcote Divorce Act of 1851, 14 and 15 Vic., c24.
28. Morris, "Incest or survival strategy?", 251–256.
29. *Moll Flanders* [1722], ed. Edward H. Kelly (New York, 1973), 71.
30. Ibid., 76.
31. Michael L. Satlow, *Jewish Marriage in Antiquity* (Princeton, 2001), 144.

32. Stephen Todd, *The Shape of Athenian Law* (Oxford, 1993), 202ff.
33. Martin Goodman, *Rome and Jerusalem: The Clash of Ancient Civilizations* (London, 2007), 223.
34. Edward Gibbon, *The History of the Decline and Fall of the Roman Empire*, vol. 8 (1776), 261.
35. Jack Goody, *The Development of the Family and Marriage in Europe* (Cambridge, 1983), 53–59, 144–146.
36. Pollock and Maitland, *History of English Law*, vol. 2, 387.
37. *Wing v. Taylor*, 2 Sw & Tr 278.
38. J. J. Scarisbrick, *Henry VIII* (London, 1968), 180–197.
39. Cited in Jason P. Rosenblatt, "Aspects of the incest problem in *Hamlet*," *Shakespeare Quarterly*, 29: 3 (1978), 359.
40. 32 Hen. 8, c 38. The complex history of Henry's statutes is still most authoritatively laid out in the judgment in *Wing v. Taylor*, 2 Sw & Tr 278.
41. S. Dugard, *The Marriages of Cousin Germans, Vindicated from the Censures of Unlawfulness, and Inexpediency* (Oxford, 1673).
42. For example, Robert Dixon, *The Degrees of Consanguinity and Affinity: Described, and Delineated* (London, 1674).
43. Már Jónsson, "Defining incest by the word of God: Northern Europe 1520–1740," *History of European Ideas*, 18: 6 (1994), 853–867. For some English examples see Hole, "Incest, consanguinity and a monstrous birth in rural England," 188–189.
44. Carlson, *Marriage and the English Reformation*, 93.
45. John Strype, *The Life and Acts of Matthew Parker* (Oxford, 1821), 551.
46. R. H. Helmholz, *The Oxford History of the Laws of England, Volume 1, The Canon Law and Ecclesiastical Jurisdiction from 597 to the 1640s* (Oxford, 2004), 544.
47. Randolph Trumbach, *The Rise of the Egalitarian Family* (New York, 1978), 19.
48. See Scarisbrick, *Henry VIII*, 163–180.
49. See Bruce Thomas Boehrer, *Monarchy and Incest in Renaissance England* (Philadelphia, 1992), chap. 2. Cf. Rosenblatt, "Aspects of the incest problem in *Hamlet*."
50. Ellen Pollak, *Incest and the English Novel, 1684–1814* (Baltimore, 2003), chap. 3.
51. Discussed by Ruth Perry, *Novel Relations: The Transformation of Kinship in English Literature and Culture 1748–1818* (Cambridge, 2004), 211. Citation in ibid.
52. John Alleyne, *The Legal Degrees of Marriage Stated and Considered* (London, 1774), 4.
53. Pollak, *Incest and the English Novel*, 55–58.
54. The rule was that "a man called his wife's relatives by the same terms as she did, and she called his relatives by the same terms as he did; and those rela-

tives used the appropriate reciprocals." Isaac Schapera, *Kinship Terminology in Jane Austen's Novels* (London, 1977), 16–19. Cf. Naomi Tadmor, *Family and Friends in Eighteenth-Century England* (Cambridge, 2001), 122ff.

55. Cited in Elizabeth Rose Gruner, "Born and made: Sisters, brothers, and the Deceased Wife's Sister Bill," *Signs*, 24: 2 (1999), 433.

56. Hansard, House of Lords, March 13, 1873, 3, vol. 214, col. 1876.

57. HC Deb, March 6, 1850, vol. 109, col. 429.

58. Cited in Susan Annes Brown, *Devoted Sisters: Representations of the Sister Relationship in Nineteenth-Century British and American Literature* (Aldershot, 2003), 114.

59. James Stuart Wortley, *Law of Marriage: The Substance of a Speech Delivered in the House of Commons, February 22, 1849* (London, 1849), 22.

60. Behrman, "The annual blister," 488.

61. *First Report of the Commissioners Appointed to Inquire into the State and Operation of the Law of Marriage, as Relating to the Prohibited Degrees of Affinity, and to Marriages Solemnized Abroad or in the British Colonies; with Minutes of Evidence, Appendix and Index,* Parliamentary Papers (hereafter P.P.), 1847–48 (973), 388.

62. Cited in Cretney, *Family Law*, 44.

63. P.P., 1847–48 (973), xxviii, x–xi.

64. P.P., 1847–48 (973), xxviii, 249.

65. Jennifer Tann, "Boulton, Matthew," *Oxford Dictionary of National Biography;* Christina Edgeworth Colvin, "Edgeworth, Richard Lovell," *Oxford Dictionary of National Biography.*

66. Jenny Uglow, *The Lunar Men* (London, 2002), 62–63.

67. Ibid., 317–318.

68. Trumbach, *The Rise of the Egalitarian Family*, 31.

69. Osbert Wyndham Hewett, *Strawberry Fair: A Biography of Frances, Countess Waldegrave 1821–1879* (London, 1956), 34.

70. This would be equivalent in purchasing power to £1.5 million in 2007 (or $2.25 million at the end of 2008). Lawrence H. Officer, "Purchasing Power of British Pounds from 1264 to 2007," MeasuringWorth, 2008. *www.measuringworth.com/ppoweruk/.*

71. Lee MacCormick Edwards, "Herkomer, Sir Hubert von," *Oxford Dictionary of National Biography.*

72. Behrman, "The annual blister," 488.

73. Ibid., 31, 32–33.

74. The letter was quoted in Parliament, HC Deb, March 13, 1855, vol. 137, CC486–518.

75. Eleanor Gordon and Gwyneth Nair, *Public Lives: Women, Family and Society in Victorian Britain* (New Haven, Conn., 2003), 173.

76. Leonore Davidoff and Catherine Hall, *Family Fortunes: Men and Women of the English Middle Class 1780–1850*, rev. ed. (London, 2002), 468.

77. Alleyne, *The Legal Degrees of Marriage*, 11–12.
78. P.P., 1847–48 (973), xxviii, x–xi.
79. Thomas Hardy, *Tess of the d'Urbervilles* (London, 1891), chap. 58.
80. P.P., 1847–48 (973), xxviii, x–xi, 66.
81. Gullette, "The puzzling case of the deceased wife's sister," 157–159.
82. William Austen-Leigh and Richard Arthur Austen-Leigh, revised by Deirdre Le Faye, *Jane Austen: A Family Record* (New York, 1989), 238.
83. Quoted in Sybil Wolfram, *In-Laws and Outlaws: Kinship and Marriage in England* (London, 1987), 33.
84. Henry James, "The Romance of Certain Old Clothes" (1868).
85. Fred Kaplan, *Dickens: A Biography* (London, 1988), 390.
86. As Valerie Sanders points out in her introduction to Harriet Martineau, *Deerbrook* (London, 2004), xx. Cf. Brown, *Devoted Sisters*, chap. 8.
87. Cited in Gullette, "The puzzling case of the deceased wife's sister," 163.
88. Wolfram, *In-Laws and Outlaws*, 39.
89. See, among others, Anon. [Felicia Skene], *The Inheritance of Evil* (London, 1849); Joseph Middleton, *Love vs Law: Or Marriage with a Deceased Wife's Sister* (London, 1855); Dinah Maria (Mulock) Craik, *Hannah*, 3 vols. (London, 1871); William Clark Russell, *The Deceased Wife's Sister* (1874); Mary Braddon, *The Fatal Three* (London, 1888). The theme crops up incidentally in a number of other Victorian novels, most famously perhaps in Anthony Trollope's *The Three Clerks* (1857) and Thomas Hardy's *Tess of the d'Urbervilles* (1891).
    There are valuable recent studies of the genre. See Brown, *Devoted Sisters*, chap. 7; Perry, *Novel Relations*; Hudson, *Sibling Love and Incest in Jane Austen's Fiction;* Gruner, "Born and Made: Sisters, Brothers, and the Deceased Wife's Sister Bill"; Gullette, "The puzzling case of the deceased wife's sister," 142–143.
90. Anon. [Felicia Skene], *The Inheritance of Evil*, 30–31.
91. Ibid., 130.
92. Craik, *Hannah*, vol. 1, 47.
93. Ibid., vol. 2, 2.
94. Ibid., vol. 2, 93.
95. Cited in Mary Jean Corbett, "Husband, wife and sister: making and remaking the early Victorian family," *Victorian Literature and Culture*, 35 (2007), 5. This citation is from Matthew Arnold, *Friendship's Garland* (London, 1871), 315.
96. Cited in Brown, *Devoted Sisters*, 114.
97. Ibid., 117.
98. Anthony Trollope, *The Way We Live Now* (London, 1875), chap. 78.
99. Wolfram, *In-laws and Outlaws*, 30–31.
100. See, for example, Abraham Hayward, *Summary of Objections to the Doctrine that a Marriage with the Sister of a Deceased Wife is Contrary to Law, Religion, or Morality* (London, 1839); Joshua Frederick Denham, *Marriage*

with a Deceased Wife's Sister Not Forbidden by the Law of Nature (London, 1847); Edward Pusey, *Marriage with a Deceased Wife's Sister* (London, 1849) and *God's Prohibition of the Marriage with a Deceased Wife's Sister* (London, 1860); W. A. Beckett, *The Woman's Question and the Man's Answer: or, Reflections on the Social Consequences of Legalizing Marriage with a Deceased Wife's Sister* (London, 1859); "An Antiquary," *An Historical View of the Restrictions Upon Marriage, Especially in Relation to England, with the True Reasons Why Marriage with the Sister of a Deceased Wife Was Prohibited* (London, 1880); Charles Cameron, *Marriage with a Deceased Wife's Sister* (London, 1883); *Debate on the Second Reading of the Deceased Wife's Sister Bill: Comments of the Press* (London, 1895).

101. Wolfram, *In-laws and Outlaws*, 31.

102. Nancy F. Anderson, "The 'Marriage With a Deceased Wife's Sister Bill' controversy: Incest anxiety and the defense of family purity in Victorian England," *Journal of British Studies* 21: 2 (1982), 68–69.

103. Cretney, *Family Law in the Twentieth Century*, 46 n.59.

104. Wolfram, *In-laws and Outlaws*, 28.

105. Louise A. Jackson, *Child Sexual Abuse in Victorian England* (London, 2000), chap. 3.

106. Ibid., 15.

107. This would be equivalent in purchasing power to £387 in 2007 (or $580 at the end of 2008). Officer, "Purchasing Power of British Pounds," *www.measuringworth.com/ppoweruk/*.

108. Discussed in Frederic Whyte, *The Life of W. T. Stead*, 2 vols. (London, 1925), vol. 1, chap. 8; for the original article, see *Pall Mall Gazette*, July 6, 1885. See D. Gorham, "The 'maiden tribute of modern Babylon' reexamined: Child prostitution and the idea of childhood in late-Victorian England," *Victorian Studies*, 21 (1978), 353–379.

109. Jackson, *Child Sexual Abuse in Victorian England*, 18–22.

110. Norman and Jeanne MacKenzie, eds., *The Diary of Beatrice Webb*, 4 vols. (London, 1982–1984), vol. 1, 244.

111. Beatrice Webb, *My Apprenticeship* (London, 1926), 275 n.; Anthony S. Wohl, "Sex and the single room: Incest among the Victorian working classes," in Anthony S. Wohl, ed., *The Victorian Family* (London, 1978). See also Victor Bailey and Sheila Blackburn, "The Punishment of Incest Act 1908: A case study of law creation," *Criminal Law Review* (1979).

112. *First Report of Her Majesty's Commissioners for Inquiring into the Housing of the Working Classes*, 3 vols., P.P., 1884–85 (C. 4402), xxx, vol. 2, Minutes of Evidence and Appendix as to England and Wales, 79, 85, 87, 121, 164, 191, 222, 225.

113. Bailey and Blackburn, "Punishment of Incest Act," 713–714.

114. Ibid., 715. This paragraph draws on their study.

115. See Anderson, "The 'Marriage With a Deceased Wife's Sister Bill' controversy," 86.

3. The Science of Incest and Heredity

1. See, for example, Gérard Delille, "Consanguinité proche en Italie du XVIe au XIXe siècle," in Pierre Bonte, ed., *Épouser au plus proche: Inceste, prohibitions et stratégies matrimoniales autour de la Méditerranée* (Paris, 1994); Raul Merzario, "Land, kinship, and consanguineous marriage in Italy from the seventeenth to the nineteenth centuries," *Journal of Family History,* 15 (1990); Jean-Marie Gouesse, "Mariages de proches parents (XVIe–XXe siècle)," in *Le Modèle Familial Européen* (Rome, 1986), 31–61.

2. For example, W. R. Wilde, *On the Physical, Moral and Social Condition of the Deaf and Dumb* (London, 1854); S. M. Bemiss, "Report on influence of marriages of consanguinity upon offspring," *Transactions of the American Medical Association,* 11 (1858), 319–425; Anon., "Des Mariages Consanguins —examen des travaux récents sur ce sujet," *Annales d'Hygiène,* 33 (1862), 222–229; J. Boudin, "Études statistiques sur les dangers des unions consanguines," *Journale de la Société de Statistique de Paris,* 3–4 (1862), 69–84, 103–120. An extensive contemporary bibliography was published: Alfred Henry Huth, "Index to Books and Papers on Marriage between Near Kin," appendix to *Report of the First Annual Meeting of the Index Society* (London, 1879).

3. Anthony Trollope, *The Small House of Allington* (London, 1863), chap. 20.

4. For example, James Gardner, "On the intermarriage of relations as the cause of degeneracy of offspring," *British Medical Journal,* 1 (1861), 290; Gilbert Child, "On marriages of consanguinity," *British and Foreign Medico-Chirurgical Review,* 29 (1862), 461–471.

5. Barbara and Hensleigh Wedgwood, *The Wedgwood Circle: 1730–1897* (London, 1980), 102.

6. Letter from Erasmus Darwin to Robert Darwin, January 5, 1792, in Nora Barlow, ed., *The Autobiography of Charles Darwin, 1809–1882* (New York, 1958), note one, 223–225.

7. Erasmus Darwin, *The Temple of Nature; or, The Origin of Society: A Poem With Philosophical Notes* (London, 1803), Additional Notes XI.

8. Barlow, ed., *The Autobiography of Charles Darwin,* 36.

9. Henry Maudsley, *Physiology and Pathology of the Mind* (London, 1868).

10. John C. Waller, "The illusion of an explanation: The concept of hereditary disease, 1770–1870," *Journal of the History of Medicine and Allied Sciences,* 57, 4 (2002), 410–448.

11. Francis Galton, *Memories of My Life* (London, 1908), 288.

12. Jane Austen, *Persuasion* (London, 1817), 1.

13. Cited in Janet Browne, *Charles Darwin: The Power of Place* (London, 2002), 471.

14. *Emma Darwin: A Century of Family Letters,* ed. Henrietta Litchfield (London, 1915), vol. 2, 238.

15. Barlow, ed., *The Autobiography of Charles Darwin,* 22.

16. Ibid., 28–43.

17. Browne, *Charles Darwin: The Power of Place,* 286.

18. Nicholas Wright Gillham, *A Life of Sir Francis Galton: From African Exploration to the Birth of Eugenics* (Oxford, 2001), chap. 13.

19. Karl Pearson, *Life and Letters of Francis Galton* (London, 1914), vol. 2, 192.

20. Charles Darwin, *The Descent of Man, and Selection in Relation to Sex,* 2nd ed. (London, 1874), 858.

21. Ibid., 860.

22. Ibid., 860–861.

23. Ibid., 944.

24. Ibid., 894.

25. Erasmus Darwin, *The Temple of Nature,* 45, notes.

26. Darwin, *The Descent of Man,* 208.

27. Erasmus Darwin, *The Temple of Nature,* Canto II.1.165.

28. Francis Galton, *Hereditary Genius* (London, 1869), Penguin edition, 1962, 187.

29. Thomas Carlyle, "Shooting Niagara, and After?" *Macmillan's Magazine,* 16 (1867), 319.

30. Cited in Gillham, *A Life of Sir Francis Galton,* 329.

31. Galton, *Hereditary Genius,* 84.

32. Ibid., 381–382.

33. Ibid., 385.

34. G. R. Searle, *A New England? Peace and War 1886–1918* (Oxford, 2004), 68–69.

35. Galton, *Hereditary Genius,* 177.

36. Janet Browne, *Charles Darwin: Voyaging* (London, 1995), 18.

37. Browne, *Charles Darwin: The Power of Place,* 277, 279.

38. Francis Galton, "Hereditary talent and character," *Macmillan's Magazine,* 12 (1865), 319.

39. George H. Darwin, "On the beneficial restrictions to liberty of marriage," *Contemporary Review,* 22 (1873), 412–426.

40. Arthur Mitchell, "On the influence which consanguinity in the parentage exercises upon the offspring," 3 pts., *Edinburgh Medical Journal,* 10 (Mar./Apr./June 1865), 1: 781.

41. Ibid., 3: 1075.

42. Ibid., 2: 907.

43. Ibid., 2: 913.

44. Charles Darwin, *The Variation of Animals and Plants under Domestication,* 2 vols. (London, 1868); *The Effects of Cross and Self Fertilisation in the Vegetable Kingdom* (London, 1876); *The Various Contrivances by which Orchids are Fertilised by Insects* (London, 1877).

45. Darwin, *Variation of Animals and Plants,* vol. 2, 144. In the revised edition he dropped the qualification "highly" before "injurious": Charles Darwin,

The Variation of Animals and Plants under Domestication, 2nd ed. (London, 1875), vol. 2, 126.

46. Ibid., 122.
47. Browne, *Charles Darwin: The Power of Place,* 282.
48. William Farr to Charles Darwin, May 21, 1868, The Darwin Correspondence, Cambridge University Library.
49. Charles Darwin to Lubbock, July 17, 1870, Darwin Correspondence, Cambridge. Reproduced in *The Life and Letters of Charles Darwin,* ed. Francis Darwin, 3 vols. (London, 1887), vol. 3, 129.
50. 44 Hansard, 3rd ser., cciii, col. 817 (July 25, 1870).
51. Ibid., col. 1009 (July 26, 1870).
52. George H. Darwin, "Marriages between first cousins in England and their effects," *Journal of the Statistical Society,* 38 (1875), 153.
53. Hansard, 3rd ser., cciii, cols. 1006–10 (July 26, 1870).
54. Farr to Charles Darwin, August 6, 1870, Darwin Correspondence, Cambridge.
55. George H. Darwin, "On the beneficial restrictions to liberty of marriage," 424.
56. George H. Darwin, "Marriages between first cousins," 153.
57. Ibid., 178.
58. Ibid., 155.
59. Ibid., 156.
60. Ibid., 162.
61. Ibid., 164.
62. Alan Macfarlane, *Marriage and Love in England: Modes of Reproduction 1300–1840* (Oxford, 1986), 250.
63. Charles Darwin to G. H. Darwin, December 6, 1874, Darwin Correspondence, Cambridge.
64. George H. Darwin, "Marriages between first cousins," 168.
65. Ibid., 168–172.
66. George H. Darwin, "Note on the marriages of first cousins," *Journal of the Statistical Society* (1875), 344–348.
67. George H. Darwin, "Marriages between first cousins," 178.
68. Darwin, *Effects of Cross and Self Fertilisation,* 2nd ed., 460–461. Cf. *The Variation of Animals and Plants under Domestication,* 2 vols. (New York, 1896), vol. 2, 104.
69. Darwin, *The Variation of Animals and Plants under Domestication,* vol. 2, 94; emphasis added.
70. Ibid., 92.
71. Barbara and Hensleigh Wedgwood, *The Wedgwood Circle,* 269.
72. Karl Pearson, *The Life, Letters and Labours of Francis Galton,* 3 vols. (Cambridge, 1914–1930), vol. 2, 188.
73. Karl Pearson, "Cousin marriages," *The British Medical Journal* (June 6, 1908), 1395.

74. See Alfred Owen Aldridge, "The meaning of incest from Hutcheson to Gibbon," *Ethics*, 61(4) (1951), 309–313.
75. Henry Maine, *Ancient Law* (London, 1861), 124.
76. J. F. McLennan, *Primitive Marriage* (Edinburgh, 1865).
77. E. B. Tylor, "On a method of investigating the development of institutions," *Journal of the Anthropological Institute*, 18 (1889), 245–272.
78. Henry Maine, *Dissertations on Early Law and Custom* (London, 1883), 228.
79. J. G. Frazer, *Folklore in the Old Testament*, vol. 2 (London, 1918), 245–246.
80. Charles Darwin, *The Descent of Man*, 2nd ed., 896.
81. Charles Darwin, *The Variation of Animals and Plants under Domestication*, vol. 2, 104–105.
82. Ibid., 124.
83. McLennan, *Primitive Marriage*, chap. 9.
84. J. G. Frazer, *Psyche's Task*, 2nd ed. (London, 1909), 47.
85. Alfred Henry Huth, *The Marriage of Near Kin: Considered with Respect to the Laws of Nations, the Results of Experience, and the Teachings of Biology* (London, 1875), v.

4. The Family Business

1. Harold Perkin, *The Origins of Modern English Society*, 2nd ed. (London, 2002), 430.
2. Quoted in Leonore Davidoff and Catherine Hall, *Family Fortunes*, 2nd ed. (London, 2002), 200.
3. David Warren Sabean, Simon Teuscher, and Jon Mathieu, eds., *Kinship in Europe* (Oxford, 2007), 188.
4. Verily Anderson, *Friends and Relations: Three Centuries of Quaker Families* (London, 1980), 182.
5. Amalie M. Kass and Edward H. Kass, *Perfecting the World: The Life and Times of Dr. Thomas Hodgkin 1798–1866* (Boston, 1988), 313–315.
6. Anderson, *Friends and Relations*, 91–92.
7. Niall Ferguson, *The House of Rothschild*, 2 vols.; vol. 2, *The World's Banker, 1849–1999* (London, 1999), xxiii.
8. Ibid., vol. 1, *Money's Prophets, 1798–1848* (London, 1998), 109.
9. Ibid., vol. 2, 238.
10. Ibid., vol. 1, 267.
11. Ibid., vol. 1, 105.
12. Ibid., vol. 1, 109.
13. David Kynastan, *The City of London*, vol. 1: *A World of Its Own 1815–1890* (London, 1995), 6.
14. Ferguson, *The House of Rothschild*, vol. 1, 268.
15. An incidental effect of the allocation of capital shares to each branch was that members of the next generation inherited more or fewer shares depending on the number of siblings they had in addition to the (fluctuating) share of their branch in the total capital.

16. Ferguson, *The House of Rothschild*, vol. 1, 74.

17. Andreas Hansert, "The dynastic power of the Rothschilds—A sociological assessment," in Georg Heuberger, ed., *The Rothschilds: Essays on the History of a European Family* (Frankfurt, 1994), 167.

18. Ferguson, *The House of Rothschild*, vol. 1, 188.

19. Cited in Pat Jalland, *Women, Marriage and Politics, 1860–1914* (Oxford, 1986), 89.

20. Ferguson, *The House of Rothschild*, vol. 1, 321–322.

21. See, for example, Ferguson, *The House of Rothschild*, vol. 1, 188; Hansert, "The dynastic power of the Rothschilds," 166.

22. See, for example, Ferguson, *The House of Rothschild*, vol. 1, 188; vol. 2, 13.

23. Barbara and Hensleigh Wedgwood, *The Wedgwood Circle, 1730–1897* (London, 1980), 11. Using the retail price index, this amount would be about £446,000 in 2007 ($645,000 at the end of 2008). Lawrence H. Officer, "Purchasing Power of British Pounds from 1264 to 2007," Measuring-Worth, 2008. *www.measuringworth.com/ppoweruk/*.

24. Ibid., 105. Half a million pounds then is today about £39 million ($56 million).

25. Ibid., 101.

26. Janet Browne, *Charles Darwin: Voyaging* (London, 1995), 111.

27. Ibid., 153–156.

28. *Emma Darwin: A Century of Family Letters*, ed. Henrietta Litchfield, 2 vols. (London, 1915), vol. 2, 2.

29. Ibid., vol. 2, 3.

30. Browne, *Charles Darwin: Voyaging*, 393. Calculating current sterling equivalent (at the end of 2007, with reference to the cost of living index), £5,000 in 1839 would be worth about £339,000 today (or $492,000 at the end of 2008), £400 would be worth £27,000 (or $39,000), £10,000 pounds would be worth £678,000 (or $985,000), and £600 would be worth £41,000 (or $60,000). Officer, "Purchasing Power of British Pounds," *www.measuringworth.com/ppoweruk/*.

31. Frederick Burkhardt, ed., *The Correspondence of Charles Darwin*, volume 2, *1837–1843* (Cambridge, 1986), 119, note.

32. B. and H. Wedgwood, *The Wedgwood Circle*, 209–210.

33. Ibid., 146.

34. Gwen Raverat, *Period Piece: A Cambridge Childhood* (London, 1960), 154.

35. B. and H. Wedgwood, *The Wedgewood Circle*, 211 ff.

36. Ibid., 261–262.

37. Ibid., 269–270, 310–316.

5. Wilberforce and the Clapham Sect

1. Kathleen Jones, *A Passionate Sisterhood* (London, 1998), 14.

2. Until late in the eighteenth century Clapham was still a village, with about a thousand mostly wealthy inhabitants. By the time Clapham became the

seat of the Sect in the 1790s it was a suburb of London, with a population of about 2,600, although the rector, John Venn, still sometimes hunted on the Common. Only four miles from Westminster Bridge and five from the City via London Bridge, it was convenient for men who worked in the City, in Parliament, or in Whitehall. A coach service ran four times a day. (A generation later, Charles Trevelyan would ride on horseback from Clapham to the Treasury during the summer months.) Clapham was nevertheless sufficiently isolated to serve as a sort of village for the Saints, although from the beginning several of their closest associates, including Hannah More, lived far from London and were only occasional visitors to the sacred common. And their leader, Wilberforce, returned to London in 1808.

3. George Otto Trevelyan, *The Life and Letters of Lord Macaulay* (London, 1876), chap. 1.

4. *The Edinburgh Review,* January 1809. £500 is equivalent in purchasing power to £27,000 in December 2007, or $39,000 in 2009. Lawrence H. Officer, "Purchasing Power of British Pounds from 1264 to 2007," MeasuringWorth, 2008. *www.measuringworth.com/ppoweruk/.*

5. See, for example, the sour obituary of Hannah More in the High Tory *Quarterly Review,* 104/52 (1834), 416.

6. Sydney Smith, *Works,* 4 vols. (London, 1839), vol. 3, 576 and 385. See the Appendix to Ernest Marshall Howse, *Saints in Politics: The "Clapham Sect" and the Growth of Freedom* (London, 1953), 188, for these and similar remarks.

7. James Stephen, "The Clapham Sect," republished in James Stephen, *Essays in Ecclesiastical Biography* (London, 1849), vol. 2.

8. James Stephen, "The Evangelical Succession," *Essays in Ecclesiastical Biography,* vol. 2, 155.

9. Stephen, "The Clapham Sect," 535.

10. Standish Meacham, *Henry Thornton of Clapham, 1760–1815* (Cambridge, Mass., 1964), 21.

11. Stephen, "The Clapham Sect," 534.

12. Meacham, *Henry Thornton of Clapham,* 60.

13. Ibid., 2.

14. E. M. Forster, *Marianne Thornton 1797–1887* (Abinger Edition, London, 2000), 22. Cf. Meacham, *Henry Thornton of Clapham,* 5–6. £2000–3000 in today's prices is worth £200–300,000 ($300–445,000), calculated with reference to the retail price index. Officer, "Purchasing Power of British Pounds," *www.measuringworth.com/ppoweruk/.*

15. James Stephen lists as the movement's "four Evangelists John Newton, Thomas Scott, Joseph Milner, and Henry Venn." Stephen, "The Evangelical Succession," vol. 2, 309.

16. Michael Hennell, *John Venn and the Clapham Sect* (Cambridge, 2003), 79.

17. Meacham, *Henry Thornton of Clapham,* 36.

18. See Friedrich Hayek, introduction to H. F. Thornton, *An Enquiry into the Nature and Effects of the Paper Credit of Great Britain* (London, 1939).
19. John Hicks, "Thornton's paper credit," in John Hicks, *Critical Essays in Monetary Theories* (Oxford, 1967).
20. Quoted in David Kynaston, *The City of London: A World of Its Own, 1815–1890* (London, 1994), 15.
21. That is, £332,000 ($540,000) on charities and £301,000 ($490,000) on personal expenses.
22. Meacham, *Henry Thornton of Clapham*, 197–198, note 26.
23. Robert and Samuel Wilberforce, *The Life of William Wilberforce*, 5 vols. (London, 1838), vol. 1, 78.
24. Reginald Coupland, *Wilberforce: A Narrative* (Oxford, 1923), 26.
25. Wilberforce and Wilberforce, *Life of William Wilberforce*, vol. 1, 158.
26. Hennell, *John Venn and the Clapham Sect*, 170.
27. Stephen, "The Clapham Sect," 522.
28. Dorothy Pym, *Battersea Rise* (London, 1934), 209.
29. Meacham, *Henry Thornton of Clapham*, 28.
30. Forster, *Marianne Thornton*, 57.
31. Trevelyan, *The Life and Letters of Lord Macaulay*, chap. 1.
32. Howse, *Saints in Ppolitics,* pp. 16–17.
33. Wilberforce and Wilberforce, *Life of William Wilberforce*, vol. 2, 234–238.
34. Hennell, *John Venn and the Clapham Sect*, 187.
35. Ibid., 185 and 186–189.
36. Ibid., 166–167.
37. Quoted in Forster, *Marianne Thornton*, 42.
38. Hennell, *John Venn and the Clapham Sect*, 172.
39. Quoted in Forster, *Marianne Thornton*, 42.
40. Meacham, *Henry Thornton of Clapham*, 39.
41. Quoted in Forster, *Marianne Thornton*, 40.
42. Stephen, "The Clapham Sect."
43. Quoted by Friedrich Hayek, introduction to H. F. Thornton, *An Enquiry into the Nature and Effects of the Paper Credit of Great Britain* (London, 1939).
44. Margaret Holland, Lady Knutsford, *Life and Letters of Zachary Macaulay* (London, 1900), 14.
45. Ibid., 5.
46. Ibid., 97.
47. Quoted in Anne Stott, *Hannah More: The First Victorian* (Oxford, 2003), 196.
48. Lady Knutsford, *Life and Letters of Zachary Macaulay*, 98–115.
49. Stott, *Hannah More*, 197.
50. John Clive, *Macaulay: The Shaping of the Historian* (Cambridge, Mass., 1987), 13.
51. Equivalent to £34,000 at the end of 2007, using the retail price index for

the calculation (or $50,000 in 2009). Officer, "Purchasing Power of British Pounds," *www.measuringworth.com/ppoweruk/*.

52. Stott, *Hannah More*, 198.
53. Noel Annan, *Leslie Stephen: The Godless Victorian* (Cambridge, Mass, 1952), 288, note.
54. Leslie Stephen, *The Life of Sir James Fitzjames Stephen* (London, 1895), 17–18; Christopher Tolley, *Domestic Biography: The Legacy of Evangelicalism in Four Nineteenth-Century Families* (Oxford, 1997), 19.
55. Stephen, *The Life of Sir James Fitzjames Stephen*, 18.
56. Robert and Samuel Wilberforce, eds., *The Correspondence of William Wilberforce*, 2 vols. (London, 1840), vol. 2, 137.
57. Coupland, *Wilberforce*, 233.
58. Stephen, *The Life of Sir James Fitzjames Stephen*, 19, 22.
59. Ibid., 20.
60. Wilberforce and Wilberforce, *Correspondence of William Wilberforce*, vol. 2, 480–482.
61. Lady Knutsford, *Life and Letters of Zachary Macaulay*, 271.
62. Ibid.
63. Wilberforce and Wilberforce, *Life of William Wilberforce*, vol. 3, 419.
64. Quoted in Forster, *Marianne Thornton*, 45.
65. Tolley, *Domestic Biography*, 44.
66. Hennell, *John Venn and the Clapham Sect*, 185.
67. Ibid., 178.
68. Meacham, *Henry Thornton of Clapham*, 51.
69. Wilberforce and Wilberforce, *Life of William Wilberforce*, vol. 3, 235.
70. Stott, *Hannah More*, 271.
71. Lady Knutsford, *Life and Letters of Zachary Macaulay*, 319.
72. Ibid., 320–321.
73. Thomas Gisborne, *An Enquiry into the Duties of the Female Sex* (1797). See Deirdre Le Faye, ed., *Jane Austen's Letters* (Oxford, 1995), 112.
74. Forster, *Marianne Thornton*, 35–36.
75. Hennell, *John Venn and the Clapham Sect*, 204.
76. Wilberforce and Wilberforce, *Life of William Wilberforce*, vol. 1, 187.
77. Ibid., vol. 1, 149.
78. Stephen, "The Clapham Sect," 579.
79. Boyd Hilton, *A Mad, Bad and Dangerous People? England 1783–1846* (Oxford, 2006), 183.
80. Stott, *Hannah More*, 297.
81. Howse, *Saints in Politics*, 57.
82. Meacham, *Henry Thornton of Clapham*, 68.
83. A Claphamite and a Saint, but older than the others, and a Unitarian, Smith was not a member of the inner circle.
84. Wilberforce and Wilberforce, *Life of William Wilberforce*, vol. 3, 298.

85. Howse, *Saints in Politics*, 75.
86. See Tolley, *Domestic Biography*, passim.
87. Meacham, *Henry Thornton of Clapham*, 43.
88. See J. A. S. L. Leighton-Boyce, *Smiths the Bankers 1658–1958* (London, 1958), 202–203, for their business links to the Wilberforce and Thornton enterprises in Hull.
89. John Venn, *Annals of a Clerical Family: Being Some Account of the Family and Descendants of William Venn, Vicar of Otterton, Devon* (London, 1904), 161–162.

6. Difficulties with Siblings

1. Thomas Babington, *A Practical View of Christian Education in Its Earliest Stages* (London, 1814).
2. E. M. Forster, *Marianne Thornton, 1797–1887: A Domestic Biography* (London [1956], 2000), 58–59.
3. Charles John Shore, Baron Teignmouth, *Reminiscences of Many Years* (Edinburgh, 1878), 1–3. See also Bruce L. Mouser, "African Academy—Clapham 1799–1806," *History of Education*, 33 (1) (2004), 87–103.
4. Christopher Tolley, *Domestic Biography: The Legacy of Evangelicalism in Four Nineteenth-Century Families* (Oxford, 1997), 21.
5. John Clive, *Macaulay: The Shaping of the Historian* (Cambridge, Mass., 1987), 489.
6. Leslie Stephen, *The Life of James Fitzjames Stephen* (London, 1895), 63.
7. Ibid., 61.
8. Ibid., 56.
9. Ibid.
10. Ibid., 128.
11. Ibid., 41.
12. Ibid., 62.
13. Ibid., 87.
14. Ibid., 44–46.
15. Paul Knaplund, *James Stephen and the British Colonial System, 1813–1847* (Madison, Wisc., 1953).
16. Stephen, *The Life of James Fitzjames Stephen*, 46.
17. Ibid., 46.
18. George Otto Trevelyan, *Life and Letters of Lord Macaulay* (London, 1881), 528.
19. Only one of James Stephen's siblings married a cousin. This was his older brother, Henry John, who joined the Chancery bar and wrote important legal textbooks. He married his father's sister's daughter, Mary Morison, herself the daughter of a lawyer and legal scholar.
20. David Newsome, *The Parting of Friends: The Wilberforces and Henry Manning* (Leominster, 1993), 5.

21. Ibid., 313.
22. Standish Meacham, *Lord Bishop: The Life of Samuel Wilberforce 1805–1873* (Cambridge, Mass., 1970), Appendix, 319–322.
23. Forster, *Marianne Thornton*, 78.
24. Ibid., chap. 3; "Letters from a young lady," *Three Banks Review* (1950), 29–46; "Henry Sykes Thornton," *Three Banks Review* (1966), 29–37; David Kynaston, *The City of London*, 4 vols. (London, 1995), vol. 1, 66–72.
25. Forster, *Marianne Thornton*, 143.
26. Ibid., 146.
27. Ibid., 147.
28. Ibid., 148.
29. Ibid., 196.
30. Ibid., 175.
31. Ibid., 177.
32. Ibid., 179.
33. Ibid., 176–177.
34. Ibid., 184.
35. Ibid., 194.
36. Ibid., 192.
37. Ibid., 264.
38. George Otto Trevelyan, *Life and Letters of Lord Macaulay*, 2nd ed., 2 vols. (London, 1877), vol. 1, 25.
39. Clive, *Macaulay*, 100. £660 would be worth about £48,000 at the end of 2007, using the retail price index for the calculation (or $70,000 at the end of 2008). Lawrence H. Officer, "Purchasing Power of British Pounds from 1264 to 2007," MeasuringWorth, 2008. *www.measuringworth.com/ppoweruk/*.
40. Clive, *Macaulay*, 248.
41. Cited in ibid., 499.
42. Ibid., 256.
43. Ibid., 266.
44. Ibid., 258.
45. Ibid., 273.
46. Ibid., 274.
47. Ibid., 271.
48. Ibid., 276.
49. Ibid., 275.
50. Ibid., 281.
51. Ibid., 279.
52. Ibid., 286.
53. William Thomas, "Macaulay, Thomas Babington," *Oxford Dictionary of National Biography*.
54. Letter to her cousin, T. G. Babington, quoted in Clive, *Macaulay*, 272.
55. William Thomas, "Macaulay."

7. The Bourgeois Intellectuals

1. In some boroughs the vote was given to men who had their own fireplace (on which they could boil a pot). At election time they were often bribed with ale, hence "drunken." And in some rotten boroughs as few as a hundred voters could return a member of Parliament.
2. Speech to Parliament, March 2, 1831. In Lord Macaulay and Lady Trevelyan, eds., *Speeches: The Complete Writings of Lord Macaulay* (London, 1866), 12.
3. Samuel Taylor Coleridge, *On the Constitution of the Church and State* (London, 1839), 46.
4. Thomas Babington Macaulay, "Milton" [1825], reprinted in *Critical and Historical Essays* (London, 1843).
5. Thomas Babington Macaulay, "Present administration," *Edinburgh Review*, 46 (1827), 252.
6. F. R. Leavis, ed., *Mill on Bentham and Coleridge* (Cambridge, 1950).
7. Coleridge, *On the Constitution of the Church and State*, 49.
8. Thomas Carlyle, *Hudson's Statue* (part 2, Latter-Day Pamphlets, no. 7; London, 1850).
9. Matthew Arnold, *Culture and Anarchy* (London, 1882).
10. Francis Galton, *Hereditary Genius* (London, 1869).
11. George Meredith, *The Ordeal of Richard Feverel* (London, 1859), vol. 5, 21.
12. Noel Annan, "The intellectual aristocracy," in J. H. Plumb, ed., *Studies in Social History: A Tribute to G. M. Trevelyan* (London, 1955), 243–287. Cf. Noel Annan, *The Dons: Mentors, Eccentrics and Geniuses* (London, 1999), chap. 1.
13. Annan, *The Dons*, 10.
14. Annan, "The intellectual aristocracy," 247.
15. Ibid., 244.
16. Ibid., 253–254.
17. Ibid., 254, 260, 273.
18. Ibid., 265.
19. Coleridge, *On the Constitution of the Church and State*.
20. This collection of seven essays by liberal intellectuals in the Church of England—among others, Benjamin Jowett, Mark Pattison, and Frederick Temple (who was to become Archbishop of Canterbury)—downplayed miracles, questioned the story of the Creation, denied the doctrine of eternal punishment, and endorsed the new German high criticism of the Bible. Its publication led to three heresy trials.
21. Janet Browne, *Charles Darwin: The Power of Place* (London, 2002), 114–125.
22. Leslie Stephen, *Some Early Impressions* (London, 1924), 70.
23. *Sir Leslie Stephen's Mausoleum Book* (Oxford, 1977), 5.
24. Leslie Stephen, *The Life of James Fitzjames Stephen* (London, 1895), 309–310.

25. Stephen, *Some Early Impressions*, 70.
26. Ibid., 54–55.
27. Ibid., 69.
28. Ibid., 124.
29. Noel Annan, *Leslie Stephen: The Godless Victorian* (London, 1984), 110. Cf. Standish Meacham, "The Evangelical inheritance," *Journal of British Studies*, 3 (1963), 88–104.
30. K. J. M. Smith, "Sir James Fitzjames Stephen," *Oxford Dictionary of National Biography*; K. J. M. Smith, *James Fitzjames Stephen: Portrait of a Victorian Rationalist* (Cambridge, 1988).
31. W. M. Thackeray, *Pendennis* (London, 1848), chap. 2.
32. *Sir Leslie Stephen's Mausoleum Book*, 7.
33. Ibid., 8.
34. Hermione Lee, *Virginia Woolf* (London, 1996), 36.
35. Stephen, *Life of James Fitzjames Stephen*, 129.
36. Ibid., 180.
37. Christopher Tolley, *Domestic Biography: The Legacy of Evangelicalism in Four Nineteenth-Century Families* (Oxford, 1997), 214–215.
38. Lee, *Virginia Woolf*, 63.
39. *Sir Leslie Stephen's Mausoleum Book*, 7.
40. Ibid., 55.
41. Henrietta Garnett, *A Life of Anne Thackeray Ritchie* (London, 2004), 68.
42. Ibid., 243–244.
43. Ibid., 81.
44. *Sir Leslie Stephen's Mausoleum Book*, 23.
45. Ibid., 22.
46. Ibid., 45.
47. Garnett, *Life of Anne Thackeray Ritchie*, 210–211.
48. *Sir Leslie Stephen's Mausoleum Book*, 45–46.
49. Ibid., 55.
50. Ibid.
51. Ibid., 34–35.
52. Garnett, *Life of Anne Thackeray Ritchie*, 144.
53. Virginia Woolf and Roger Fry, *Introduction to Victorian Photographs of Famous Men and Fair Women* (London, 1926), 1.
54. Ibid.
55. Lee, *Virginia Woolf* (London, 1996), 88.
56. Cited in ibid., 89. Herbert Fisher (1848–1925) was a historian and liberal politician. One of his sisters was married first to F. W. Maitland and then to Francis Darwin, a son of Charles Darwin. Another sister was the first wife of the composer Ralph Vaughan Williams.
57. *Sir Leslie Stephen's Mausoleum Book*, 26.
58. Ibid., 30.

59. Virginia Woolf, *Moments of Being: Autobiographic Writings,* ed. Jeanne Schulkind (London, 2002), 99.
60. *Sir Leslie Stephen's Mausoleum Book,* 28.
61. Garnett, *Life of Anne Thackeray Ritchie,* 224.
62. Laura Trevelyan, *A Very British Family: The Trevelyans and Their World* (London, 2006).

8. The Bloomsbury Version

1. S. P. Rosenbaum, ed., *The Bloomsbury Group* (Toronto, 1975), 25.
2. Ibid., 25–26.
3. £500 a year in 1929 is the equivalent in purchasing power to roughly £22,000 in 2007 (or $32,000 at the end of 2008). Lawrence H. Officer, "Purchasing Power of British Pounds from 1264 to 2007," Measuring-Worth, 2008. *www.measuringworth.com/ppoweruk/.*
4. J. M. Keynes, "Am I a Liberal?" [1925]; reprinted in *The Collected Writings of John Maynard Keynes* (London, 1972), 297.
5. Rosenbaum, ed., *The Bloomsbury Group,* 4.
6. Ibid., 165.
7. Raymond Williams, "The significance of 'Bloomsbury' as a social and cultural group," in Derek Crabtree and A. P. Thirwall, eds., *Keynes and the Bloomsbury Group* (London, 1980), 61.
8. Leonard Woolf, *Beginning Again* (London, 1964), 25.
9. Quoted in S. P. Rosenbaum, *Victorian Bloomsbury* (London, 1987), 246.
10. Leonard Woolf, *Beginning Again,* 25.
11. Rosenbaum, *The Bloomsbury Group,* 21.
12. Ibid., 165.
13. Ibid., 203.
14. Paul Levy, ed., *The Letters of Lytton Strachey* (London, 2005), 624.
15. Virginia Woolf, *Moments of Being* (London, 2002), 79. This sense of continuity was passed on to the next generation. Julian Bell, the son of Virginia's sister Vanessa, wrote in his poem "Autobiography" that he was
    . . . the product made
    By several hundred English years,
    Of harried labourers underpaid,
    Of Venns who plied the parson's trade,
    Of regicides, of Clapham sects,
    Of high Victorian intellects,
    Leslie, FitzJames.
16. Leonard Woolf, *Sowing: An Autobiography of the Years 1880–1904* (London, 1960), 190.
17. Michael Holroyd, *Lytton Strachey* (London, 1968), 31.
18. Victor Hilts, "A guide to Francis Galton's *English Men of Science,*" *Transactions of the American Philosophical Society,* 65, Part 5 (1975), 69–70.

19. David Gilmour, *The Ruling Caste: Imperial Lives in the Victorian Raj* (London, 2005), 31.
20. Virginia Woolf, *Moments of Being*, 149.
21. Ibid., 150.
22. Lytton Strachey, "Lancaster Gate," in Michael Holroyd, ed., *The Shorter Strachey* (Oxford, 1980), 10.
23. Levy, ed., *The Letters of Lytton Strachey*, 6.
24. Holroyd, *Lytton Strachey*, 52.
25. Virginia Woolf, *Moments of Being*, 33.
26. Hermione Lee, *Virginia Woolf* (London, 1996), 55–56.
27. Virginia Woolf, *Moments of Being*, 131.
28. Barbara Caine, *Bombay to Bloomsbury: A Biography of the Strachey Family* (Oxford, 2005), 104–113.
29. Virginia Woolf, *Moments of Being*, 44–45.
30. Strachey, "Lancaster Gate," 3.
31. Ibid., 5.
32. Ibid., 6–7.
33. Virginia Woolf, *Moments of Being*, 31–33.
34. Ibid., 34.
35. Ibid., 106.
36. Introduction by Alan Bell to *Sir Leslie Stephen's Mausoleum Book* (Oxford, 1977), xxvi.
37. *Sir Leslie Stephen's Mausoleum Book*, 77.
38. Virginia Woolf, *Moments of Being*, 19.
39. Introduction by Alan Bell to *Sir Leslie Stephen's Mausoleum Book*, xxvi.
40. *Sir Leslie Stephen's Mausoleum Book*, 59, note.
41. Virginia Woolf, *Moments of Being*, 19.
42. *Sir Leslie Stephen's Mausoleum Book*, 97.
43. Virginia Woolf, *Moments of Being*, 27.
44. Ibid., 145.
45. Ibid., 148.
46. Ibid., 33.
47. Ibid., 42.
48. Lee, *Virginia Woolf*, 153–159.
49. Virginia Woolf, *Moments of Being*, 171.
50. Ibid., 44.
51. Ibid., 82.
52. Lee, *Virginia Woolf*, 125–127.
53. Leonard Woolf, *Downhill All the Way* (London, 1967), 68.
54. Nigel Nicolson, ed., *The Letters of Virginia Woolf* (London, 1976), vol. 2, 546–547.
55. W. C. Lubenow, *The Cambridge Apostles, 1820–1914* (Cambridge, 1998).
56. Rosenbaum, ed., *The Bloomsbury Group*, 180.

57. Robert Skidelsky, *John Maynard Keynes, Hopes Betrayed, 1883–1920* (London, 1983), 125.
58. Bertrand Russell, *The Autobiography of Bertrand Russell, 1872–1914* (London, 1967), 74.
59. Quoted in Lubenow, *The Cambridge Apostles,* 52.
60. Russell, *The Autobiography of Bertrand Russell,* 70.
61. Ibid., 70–71.
62. Ibid., 68.
63. Levy, ed., *The Letters of Lytton Strachey,* 17.
64. J. M. Keynes, "My early beliefs," in *Essays in Biography* (London, 1972), 435.
65. Ibid., 436.
66. G. E. Moore, *Principia Ethica* (Cambridge, 1903), 237–238.
67. Michael W. Pharand, "Bloomsbury and France: Art and friends (review)," *Comparative Literature Studies,* 38: 2 (2001), 169.
68. E. M. Forster, *Two Cheers for Democracy* (London, 1951), 66.
69. David Garnett, *The Golden Echo* (London, 1953), 270.
70. A successful businessman, Charles Booth was a social reformer and a pioneer of social research. His wife was a niece of Thomas Babington Macaulay.
71. Virginia Woolf, *Moments of Being,* 46–47.
72. Leonard Woolf, *Beginning Again,* 16.
73. Quentin Bell, *Virginia Woolf: A Biography* (New York, 1974), vol. 1, 243.
74. Quoted in Lee, *Virginia Woolf,* 213.
75. Virginia Woolf, *Moments of Being,* 53.
76. Sarah M. Hall, *Before Leonard: The Early Suitors of Virginia Woolf* (London, 2006), 42.
77. Garnett, *The Golden Echo,* 251–252.
78. Quoted in Lee, *Virginia Woolf,* 238.
79. Quoted in Peter Stansky, *On or About December 1910* (Cambridge, Mass., 1997), 115.
80. Rosenbaum, *The Bloomsbury Group,* 79.
81. Virginia Woolf, "Old Bloomsbury," in *Moments of Being,* 173–174.
82. Anne Olivier Bell, ed., *The Diary of Virginia Woolf* (New York, 1977), vol. 1, 11, note.
83. Leonard Woolf, *Beginning Again,* 35.
84. Virginia Woolf, *Moments of Being,* 54.
85. Hall, *Before Leonard: The Early Suitors of Virginia Woolf.*
86. Bell, *Virginia Woolf,* vol. 1, 129.
87. Victoria Glendinning, *Leonard Woolf: A Life* (London, 2006), 93.
88. Ibid., 153.
89. Bell, *Virginia Woolf,* vol. 1, 247.
90. Rosenbaum, ed., *The Bloomsbury Group,* 28.

91. Levy, ed., *The Letters of Lytton Strachey*, 99.
92. The details are complicated but typical of the intricate family bonds in this milieu. Richmond Ritchie, who married Anny Thackeray, Leslie Stephen's sister-in-law, was Molly's mother's brother. Moreover, Molly's younger sister, Cecilia, married William Fisher, the son of Virginia Woolf's mother's sister. William Fisher's sister married F. W. Maitland, Leslie Stephen's biographer, and their daughter married the Bloomsberry Gerald Shove.
93. Hugh and Mirabel Cecil, *Clever Hearts: Desmond and Molly MacCarthy, A Biography* (London, 1990), 132–142, 150–151.
94. Leonard Woolf, *Sowing*, 263.
95. Leonard Woolf, *Downhill All the Way*, 114.
96. Levy, ed., *The Letters of Lytton Strachey*, 452–453.
97. Quoted in Rosenbaum, *The Bloomsbury Group*, 165.
98. Skidelsky, *John Maynard Keynes*, 333.
99. Quoted in Cecil and Cecil, *Clever Hearts: Desmond and Molly MacCarthy*, 202.
100. Leonard Woolf, *Downhill All the Way*, 114.
101. Quoted in Cecil and Cecil, *Clever Hearts: Desmond and Molly MacCarthy*, 264.
102. Ibid., 265.
103. Glendinning, *Leonard Woolf*, 249.
104. Ibid., 237.
105. Skidelsky, *John Maynard Keynes*, vol. 1, 247.
106. Edith Sitwell, *Taken Care Of* (London, 1965), 81–82.
107. Cecil and Cecil, *Clever Hearts: Desmond and Molly MacCarthy*, 115.
108. Lee, *Virginia Woolf*, 268.
109. Rupert Brooke's group was also virulently racist and anti-Semitic. Brooke used to refer to the Woolfs as "the Jew and his wife." His mistress, Noel Olivier, reassured him: "You need have no fear of slug-like influences from the people Jacques [Raverat] calls 'the Jews': (they comprise the Bloomsbury household and the Stracheys, I believe)." Cited in Lee, *Virginia Woolf*, 293.
110. Quoted in Stansky, *On or About December 1910*, 123.
111. Quoted in Sandra Jobson Darroch, *Ottoline* (New York, 1975), 255, note.
112. Levy, ed., *The Letters of Lytton Strachey*, 588.
113. Quoted in ibid., 176.
114. Caine, *Bombay to Bloomsbury*, 162–167.
115. Bell, *Virginia Woolf*, vol. 1, 169.
116. Nicholas Murray, *Aldous Huxley* (London, 2002).
117. Levy, ed., *The Letters of Lytton Strachey*, 288.
118. Angelica Garnett, *Deceived with Kindness: A Bloomsbury Childhood* (London, 1985), 33.
119. Quoted in Douglas Blair Turnbaugh, *Duncan Grant and the Bloomsbury Group* (Secaucus, N.J., 1987), 60.

120. Garnett, *Deceived with Kindness: A Bloomsbury Childhood*, 55.
121. Lee, *Virginia Woolf*, 547.
122. Levy, ed., *The Letters of Lytton Strachey*, 441.
123. Anthony Powell, *Books Do Furnish a Room* (London, 1971), 119.
124. S. C. Roberts, *Adventures with Authors* (Cambridge, 1966), 121.
125. Glendinning, *Leonard Woolf*, 359.
126. Noel Annan, *Leslie Stephen: The Godless Victorian* (London, 1984), 121.
127. Ibid., 123.
128. Keynes, "My early beliefs," 436–438.
129. Henrietta Garnett, *Family Skeletons* (London, 1986).

Coda

1. David Warren Sabean, Simon Teuscher, and Jon Mathieu, eds., *Kinship in Europe: Approaches to Long-Term Development (1300–1900)* (Oxford, 2007), passim. See also Jean-Marie Gousse, "Mariages de proches parents (XVIe–XXe siècle)," in *Le modèle familial européen. Actes des séminaries organisés par l'école française de Rome*, 90 (Rome, 1986), 31–61, for Spain, France, and Italy; and Harold James, *Family Capitalism* (Cambridge, Mass., 2006), 14–16 and passim, for kin marriages in Rhineland industrial families.
2. Johann Wolfgang von Goethe, *The Man of Fifty*, trans. Andrew Piper (London, 2004). The quotations in the text are taken from this edition.
3. André Gide, *Strait is the Gate*, trans. Dorothy Bussy (London, 1924).
4. Martin Oppenheimer, *Forbidden Relatives: The American Myth of Cousin Marriage* (Urbana, Ill., 1966), 27.
5. Russell M. Reid, "Church membership, consanguineous marriage, and migration in a Scotch-Irish frontier population," *Journal of Family History*, 13 (1988).
6. Susan R. Frankenberg, "Kinship and mate choice in a historic eastern Blue Ridge community, Madison County, Virginia," *Human Biology*, 62: 6 (1990), 817–835.
7. Peter Dobkin Hall, "Family Structure and Class Consolidation among the Boston Brahmins" (doctoral dissertation, State University of New York at Stony Brook, 1973), 23; Peter Dobkin Hall, *The Organization of American Culture, 1700–1900: Private Institutions, Elites, and the Origins of American Nationality* (New York, 1982), 64.
8. Hall, *The Organization of American Culture*, 66–68.
9. Bernard Farber, *Guardians of Virtue: Salem Families in 1800* (New York, 1972), 130–133.
10. Hall, "Family Structure and Class Consolidation among the Boston Brahmins," 170, 176, 179.
11. Ibid., 170.
12. Ibid.
13. Cited in Hall, *The Organization of American Culture*, 73.
14. S. M. Bemiss, "Report on influence of marriages of consanguinity upon

offspring," *Transactions of the American Medical Association,* 11 (1858), 319–425.

15. Oppenheimer, *Forbidden Relatives,* 54–57.
16. Michael Grossberg, *Governing the Hearth: Law and the Family in Nineteenth-Century America* (Chapel Hill, N.C., 1985), 144–146.
17. Ibid., chap. 4.
18. Ibid., 126–140.
19. See Margareth Lanzinger, "The 'bonds of blood': Kin marriages and a blood discourse in the 19th century," paper presented to the European Social Science History Conference, Lisbon, 2008.
20. Thomas Trautmann, *Lewis Henry Morgan and the Invention of Kinship* (Berkeley, 1987), 244.
21. Leonard Darwin, *What Is Eugenics?* (London, 1928), 86–87.
22. J. B. S. Haldane, *Heredity and Politics* (London, 1938), 89–91; Daniel J. Kevles, *In the Name of Eugenics* (Cambridge, Mass., 1985), 177.
23. Thomas Hardy, *Jude the Obscure* (London, 1896), chap. 2.
24. John Galsworthy, *To Let* (London, 1921), chap. 5.
25. Ford Madox Ford, *Some Do Not . . .* (London, 1924), part 2, chap. 3.
26. See Alan A. Bittles, "Genetic aspects of inbreeding and incest," in Arthur Wolf and William Durham, eds., *Inbreeding, Incest, and the Incest Taboo* (Stanford, 2005), 38–60; Oppenheimer, *Forbidden Relatives,* 116–133.
27. Alan H. Bittles and Udi E. Makov, "Inbreeding in human populations: Assessment of the costs," in C. G. N. Mascie-Taylor and A. J. Boyce, eds., *Human Mating Patterns* (Cambridge, 1988), 164.
28. R. L. Bennett, A. G. Motulsky, L. Hudgins, et al., "Genetic counselling and screening of consanguineous couples and their offspring," *Genetic Medicine,* 1 (2002), 286–292.
29. Diane B. Paul and Hamish G. Spencer, "'It's OK, We're not cousins by blood': The cousin marriage controversy in historical perspective," *PLoS Biology* (December, 2008), www.plosbiology.org.
30. Medical Research Council, *Annual Report* (London: 1935/36), 139–140; (1936/37), 157–158; (1938/39), 81.
31. Raymond Firth, Jane Hubert, and Anthony Forge, *Families and Their Relatives: Kinship in a Middle-Class Sector of London* (London, 1970), 191–193.
32. P. L. Cottrell, "Domestic finance, 1860–1914," in Roderick Floud and Paul Johnson, eds., *The Cambridge Economic History of Modern Britain* (Cambridge, 2004), vol. 2, 261–270.
33. J. M. Keynes, *The Economic Consequences of the Peace* (London, 1920), 254.
34. G. R. Searle, *A New England? Peace and War, 1886–1918* (Oxford, 2004), 779.
35. Ibid., 795.
36. Michael Anderson, *Approaches to the History of the Western Family, 1500–1914* (Cambridge, 1995), 7. See Zhongwei Zhao, "The demographic transition in Victorian England," *Continuity and Change,* 11:2 (1996), 245–246.

37. K. Theodore Hoppen, *The Mid-Victorian Generation 1846–1886* (Oxford, 1998), 317.
38. The table in the text shows the age at marriage and fertility for different cohorts. This table is drawn from the genealogies I collected as part of the research for this book. The families documented were chosen as they linked into the case studies I investigated.
39. For the general population see Zhao, "The demographic transition in Victorian England," 256.
40. E. M. Forster, "The early novels of Virginia Woolf," in *Abinger Harvest* (London, 1936), 106.
41. Hermione Lee, *Virginia Woolf* (London, 1996), 375.
42. Virginia Woolf, *Night and Day* ([1919] Oxford, 1992), 34–35.
43. Ibid., 32.
44. Ibid.
45. Gwen Raverat, *Period Piece* (London, 1960), 175.
46. Mary Wesley, *The Camomile Lawn* (London, 1984).

Index